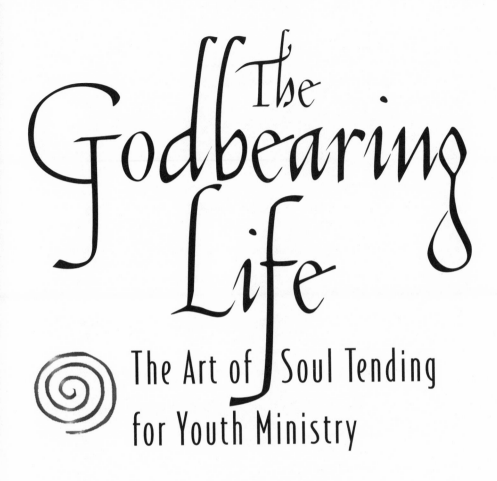

The Godbearing Life

The Art of Soul Tending
for Youth Ministry

Kenda Creasy Dean and Ron Foster

UPPER
ROOM BOOKS®
NASHVILLE

THE GODBEARING LIFE
THE ART OF SOUL TENDING FOR YOUTH MINISTRY

The Upper Room Web site: www.upperroom.org

UPPER ROOM®, UPPER ROOM BOOKS® and design logos are trade-
marks owned by The Upper Room®, Nashville, Tennessee. All rights reserved.

At the time of publication all Web sites referenced in this book were valid.
However, due to the fluid nature of the Internet some addresses may have
changed or the content may no longer be relevant.

Cover design: Bruce Gore
Seventh printing: 2004

Page 222 constitutes an extension of this copyright page.

Library of Congress Cataloging-in-Publication

Dean, Kenda Creasy, 1959–   .
    The godbearing life: the art of soul tending for youth ministry / by Kenda
Creasy Dean and Ron Foster.
            p.   cm.
    ISBN 0-8358-0858-0
    1. Church work with teenagers. 2. Teenagers—Religious life. 3.
Christian life. direction. I. Foster, Ron, 1961–   . II. Title.
BV4447.D39   1998   98-15998
259'.23—dc21   CIP

Printed in the United States of America

For Holly and Kevin
You tend our souls.

ontents

Prayer is needed for children.
Whatever religion we are, we must pray together.
Children need to learn to pray, and they need
to have their parents pray with them.
If we don't do this,
it will become difficult to become holy,
to carry on,
to strengthen ourselves in faith!

Mother Teresa, 1910-1997

Preface

THIS PROJECT was born out of two convictions. The first: Adolescents are looking for a soul-shaking, heart-waking, world-changing God to fall in love with; and if they do not find that God in the Christian church, they will most certainly settle for lesser gods elsewhere. The second conviction: So will we.

The risks facing contemporary teenagers bear solemn testimony to the church's ineffectiveness at addressing adolescence. Youth look to the church to show them something, Someone, capable of turning their lives inside out and the world upside down. Most of the time we have offered them pizza. We are painfully aware that we have sold them short. We have tended to their situations more effectively than their souls, and we have the statistics to prove it. In the meantime, our own wells have run dry. We are running out of ideas. And steam. And hope.

Ministry, least of all youth ministry, was never intended to be a service profession. Ministry is the grateful response of God's people, whose activity in the world and with one another suggests a new way of being alive. Ministry is not something we "do" to someone else. It is a holy way of living toward God and toward one another. Somehow in the din of modernity, this distinctive way of life—variously called the sanctified life, Christian perfection, or "holiness," depending upon theological perspective—often got lost along the way. We traded holiness for effectiveness, charisms for careers, soulfulness for savvy. In the meantime, youth got lost. So did many adults.

This book is our attempt to rechart a course for youth ministry in a way that fuels the faith of both young people and the adults who love them. It is also a not-very-well-disguised attempt to rechart a course for *ministry*, period, in similar directions. Our own involvement in this project evolved out of friendship and a mutual passion for God, youth and the church. We met by chance between the business sessions of the

Baltimore-Washington Annual Conference of The United Methodist Church in 1991 and discovered a shared a sense of vocation that tries to bring these passions together. Ron serves a congregation in Bethesda, Maryland, as pastor; Kenda, a youth minister-turned-academic, teaches at a mainline Protestant seminary in New Jersey. Over the past eight years we have relied on our friendship to help each other stay spiritually honest and theologically grounded both because of and in spite of our job descriptions.

We have worked together and separately on behalf of youth and the church; and while writing with shared convictions, we write with different voices and experiences. We chose not to homogenize our writing styles, which allows us to convey our individual perspectives more candidly. Every now and then you may experience a stylistic speed bump when the narrative shifts gears. We hope you will use these bumps to slow down long enough to insert your own perspective into the conversation.

We are grateful for the many people who have supported this project so enthusiastically. Special thanks belong to the participants in the Princeton Forums on Youth Ministry, who helped us hone many ideas in this book that originated in our teaching. We are also grateful for the unwitting support of the waitstaff at the Ball Park Restaurant and the staff members of Bel Air United Methodist Church, who had no idea they were serving as midwives to this project during our many meetings at these "halfway stops" between our homes.

Special thanks also go to Amy Vaughn, Emily Anderson, Laurel Brown, and Dave Stum, colleagues who offered (very) honest feedback on this book-in-process, and to Dayle Gillespie and Mike Selleck who gave the final draft a perceptive once-over. These people are treasured conversation partners in our lives and our ministries, people who exemplify the God-bearing life for us. Alice Caltrider, Pat Dinsmore, Tom Brown, and Paul Barrett provided the critical and good-humored secretarial and research support. Paul devoted a perfectly good summer to spelunking in the library for footnotes (most of which were cut from the final version), bringing his own deep love for youth, God, and the church to every page.

Above all, thanks must go to the youth who have pastored us over the course of our ministries. We have been loved and shaped by the extraordinary faith of young people who have fearlessly shot down our most valued ideas, pushed us with questions we would rather avoid, and set us on fire with their passion for God. And to our spouses, Holly and Kevin, and to our children Christine and Sara, Brendan and Shannon, your loving support was this venture's vital ingredient. We love you even more now than when we first began. You are Godbearers, every one.

INTRODUCTION

A Parable for a Paradigm Shift

Toto, I've a feeling we're not in Kansas anymore.
—Spoken by Judy Garland, The Wizard of Oz

J ENTERED PARISH life in the 1980s with a raft of ideas on how to do youth ministry that would "attend" to Jesus Christ in our contemporary cultural climate. As a pastor, my Achilles' heel was (and is) "ideas." A part of me has always identified with those old Judy Garland/Mickey Rooney movies. Whenever the kids in their neighborhood got bored, Mickey or Judy would chirp, "Hey, kids! I've got an idea…!" Like a lot of youth leaders, I have millions of ideas. Not little ones either. I can take a perfectly good small idea and whip it up into monumental proportions in no time.

I worked hard at maintaining integrity in my ideas for youth ministry; I stressed the importance of worship, avoided gimmicks without theological purpose, never built a program around the egg-in-armpit relay, tried to involve youth in the total mission of the church. I had dozens of ideas for focusing on relational ministry alone—not to mention the service projects, the Bible studies, the peer counseling training, the homeless shelter development group, the covenant discipleship meetings, and the music and drama programs. I devoured literature on the problems facing contemporary youth. I had ideas on how to do youth ministry with all of them.

Then one Sunday an eighth-grader accidentally pointed out that God had not called me to "do" youth ministry. Michelle was like a lot of thirteen-year-olds. She wanted to be a "good" kid but was drawn to dangerous friendships. She loved her parents but could not seem to establish her own autonomy without furious rebellion against them. She attended church with her family but basically could have cared less. She slid in and out of our youth program at a time when I was in the habit

11

of asking each youth, "What shall I pray for you this week?" It was one of those questions I wasn't sure anybody ever heard. It always got lost in the cracks somewhere between volleyball and Bible study. Occasionally someone would pacify me with a prayer request for his or her grand-mother, and I would promise to pray and get back about it.

Then one Sunday, as I was greeting parishioners after worship, Michelle leveled the playing field. As I was shaking her hand, she pulled me close and whispered, "What shall I pray for *you* this week?" Sur-prised, I suggested something. As her parents yanked her out the door, she looked back at me and hollered, "I'll get back to you on that!" And with a grin she was gone.

Michelle turned out to be embarrassingly true to her word. She pummeled me for prayer requests and checked back on every one of them from that day forward. But Michelle's question—my own ques-tion, heard anew—suddenly made me realize that the last thing Mi-chelle needed was another "idea." Suddenly a lot of my youth ministry "ideas" seemed just plain irrelevant. What Michelle had responded to—out of the entire smorgasbord of options available to youth in our con-gregation—was the simple question of a pastor. When Michelle donned the role of pastor herself, participating in a practice of ministry that until then had only been practiced on her behalf, Michelle's sense of who God was calling her to be began a slow but relentless transformation. And my sense of who God was calling *me* to be began a metamorpho-sis as well.

A *pastor* (the word comes from a Latin root meaning "to feed" or "to pasture") is simply somebody, anybody, with a flock. Modern churches redefined the term to serve institutional ends, but pastors are basically shepherds, people who care for sheep that belong to Someone Else. Clearly God intended this thirteen-year-old spiritual train wreck of a girl to care for her flock every bit as much as God intended me to care for mine—and what's more, Michelle's flock included me. The word *pastor* began to "morph" into something much larger than my profes-sional identity or training had suggested. I began to see my vocation less as a noun and more as a verb. I was not "a" pastor as much as someone who pastors—and what I pastored was people, not "a" church. Ideas are for those who do youth ministry. My charge had less to do with the oversight of various "ministries" (which, according to my job description, included youth) than with the oversight of souls, people who needed to be in a community of prayer far more than they needed to be part of a youth fellowship group.

After that Sunday, I tried pastoring youth instead of "doing" youth ministry—a shift in my self-understanding that proved to be as disorienting as freeing. There were subtle changes in my calendar:, I stopped showing up at youth group meetings every Sunday and started showing up at school cafeterias. I asked others to plan the beach retreat and signed on as a driver in order to have six hours locked in a car with three talkative tenth graders. I started paying real attention to the ministry I had with youth from the pulpit and at the mall, as well as in the traditional "youth ministry" venues of Sunday school, youth group, and confirmation. I invested heavily in teaching youth—and myself—how to pray.

Above all, I began spending the bulk of my "relational ministry" helping youth, even unchurched ones, develop a vocabulary of faith. I learned that pastors have permission, and even an obligation, to ask questions others do not ask. So I quit beating around the bush and asked up front: "What's going on between you and God? How goes your spiritual life?" We struggled to discern the difference between a language of deep faith and too-facile "God-talk" and found ways to risk using that language to describe ourselves and our place in the world. Together we tried to notice and critique the theology present in the hallways at school, in the kitchen at home, and in the nagging omnipresent question of both adolescents and Jesus Christ: "Who do you say that I am?"

Truth be told we continued most of our regular "youth activities" at church. But now I viewed them as subversive acts, vehicles to hot-wire for smuggling Christ into culture. I tried mightily (if haltingly) to get my own practices of prayer in order so that I could honor with real depth youth's prayer requests. I found excuses—lunch at McDonald's, nail-pounding at a work project, long walks of consolation—to ask youth about their prayers and about what they thought God was up to in their life. Every single teenager willingly talked.

Zooming In: Teenagers Entering a New Era[1]

In the years since, I have come to believe that these youth were not unique. If today is an average day, more than one-third of American teenagers will spend their free time this evening visiting with their friends.[2] In a town with 1,000 girls between the ages of eleven and seventeen, 830 will call their friends on the telephone. If this town has 1,000 boys of the same age, 400 of them will have a computer at home and about half will communicate by going on-line.

If today is an average day, the vast majority (96 percent) of teenagers—despite what we might think—will say they get along well with their parents (although they will intimate that this is not true for their best friends). Twice as many teens will admit they get along better with mom than with dad. At dinner tonight, three-fourths of them will talk about school with their parents and about half will discuss family matters or current events. If a visitor at the table were to ask, "What is the the biggest problem facing your generation?" they would probably say drugs, followed by peer pressure and AIDS. Yet if asked about the biggest problem facing them personally, most would reply, "Grades at school." Slightly more than half of these teenagers will say they attended worship this week, most of them because they wanted to.[3] Ninety-five percent of them believe in God. Nearly all of them recycle.

Still, if today is an average day, the stakes involved in being a teenager are extraordinarily high. Some pressures are perennial: About half of American students admit to cheating; one in five get drunk regularly; more than half drive recklessly.[4] But adolescents inevitably bear the scars as well as the triumphs of their generation. One out of four of them live in poverty, up 16 percent from 1978.[5] Half of all families know the devastation of divorce firsthand. Most parents work, and today's teenagers have less adult contact than any generation in human history.[6] On any given day, half of American ten- to seventeen-year-olds are in danger either of not growing up healthy or of not growing up at all.[7] For instance, in our town of 1,000 teenage girls, almost a quarter of them will become pregnant this year, and one in four new HIV infections reported by local health authorities will be diagnosed in teenagers.[8]

Teenagers today live in a world where violence and sex are givens. One-tenth of teenage boys and almost twice as many girls harbor memories of at least one botched suicide attempt.[9] Physical assault has more than doubled in American schools since 1985, with nonwhite youth the most likely victims. A quarter of all middle- and senior-high students will attend school today fearful for their safety. One in three youth over the age of ten is sexually active;[10] by age nineteen, three-fourths of white females, 85 percent of white males, 83 percent of black females, and 96 percent of black males will have had coitus at least once.[11] Most of the girls regret it.[12]

The Aweless Generation

On the whole, those of us in churches are agonizingly aware of our inability to influence America's young people significantly, especially youth at the margins. Almost three out of four religious youth workers say reaching out to youth who are living "at risk" (those in significant physical and/or emotional jeopardy) is important, but only 9 percent say they reach out to these teenagers effectively.[13] Part of what puts adolescents in harm's way is an unprecedented number of choices: paper or plastic, cable or cyberspace, brand of tofu, flavor of coffee, live with mom or dad—the array of options available to contemporary youth boggles the mind. At the same time, educating youth to discern among these choices is still a novelty for churches as well as school systems, and educating youth for theologically responsible discernment is rarer still.

The hypertext generation has made it excruciatingly clear that evangelization must aim for Christian discernment, not simply Christian information. Believing in God is not the issue; believing God *matters* is the issue. The signature quality of adolescence is no longer lawlessness but awelessness. Inundated with options and the stress that comes from having to choose among them, contemporary adolescents have lost their compass to the stars, have forgotten the way that points to transcendence. With so much vying for young people's finite attention, the responsibility of choosing among endless alternatives is overwhelming, and the path to transcendence disappears beneath a bramble of competing claims on the the soul. So go ahead, youth say to the church, impress me. When everything is true, nothing is true. Whatever.

Christian faith, on the other hand, strives for a life of discernment. Faithfulness grows in the presence of people who practice discerning the One voice among the many and who by "attending" to Jesus Christ find themselves transformed and marked as his followers. Catechesis means impressing upon youth a Life, not a religion. In the life, death, and resurrection of Jesus Christ, Christian faith offers a center that holds and not just one more alternative from which to choose.

Tending the Soul as a Paradigm for Ministry with All People

During my years of parish youth ministry I learned that pastoring teenagers is not about "youth ministry"; it is about ministry, period. Tending to the souls of the young taught me how to listen more deeply to the needs of people—*all* people—young and old alike. Ministry that addresses adolescents' most deep-seated, acted-out passions touches something fundamental to being human, not just fundamental to being a teenager. All of us long for a god, something trustworthy toward which we can direct our entire being. "To be a self," wrote H. Richard

Niebuhr, "is to have a god"[14]—although, admitted Niebuhr, sometimes we choose the God of Jesus Christ, and sometimes we choose the god of job, family, or football instead.

Choosing a god is fundamental to the process of identity formation, and we soon discover that not just any god will do. Power and status, money and education, drugs and alcohol, even friends and family are common gods toward which we direct our lives. Yet what human beings crave is an *un*common god. We hunger for a God who is bigger than the self. Choosing an inadequate god, a god too small to transcend our limitations and who therefore can neither save nor transform us, drives us to keep hunting. The difference between youth and adults often is simply that adults have stopped acting out this search, maybe because we have settled for lesser gods instead.

Some years ago Ron introduced me to the writings of Eugene Peterson, who showed me that what I was really up to with Michelle was reconceiving ministry as spiritual direction.[15] It was, and still is, an awkward transition. Resources exist for "doing" youth ministry but few are available for pastoring youth. Like many other youth leaders who instinctively have charted the same course, I regret that people I have pastored—young and old alike—have borne the bruises of ministerial bumps in the night and wrong turns earnestly taken. When Search Institute asked more than 500 religious youth workers what kind of training they most desired, more than four out of five (83 percent) said they wished they had training in ways to nurture spiritual growth—a higher percentage than any other content area.[16] Not that youth leaders are blind to the social pressures facing youth as well: Christian youth leaders are more likely to desire training in *any* aspect of their ministry than their counterparts in other church vocations.[17]

But anyone who works closely with young people—parent, pastor, educator, youth minister, coach, Scout leader, guidance counselor, community volunteer—quickly recognizes an undeniable link between social distress and spiritual famine. We wonder how to pastor a generation that trades social survival for moral suicide, youth for whom adolescence means life-and-death decisions every day. Our own faith is often desperately undernourished, and we question the integrity of sharing scrawny faith with teenagers who know the difference between Chicken McNuggets and a full-course meal and who are starved for the latter. We know how quickly teenagers rip through thin faith. Teenagers can find thin gods anywhere, and if the God of Jesus Christ isn't more awesome and substantial than the seething rush of the mosh pit, the ecstasy of LSD, the mystery of sexual intercourse, the security of cash, the affirmation of the *A* or the adulation of the cheering crowd in the gym—then why bother with Christianity at all? Thin gods are available by the dozen, and teenagers see right through them. If we're honest, so do we.

Godbearing Ministry: Improbable Pastoring

The fundamental assumption behind this book is that youth ministry is not only for youth. Youth ministry is more about ministry than about youth, for Jesus Christ calls young people—like all of us—into ministry and not into a youth program. Authentic ministry with youth is not just about spiritual discipline; it is a spiritual discipline. Youth ministry, like all ministry, requires and provides spiritual nourishment for pastors as well as for young people. In practice, this means that when our own life with God catches fire, the souls of youth and our congregations ignite as well. An overlooked irony of youth ministry is that however disjointed it may seem to those of us involved at close range, adults often envy the quality of pastoring available to the young. The reason is simple. Adults long for a circle of friends and a rhythm of life that will set their faith ablaze. Even as we celebrate young people's easy combustibility before God, we often wish those God-sparks would fall upon us.

Pastoring young people can teach us volumes about pastoring people of all ages, for youth ministry ultimately is not limited to what the church has to offer youth. It includes what youth offer us as well: a way of being "church" that takes seriously the search for God that is so acute during adolescence but so necessary for us all.

Youth ministry, therefore, is primary—not secondary—ministry, for youth are called to bear the gospel in their own right. Christians who work with young people know that authentic ministry is more than a defensive posture, despite the fact that we inherit more than a century of youth ministry traditions designed to save youth from the evils of culture and to preserve "the church of tomorrow" (see Appendix A). Adolescents have their mission fields as well as we do, and they look to the church for guidance in how to be the person God calls them to be—both in and in spite of their own culture.

Luke's Gospel tells us that a teenager named Mary came to understand her call to ministry in precisely this way. The Eastern Orthodox tradition calls Mary *Theotokos*, or "Godbearer," because she (quite literally) brought God into the world. In the biblical witness, God seems especially fond of calling upon unlikely suspects for such missions. Young people—impetuous, inexperienced, improbable choices by all accounts—figure prominently among God's "chosen" in both the Hebrew Scriptures and the New Testament. And while God does not ask any of us to bring Christ into the world as literally as did Mary, God calls each of us to become a Godbearer through whom God may enter the world again and again.

Using This Book

This book (we hope) will provoke your thinking about what a God-bearing ministry with, for, and by adolescents might look like. You may get a few "ideas" along the way. But what we really hope is that you will come away convinced that when we develop ministry based on practices that feed our own famished faith, we cannot help but pastor a "flock" as well, regardless of the age of the sheep.

Although we write as United Methodist clergy, we think "the God-bearing life" is an apt metaphor for the ministry of all Christians who work with youth in families, churches, schools, and communities, as well as for the vocation of youth themselves. By focusing on spiritual disciplines, we want to emphasize every pastor's need—no matter what the flock—to nourish his or her own soul in order to lead others to the table. The soul food we are talking about is not the disembodied, ethereal kind. Through the centuries Christian spirituality has always trafficked in the concrete details of particularity, anchored in the messy and holy weave of practices and relationships that constitutes the community of faith.

You may choose to read the four parts together or one at a time as fodder for discussion and study. In Section 1, "Redefining Youth Leadership," we define youth ministry in view of a shift taking place in youth ministry in the late twentieth and early twenty-first centuries. This shift relocates youth ministry in significant relationships between youth and adults and moves away from "programs" as the primary vehicles for youth ministry. Not only does this movement affect the nature of youth ministry, but it also has profound consequences for the identity and expectations of the youth minister. Specifically, this shift calls the youth pastor to be a Godbearer rather than a program leader.

Section 2, "Soul Tending on Holy Ground," examines the goals of Godbearing youth ministry: where it takes root and who it involves. Among the places we find God's counsel for soul tending is in the biblical story of Moses, whose initial reluctance and later frustration with his charges sound surprisingly familiar. In God's response to Moses we hear God address our own hesitancy to lead and our frustration with ministry.

Section 3, "Ingredients of the Godbearing Life," suggests the pieces composing a faithful ministry with youth: a set of holy practices and a circle of spiritual friends who draw us nearer to God and to one another. These ingredients have governed spiritual life for more than two thousand years; Jesus himself practiced them. In Section 4, "Godbearing Practices for Youth Ministry," we offer six approaches to practices that inform Godbearing ministry with youth but that are equally important for our own faith maturity as adults.

We hope the questions, exercises, and meditations at the end of each chapter will assist your vocational identity as a "Godbearer" for the youth God has entrusted to you for spiritual oversight. We intend this section to aid personal reflection and to provide learning tools for use in classrooms, youth leader support groups, leadership training events, and congregational youth ministry programs. For those of you serving as facilitators for other adult leaders, "Ideas for the Road" actively engages chapter themes in a group experience that might spark further discussion. Finally, because this book is for "people who pastor the young" and not only youth ministry "professionals" (who we hope also pastor the young), people besides those on the church payroll—parents, Scout leaders, parachurch staff people, volunteers, men's and women's groups, and teenagers—may begin to see themselves as "Godbearers" as well. And that would be a wonderful thing.

QUESTIONS AND EXERCISES

1. What flock(s) is God calling you to pastor at the moment? Which "souls" are relying on you for nourishment? If you begin to envision yourself as "pastor" to them, how will that concept change your interaction with these people?

2. List by name the youth in one of your flocks. Name a talent God has given each of them.

3. Do the youth in your flock realize that you notice their giftedness? How can those within congregations acknowledge the gifts of youth and encourage them to use those gifts to pastor others?

IDEA FOR THE ROAD

Pass out "shepherd staffs" (candy canes) to remind youth and adults that anyone with a flock is a pastor.

FARE FOR THE SOUL

Train yourself in godliness, for, while physical training is of some value, godliness is valuable in every way, holding promise for both the present life and the life to come. The saying is sure and worthy of full acceptance. For to this end we toil and struggle, because we have our hope set on the living God, who is the Savior of all people, especially of those who believe. These are the things you must insist on and teach.

—1 Timothy 4:7-11

I am no longer my own, but thine.
Put me to what thou wilt, rank me with whom thou wilt.
Put me to doing, put me to suffering.
Let me be employed by thee or laid aside for thee,
exalted for thee or brought low by thee.
Let me be full, let me be empty.
Let me have all things, let me have nothing.
I freely and heartily yield all things
to thy pleasure and disposal.
And now, O glorious and blessed God,
Father, Son, and Holy Spirit,
thou art mine, and I am thine. So be it.
And the covenant which I have made on earth,
let it be ratified in heaven. Amen.[18]

—*A Covenant Prayer in the Wesleyan Tradition*

Notes

1. We use the terms *youth, teenagers, adolescents,* and *young people* synonymously, since they all had fluid connotations over the past century. *Adolescent* usually refers to anyone who has reached puberty but who has not yet made the vocational or ideological commitments of young adulthood. The chronological age of adolescence is expanding—puberty occurs earlier and adult vocational and ideological commitments are increasingly postponed in the U. S.

2. These statistics are extrapolated from the most recent Gallup Youth Survey of 1,000 youth on more than 200 issues of ongoing social importance. The results of this survey are published in Robert Bezilla, ed., *America's Youth in the 1990s* (Princeton: George H. Gallup International Institute, 1993).

3. George H. Gallup Jr. and Robert Bezilla, *The Religious Life of Young Americans: A Compendium of Surveys on the Spiritual Beliefs and Practices of Teen-agers and Young Adults* (Princeton: George H. Gallup International Institute, 1992), 38.

4. Statistics on drinking and reckless driving and riding are taken from Search Institute statistics reported by Eugene C. Roehlkepartain and Peter C. Scales in *Youth Development in Congregations: An Exploration of the Potential and Barriers* (Minneapolis: Search Institute, 1995), 37. "Vehicle recklessness" is defined as drinking and driving, riding with a drinking driver, or failing to use seat belts. Alcohol abuse is common in early adolescence as well as late adolescence: 77 percent of eighth graders report having used alcohol, and one in four (26 percent) say they have had five or more drinks within the past two weeks (*A Matter of Time: Risk and Opportunity in the Nonschool Hours* [New York: Carnegie Corporation, 1992], 26).

5. Nearly 30 percent of all adolescents live in rural areas, and one in four rural youth are poor (*A Matter of Time*, 26).

6. Parents spend 40 percent less time with their children (the equivalent of 10–12 hours a week) than they did a generation ago. See Mary Pipher, *The Shelter of Each Other: Rebuilding Our Families* (New York: Grosset/Putnam, 1996), 231.

7. Joy G. Dryfoos, *Adolescents at Risk: Prevalence and Prevention* (New York: Oxford University Press, 1990), 107.

8. According to "Sex and America's Teenagers," a report by the Alan Guttmacher Institute, roughly one million unmarried teenage girls become pregnant each year—11 percent of all women under the age of 20. The Office of National AIDS Policy reports that one-fourth of all new HIV infections occur among those under age 21. Reported by David Friedman, "Look Who's Teaching Sex," *Good Housekeeping* (November 1996): 74–78.

9. Neil Howe and Bill Strauss, *13th Gen: Abort, Retry, Ignore, Fail?* (New York: Vintage, 1993), 83.

10. Roehlkepartain and Scales, 37.

11. C. E. Irwin and M. Shafer, "Adolescent Sexuality: Negative Outcomes of a Normative Behavior," in E. E. Rogers and E. Ginzberg, *Adolescents at Risk* (Boulder: Westview Press, 1992), 37. Quoted in David Elkind, *Ties That Stress* (Cambridge: Harvard University Press, 1994), 154–55.

12. A survey conducted by *Seventeen* found that 73 percent of girls agreed to have sex with their boyfriends in order to please the boy, but 81 percent of these girls said they later regretted giving in ("Girls Just Wanna Have Fun?" *Youthworker Update* 10 [June 1996]: 7). When Emory University's Marion Howard, who directs a teen services clinic at Atlanta's Grady Memorial Hospital, asked 1,000 sexually active girls what they really wanted to know about sex, she was surprised when 84 percent said they wanted to learn "how to say no without hurting the other person's feelings." Howard's research led to the development of a national program in peer-led sex education called "Postponing Sexual Involvement" for young adolescents in public schools (Friedman, 74).

13. Peter C. Scales et al., *The Attitudes and Needs of Religious Youth Workers: Perspectives from the Field* (Minneapolis: Search Institute, 1995); 14, 17. The term *at risk* has been called into question by many youth workers because it may label adolescents unfairly. Our assumption is that all youth live "at risk" by virtue of the fact that they are adolescents, recognizing that some combinations of external and internal liabilities create the potential for higher incidences of risky behavior.

14. H. Richard Niebuhr, *The Meaning of Revelation* (New York: Collier, 1941), 59.

15. Eugene H. Peterson, *Working the Angles: The Shape of Pastoral Integrity* (Grand Rapids: Wm. B. Eerdmans, 1987), 150.

16. Scales et al., *Attitudes and Needs*, 19.

17. Ibid., 5.

18. *The United Methodist Hymnal* (Nashville: The United Methodist Publishing House, 1989), 607.

Section 1

Redefining Youth
Leadership

ONE

From Programs to People

The most important thing about Christianity isn't "what" but "Who."

The most important thing about youth ministry isn't "what" but "Who."

$\mathcal{Y}$OUTH MINISTRY is undergoing a fundamental paradigm shift. This shift calls us back to our roots in the first-century missionary movement, when the first instance of youth ministry went on record. Without so much as a ski trip or a slice of pizza, a young man named Timothy became the protégé of a missionary named Paul. Acts 16 offers a glimpse of Paul's ministry with young Timothy who, in all likelihood, was a teenager when he joined Paul in his travels. While visiting Lystra in Asia Minor, Paul

> found a disciple there by the name of Timothy, son of a devout Jewish mother and a Greek father. Friends in Lystra and Iconium all said what a fine young man he was. Paul wanted to recruit him for their mission, but first took him aside and circumcised him so he wouldn't offend the Jews who lived in those parts. They all knew that [Timothy's] father was Greek (Acts 16:1-3, THE MESSAGE).

This brief passage merits a closer look, for Paul's ministry with Timothy says much about our own ministry with youth. In the first place, Paul does not consider Timothy an *object* of mission to be won and counted. Paul desires this young man's involvement in the church as a missionary in his own right. Nor does Paul view Timothy merely as an *instrument* of mission, a useful tool for promoting the gospel. Paul clearly is interested in Timothy's own transformation as well as in his potential for leadership. After all, Paul circumcises him—a visible sign of God's covenant with Abraham—and then apprentices Timothy before turning him loose for ministry in the larger church.

What Paul sees in Timothy is an agent of mission, a young man transformed by the gospel who can convey this transforming good news to others. Paul considers Timothy a reliable source of strength and encouragement for the body of Christ in a pagan culture. But Paul also sees Timothy as a person capable of spreading the gospel within his own culture, namely among the Jews living in Asia Minor. While Timothy's father was Greek, his mother was Jewish. According to Jewish law, Timothy was also a Jew despite his uncircumcised status. Paul did not consider circumcision necessary for Gentile converts; yet before he allows Timothy to join the missionary movement, Paul circumcises him. Why?

Paul knows that Timothy's credibility among his own people, in his own culture, must be impeccable. While Paul mentored many Gentile disciples in the early church, he was painfully aware that no one could bring the gospel to the Jews better than another Jew. In short, Paul views Timothy as someone capable of ministry to the Gentiles but also uniquely equipped to share the gospel credibly in the Jewish culture of his youth.

Recovering Relational Ministry

Paul's ministry with Timothy suggests an approach to youth ministry that churches are rediscovering. When we tend to our relationships with young people, we impart the gospel in a way that prepares them for mission. God needs their prophetic voices in the church, in the culture, and in the families they call their own. To vastly oversimplify the paradigm shift in youth ministry with one vast oversimplification: "program" is out; "relational ministry" is in. Please don't misunderstand us here. Youth programs are not the villains in this story. "Relational ministry"—contact ministry, showing up, hanging out, earning the right to be heard, or whatever you may call it—is nothing more than good-fashioned pastoral visitation in Nikes™. Furthermore, youth programs—whether in the form of youth fellowships, teen choirs, Sunday schools, club meetings, or Bible studies (to name a few)—continue to supply the pulse of most churches' youth ministry. As long as these programs integrate young people into the overall mission of the church and build significant relationships between youth and Christian adults and peers, we're all for them. Small groups of significant others are crucial for adolescents who need close primary groups beyond their families to help them test "who they are" in the process of identity formation.

However, youth ministry sets out to introduce teenagers to a *particular* relationship—namely, a relationship with Jesus Christ. In a culture where young adolescents say the ideal youth program is, among other things, physically "safe,"[1] wholesome activity has much to commend it. But *ministry* seeks more than wholesome activity. Cognitive psychology teaches us that significant relationships are the adolescent equivalent of a transitional object. Significant relationships become the "blankies" youth carry with them to mediate their passage from the familiar territory of the primary family into the public and sometimes scary world of adulthood. In these relationships, adolescents discover who they are through the eyes of trusted others. James W. Fowler has described the adolescent thought process in terms of the couplet, "I see you seeing me; I construct the *me* I think you see."[2] In the protected space of friendship, teens may safely try on various selves until they find one that fits. Of particular importance to adolescents is friendship with an adult who sees in them potential they do not necessarily see in themselves. Studies consistently indicate that a relationship with such an "adult guarantor" during adolescence outweighs all other forms of youth ministry in terms of positive influence on youth development.[3]

Therefore, most youth ministry literature argues vehemently for churches to engage in "relational ministry" on behalf of young people because teenagers *need* relationships. No question. But using relationships for the sake of meeting developmental needs represents a misguided concept of church. Youth *ministry* focuses on relationships, not only because of who teenagers are but because of who God is. God is a relationship—Christian tradition uses the relational language of Father, Son, and Holy Spirit to describe the persons of the Trinity—and this God's love is so generous the Godhead alone cannot contain it. Significant relationships with other Christians matter because they teach us something about what *God* is like—the One who can love us in spite of ourselves and who loves us passionately enough to suffer willingly on our behalf.

For this reason, we prefer the term *incarnational* to *relational* when we speak of ministry. Anybody can have a relationship, but only God takes on flesh in the incarnation of Jesus Christ. I once saw a painting of the crucifixion in which John the Baptist stands in the corner of the canvas pointing to Jesus on the cross. The image caught me. As Robin Maas has pointed out, youth ministers are John the Baptists, people who point to Jesus Christ (and who are often thought strange for doing so). They prepare the way for the Lord, clearly acknowledging that Jesus is Lord and they are *not*.[4] This reminder that I am only a John the Baptist and not a savior relieves me at first. But then I remember the ruthless constancy teens expect of those they trust. I am only human, but I may be the most convincing witness to Jesus Christ many of these young people have ever had. My responsibility to "point" them to Jesus Christ looms large.

Are we suggesting that *we* can be *Christ* to these teenagers? No. Pastors who confuse themselves with the Savior (and there are plenty) are in serious trouble, both theologically and professionally. Anyway, teenagers know we are conning them. Karl Barth preferred the term *witness* to describe the kind of ministry we are suggesting, reserving the term *incarnation* for God alone.[5] Barth's point is well taken, especially in light of many popular youth ministry texts that imply that incarnational ministry calls adults to "model" Jesus Christ for young people, something well beyond our sinful capabilities even on our best days.

The point of incarnational ministry is not to model Christ so youth will follow *us* but—to use Martin Luther's language—to become "Christs" for our neighbor, incarnating Christ's love transparently so that youth will follow *him*.[6] Paul put the matter succinctly: "It is no longer I who live, but it is Christ who lives in me" (Gal. 2:20). Incarnational language underscores the fact that we cannot point to Christ on our own. Our arms get tired; our compasses are off; we point to impersonators rather than the true Son of God. Only the power of the Holy Spirit makes ministry possible at all, and the presence of the Spirit transforms us into an "incarnation" of another sort: the "flesh and bones" of the church, the body of Christ. As John Wesley argued, the fact that you and I are also "children of God" in no way compromises the unique position of Jesus Christ as God's only begotten Son. But it does imply that we unashamedly bear the "marks" of a Christian, those family resemblances that make Christ recognizable through us.[7]

And so, while there is only one Incarnation, we cannot get around the fact that Christ expects each of us to "incarnate" his love relentlessly to the young. Most of us have someone in our lives who has incarnated Jesus, someone who has put flesh and bones on God's love for us. Most of us can't remember what we learned in Sunday school or youth group, but we have an indelible memory of *people* who taught us. To paraphrase a wise professor, curriculum doesn't teach; people do. Denying that we are the Christ (which all John the Baptists vigorously and rightly deny) does not change the fact that we are called to be Christ*like*, to bear that family resemblance that causes all who meet us to see God's face in us and to know immediately to Whom we belong. At the end of the day, it is still true that God chooses human beings over "ministries" as God's preferred means of witness.

Ousting the One-Eared Mickey Mouse

The point of incarnational ministry is that the Person *is* the program. This shift in youth ministry represents a radical historical departure. For over a century, Euro-American, middle-class congregations—which for all their limitations have defined youth ministry literature since the early 1900s—have equated youth ministry with youth groups (see Appendix A). During a youth ministry consultation for a cluster of Maryland churches, one pastor asked if I might meet with his small congregation individually. "We're so much smaller than the rest of these churches," he said. "We only have one hundred people in worship on Sunday morning. But we have a lot of teenagers—about thirty every Sunday in worship, about the same number in Sunday school—and so we really need to do youth ministry."

Needless to say, I was thinking: *One-third of the people in the pews every Sunday are teenagers? Why don't you come and consult with me!* This pastor assumed that because his congregation did not have a youth group, his church did not "do" youth ministry. During our conversation, he quickly realized that his congregation had a great deal to offer this cluster of churches in terms of youth ministry. Besides a cadre of caring adults who knew every teenager in the congregation by name, this church's youth "program" turned out to be regular and intergenerational responses to crises. After a hurricane, flood, or fire, the congregation—teens included—loaded up a caravan of tents and supplies and headed to the crisis site. They camped out and served meals to local relief workers and persons in need. These weekends became high points in the life of the congregation and reminded youth and adults alike of their unique calling as Christians to a troubled world.

Since the late nineteenth century, when Christian Endeavor popularized the "youth group" model of ministry, church youth fellowships have represented efforts to protect young people from the seductions of popular culture, a movement that began in the 1840s with the YMCA's response to teenagers lured to the cities by industrial jobs. By 1900, psychology recognized adolescence as a distinct and highly spiritual stage in the life cycle, and youth organizations sprang up—first in churches and soon after in schools—in order to disciple teenagers through the "storm and stress" of sexual maturation. The most prominent youth organization by far in the early twentieth century was the church youth group. These youth groups promised Christian friendship and a wholesome environment for youth, assuming they would later spring fullgrown into adult church membership. Such programs did provide a degree of protection from risky behavior. Even today, youth involved in religious programs are somewhat less "at risk" than youth in the general population, although whether this protection stems from the religious nature of these programs, or simply from their availability, remains unclear.[8]

The problem, we have discovered after a hundred years of youth groups, is that the youth group is notoriously unreliable for fostering ongoing *faith*. The youth group model—sometimes referred to as the "one-eared Mickey Mouse"[9] model of ministry—created an environment in which youth, isolated in an "ear" on top of Mickey's head, had only marginal contact with the rest of the body of Christ. The congregation worshiped in the sanctuary; youth met in the basement. The congregation gathered on Sunday mornings; youth gathered on Sunday nights. The congregation listened to sermons; youth heard "youth talks." The congregation had Bible study; youth had devotions. The congregation had a budget; youth had a bake sale.

Nothing that happened in the life of the congregation as a whole looked even vaguely familiar to youth ghettoized in youth groups and vice versa. In parachurch ministries, the gap between youth group and congregation widened further. Although parachurch ministries preserved certain theological foci commonly lost in congregational youth groups (for instance, the emphasis on repentance and personal salvation), parachurch clubs met at school or in homes during the week, and most had only minimal connections—if any—to a worshiping congregation.

The upshot of the overwhelming dominance of youth-group models of ministry was a deepening chasm between youth ministry and the theology of the church as a whole. When youth graduated from the "youth group"—the only form of ministry many young people had ever experienced—they effectively graduated from church as well. Those who returned to church as adults often found worship an alien experience, a distant second to the warmth and intimacy they remembered from the youth ministry of their teen years.

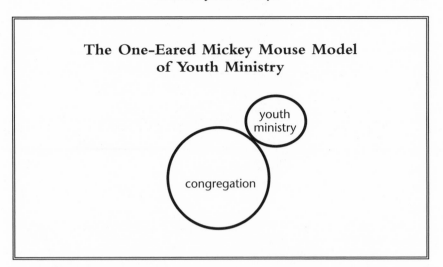

The One-Eared Mickey Mouse Model
of Youth Ministry

By now the exodus of adolescents from mainline churches is both legendary and sobering. About half of Christian youth workers report having "some" trouble keeping ten- and eleven-year-olds involved in church; 70 percent report having "a great deal of trouble" retaining seventh through ninth graders. Nearly all of youth workers report a great deal of trouble involving tenth through twelfth graders.[10] Most of these youth do not drop out to attend other churches; the majority of these youth attend no church at all.[11] Eighty percent of American adults report having dropped out of church (60 percent) or diminished their participation (20 percent) for two or more years during their own adolescence, a pattern visited doubly upon their sons and daughters. Today more than half of the youth who attended church as children have disappeared from church involvement by the time they are seventeen.[12] Even youth who go through confirmation tend to view the ceremony not as a rite of passage into the life of the church but as graduation out of it.[13]

Entering the Mission Field of Adolescence

Incarnational youth ministry requires us to view adolescence as a mission field. In this case, the mission field is a life stage rather than a spot on the globe, but it is often every bit as foreign to us as unfamiliar geography. We, like Paul, need to understand the term *missionary* theologically rather than historically. Fearful of the ideological baggage that often accompanied missionary movements throughout the church's history, many mainline churches have shunned "mission" talk, hoping to shed its colonial connotations. But *missionary* simply means "one who is sent," especially one who is sent across boundaries. The early church believed that the archetypal "mission" was the Triune God's "sending" of the Son to earth—an act of love that crossed every human boundary imaginable: life and death, divinity and humanity, space and time.

It helps me to imagine a continuum to describe my self-image on this score. Posted on one end of the continuum is a snapshot of me in my best "missionary" attire; on the other end is a picture of my "program director" self. I don't intend to sacrifice my missionary call for the cruise director status of program director. It sneaks up on me while I am doing my best work. I am terribly busy; I'll pray next week. I am unfailingly enthusiastic; I just have to recruit a few more volunteers before I can take a day off. I have limited time and energy; I suppose I should concentrate on the youth who are already "in" the church. I am convincingly well-organized; with parental involvement and youth meetings planned from now until Pentecost, I can let go of this program and go on to another.

We have such good reasons for being program directors—which is the point. There are no good reasons for being missionaries, only faithful ones. Mission work requires a different way of thinking about our task than program ministry does. To begin with, mission work insists on careful study of theological identity questions:

- Who is God?
- Who is the other?
- Who am I?

These questions circumscribe the scope of a missionary's ministry. Missionaries' own faith authorizes their credibility. They know Christ well enough to introduce him around. Missionaries also must genuinely respect and participate in a non-Christian culture without being co-opted by it and have a deep and sympathetic understanding of those served. Like every Peace Corps volunteer, youth leaders need to enter our mission field armed with substantial anthropological data and language facility. Youth ministry compels us to *inhabit* an alien culture rather than just visit and pose for snapshots. This habitation does not mean that we *adopt* youth culture as our own. One sign of healthy adult leadership is the ability to be one *with* youth without becoming one *of* them (see Appendix B). These missionaries know where "self" stops and "other" begins. They know how and when to say unapologetically, "You're fourteen; I'm not."

Suppose, for instance, a man named Eric responds to Emmanuel Church's plea for a youth director. Eric "comes in" and promptly receives a specific task: the oversight of youth ministry in the congregation. The education and age-level ministry committees in the congregation support "the youth" by sponsoring occasional fundraisers on their behalf. Members of these committees inquire with interest about what Eric is doing to meet the needs of young people, needs they recognize as being acute. All concerned affect a "causal" attitude: what Eric does (*a*) will cause *b* to happen (or in retrospect: if only Eric had done *x*, we could have avoided *y*). Eric's relationship with youth will "cause" them to develop an interest in Christ; the youth's involvement in Sunday school will "cause" them to know the Bible; their experience in youth group will "cause" them to mature in their faith, and so on. The congregation has confidence in Eric. Church members expect him to get youth ministry "done," although because of their progressive thinking, they do not expect him to do it alone. They believe his task is finite; once he completes it, Eric may go home (which, of course, he seldom does).

Emmanuel Church recruited Eric because of his obvious love of teenagers as well as for his enthusiasm, organizational abilities, responsibility, and initiative. All of his references described him as a "self-starter." Under Eric's leadership, the youth will become enthusiastic and responsible church members, familiar with the congregational culture and more visible in the pews. The church members perceive Eric as an electric current that youth can readily "plug into." One of Eric's few obvious faults is his tendency to set aside personal relationships in order to have more time to respond to youth who find themselves in life-threatening situations and who respond well to his counsel. Ultimately Eric reports to the personnel committee of the congregation. As long as the committee is happy, Eric may pursue ministry any way he chooses—unless, of course, he is like the majority of youth ministers who quit after eighteen months (or less) out of sheer exhaustion and spiritual, social, and vocational isolation. We all know an Eric: He had a great time in ministry while it lasted, but now he works at the bank.

But what if Emmanuel Church had approached their youth minister more like the mission-minded All Saints' Church down the street? All Saints' recently gave over the reins of the congregation's youth ministry to a woman named Emily. All Saints' did not invite Emily to "come in" to the church to "do" a ministry; they sent her *out* from the congregation into a mission field defined as the local junior-high and senior-high schools. This mission is supported by the entire church, not just the education department. Emily's ministry, in fact, extends the church's mission as a congregation and therefore is supported by the whole spectrum of subgroups within the congregation. This support includes but is not limited to monetary assistance. Emily understands youth ministry as a life work, not a career. Perhaps her youth ministry will be as a parent or senior pastor someday, or perhaps at some point she will use her pastoral gifts in a secular role as a teacher, social worker, or health care professional. The point is that Emily believes she is called to youth ministry, not assigned to it, and that this ministry—in whatever context—has been handed her by God, not by a hiring committee.

Neither Emily nor the All Saints' congregation harbors any illusions about getting youth ministry done. They recognize that youth ministry, like all ministry, is an ongoing state of readiness, not a task with a beginning and an end. As a result, Emily spends far less time planning to meet teenagers' needs than she does figuring out how to be present with them, how to be available in the dark corners as well as on the broad plains of adolescence. As a missionary, Emily knows she can never adequately feed all the adolescent hunger that surrounds her. She is perennially underresourced. Experience has taught her that nothing she plans will "cause" faith, and a good deal can happen that actually obstructs it. Still, in spite of everything, she has learned that Christ prevails where she cannot. For this reason, Emily's faith and sense of vocation are the credentials that won her the mantle of "youth minister," not her educational pedigree or her desire to volunteer.

Emily's relationship with Christ informs everything she does in ministry. She treasures and nurtures her prayer life both privately and "in the field." The congregation gives her one day a month for spiritual direction and encourages her to spend her continuing education time developing her pastoral identity as well as skills for working with youth. Youth meetings, retreats, and Bible studies all figure into her schedule; and she places worship at the center of youth ministry.

Yet Emily leaves room to introduce youth to Jesus Christ implicitly as well, serving as the church's visible presence at band concerts, beach parties, and a local halfway house for recovering teen alcoholics. Emily sees herself as an electric wire, not its current—she knows her ministry's value depends upon remaining solidly connected to Jesus Christ on one end and to teenagers on the other. She knows she bears a current much stronger than she. Emily believes in *youth's* ministry, and she looks for ways youth can minister in their own right, serving as missionaries in their families, schools, and culture.

A Continuum for Youth Ministry

	Program leader	Missionary
Relationship to congregation	Comes in ━━━━━━━	Sent out
Relationship to task	Assigned ━━━━━━━	Called
Support system	Age-level ministry ━━━	Entire congregation
Educational concern	What (activity) ━━━━━	Who (incarnation)
Purpose	Meet needs ━━━━━━	Love people in Christ's name
Attitude	Therefore ━━━━━━	Nevertheless
Commitment	Limited (task completion) ━━	Radical (life work)
Adjective	Responsible ━━━━━━	Faithful
Theological method	Socialization ━━━━━	Evangelization
Self-image	Electric current ━━━━━	Electric wire
Accountability	Congregation ━━━━	God

Reality Check

In real life, of course, no clear line divides the work of a missionary and a youth director. Our ministries—and our church's expectations—inevitably fall somewhere between these poles. Many times we see ourselves as missionaries while our congregations see us as program directors *par excellence*. Then our task becomes helping the congregation reconceive youth ministry as mission. The images of missionary and program director serve us best as compass arrows, guiding us toward some paths of ministry and away from others even while we face daily realities like finding an extra driver and fixing the temperamental VCR.

The image of the missionary goes before us like a pillar of fire, remind-ing us to fix our attention on Yahweh even when the desert seems to stretch on forever.

What is at stake in the missionary/program director distinction is, in the words of Eugene Peterson, following a holy vocation instead of a religious career.[14] It is easy to "fake" ministry. Unlike being an electri-cian, where incompetence becomes obvious when you turn on the lights, most of us can "get by" in ministry. The ability to say grace in public and a modicum of interpersonal savvy suffice, at least for a while. We do not intend to fool people. We have good instincts, and on most days we can rid ourselves of the nagging suspicion that we might be frauds. Anyway, the church rewards us. Members celebrate our energy, commend our creativity, and admire our busyness. People wonder how we do it. Amazing, they say, how well we "relate" to the youth.

But relating to youth is a far cry from taking responsibility for their souls. People who pastor youth have signed on with God to be held accountable, not for teenagers' wholesomeness but for their *holiness*. With each passing Sunday school lesson we bide our time, but we are like chil-dren playing catch with hand grenades in the garage, blithely unaware of the power—and the danger—in our hands. The indictment to which contemporary youth ministry is vulnerable is careless handling of the soul. We have related to youth admirably; we play catch exceptionally well. But in teaching youth to navigate culture, we have failed to enlist them in the missionary movement of Jesus Christ.

In Search of Timothy

At some level, we know our job is to tend seeds. According to the para-ble, the seed is the word of God (Luke 8:11)—and God alone plants it. The question is what kind of soil will nourish it? Christ creates the con-verts, but he has left us in charge of preparing the land. Obviously some soil takes more work than others, and some is downright hostile. A lot of days we scan the "Want Ads" for saner employment. However, if we do our job faithfully, we not only prepare the earth to receive the seed; we fertilize it so that it bears fruit. Youth ministry as mission creates mis-sionaries, healthy seedlings to be sure, but also Christians who, like Timothy, will mature to bring God's good news to their own culture.

It is worth pointing out that, for all the trust Paul invested in Tim-othy's youthful capabilities, Timothy's ministry had its share of problems. Paul had to bail Timothy out of trouble at least once with the divisive church at Corinth. Paul intervened himself and finally sent Titus to resolve the problem (see 1 Cor. 4:17; 2 Cor. 12:18). Paul's most famous words to Timothy admonish him to stop doubting his effectiveness as a young person in ministry:

> Don't let anyone put you down because you're young. Teach believers with your life: by word, by demeanor, by love, by faith, by integrity. Stay at your post reading Scripture, giving counsel, teaching. And that special gift of ministry you were given when the leaders of the church laid hands on you and prayed—keep that dusted off and in use (1 Tim. 4:12-14, THE MESSAGE).

Teenagers need faithful adults to represent the gospel, to shore up their faith, and to guide them in mission. We do not know the genesis of Paul and Timothy's relationship, and it is fair to assume that they did not spend every waking moment deep in the throes of theological discussion. But Paul did not win Timothy for God's mission with endless variations of broomball either. Paul's relationship with Timothy underscores a kind of youth ministry that we are rediscovering: Youth ministry is less about counting converts than about creating missionaries capable of teaching the believers with their lives because others have taught them with *their* lives first.

QUESTIONS AND EXERCISES

1. Years ago I participated in a seminar where educator and youth pastor David Stone led this exercise to illustrate incarnational ministry. Think back to the one person, besides your parents, who most positively influenced you during your teenage years. In one sentence, state the person's name and his or her meaningful influence in your life. (I often lead this exercise by sharing my own sentence: "Reverend John believed in me.") Now repeat the same sentence, substituting the name "Jesus" for the person you remember. (Now my sentence is "Jesus believed in me.") After repeating the sentence a second time, reflect on the statement: "Incarnational theology means that God always comes to us through a person." What advantages does this theology offer youth ministry? What dangers do you foresee?

2. Locate yourself on the "Continuum for Youth Ministry" on page 35. How would your ministry be different if you approached your role as a missionary?

3. Evaluate the status of your own "healthy adulthood." Answer the questions in Appendix B ("Guidelines for Healthy Adult Leaders of Youth"). With a trusted partner, discuss the points at which you feel most comfortable and most uncomfortable.

IDEA FOR THE ROAD

Write a note to the person you named in #1 or (if no longer living) to someone close to that person. Share your thanks for his or her witness (intentional or unintentional).

FARE FOR THE SOUL

The whole concept of God taking on a human shape,…had simply never made any sense to me. That was because, I realized one wonderful day, it was so simple. For people with bodies, important things like love have to be embodied. That's all. God had to get embodied, or else people with bodies would never in a trillion years understand about love.[15]

—Jane Vonnegut Yarmolinsky, *Angels without Wings*

Notes

1. *A Matter of Time: Risk and Opportunity in the Nonschool Hours* (New York: Carnegie Corporation, 1992), 77.

2. James W. Fowler, *Stages of Faith: The Psychology of Human Development and the Quest for Meaning* (New York: Harper and Row, 1981), 73.

3. See Kenda Creasy Dean, "A Synthesis of the Research on, and a Descriptive Overview of, Protestant, Catholic, and Jewish Religious Youth Programs in the United States," working paper (Washington, D.C.: Carnegie Council on Adolescent Development, February 1991), 51.

4. Robin Maas developed this theme eloquently in "Christ and the Adolescent: Piper or Prophet?" *Christ and the Adolescent: A Theological Approach to Youth Ministry* (Princeton: Princeton Theological Seminary, 1996), 35–47.

5. See Karl Barth, chap. 16 in *Church Dogmatics IV: The Doctrine of Reconciliation*, vol. 1, trans. G. W. Bromiley (Edinburgh: T. & T. Clark, 1962).

6. Martin Luther, "The Freedom of a Christian" (1520), *Martin Luther: Selections from His Writings*, ed. John Dillenberger (Garden City, N.Y.: Anchor Books, 1961), 75.

7. See John Wesley, "The Witness of the Spirit," *Sermons on Several Occasions* (London: Epworth Press, 1980), 111–123.

8. Dean, "Synthesis"; 19–20, 22–28.

9. Stuart Cummings-Bond, "The One-Eared Mickey Mouse," *Youthworker* 6 (Fall 1989): 76.

10. Peter C. Scales et al., *The Attitudes and Needs of Religious Youth Workers: Perspectives from the Field* (Minneapolis: Search Institute, 1995), 13.

11. Wade Clark Roof and William McKinney, *American Mainline Religion: Its Changing Shape and Future* (New Brunswick, N. J.: Rutgers University Press, 1987), 18.

12. Dean R. Hoge, Benton Johnson, and Donald A. Luidens, *Vanishing Boundaries: The Religion of Mainline Protestant Baby Boomers* (Louisville: Westminster John Knox, 1994), 75.

13. See Richard R. Osmer, *Confirmation: Presbyterian Practices in Ecumenical Perspective* (Louisville: Geneva Press, 1996), 4.

14. Eugene H. Peterson, *The Contemplative Pastor: Returning to the Art of Spiritual Direction* (Grand Rapids: Wm. B. Eerdmans, 1989), 41.

15. Jane Vonnegut Yarmolinsky, *Angels without Wings: A Courageous Family's Triumph over Tragedy* (Boston: Houghton Mifflin, 1987), 74.

TWO
From Gung-Ho to Godbearer

Here am I, the servant of the Lord.
Let it be with me according to your word.
—*Mary, a teenage girl*

M Y SUPERVISING pastor in seminary was a seasoned Southern parson named Sam Stanley. Sam pastored a little chapel in Arlington, Virginia, and people packed it to the gills every Sunday. You could easily underestimate Sam because of his laid-back style and bone-deep gentility. He wore his considerable clout like an undershirt, unconscious of it. Yet Sam was both the strongest and most subtle pastor I have ever known. Despite his determined opinions, he seldom spoke at meetings. He made himself available for appointments or counseling or coffee. He was an ace preacher; worship was memorable and moving. He and his wife Ruth ate lunch together every day.

But Sam had an ear to the ground like a Cherokee warrior. The least vibration in the grass sent him flying to his Volkswagen Rabbit, which had about four million miles on it. A minute's time would find him standing at a parishioner's front door (unannounced) to "check in," as he put it. "There's really only time for two things in ministry," he drawled one afternoon as we zipped around the beltway to "check in" —without warning—on the fifth or sixth person that afternoon. "Lead a fine worship. Visit the people. The program, leave to volunteers and gung-ho seminarians."

As a gung-ho seminarian at the time, I wasn't sure what to make of that remark. I liked programs; I was good at them. Yet whether he intended to or not, Sam gave me a great gift that day: permission to place the worship of God and the daily needs of human beings at the center of ministry—permission, in other words, to be a pastor instead of somebody bound by a job description. *Being* a pastor, I have come to discover, is infinitely harder than *doing* ministry. And yet who I am with youth, and not what I do with them, is what they will remember twenty years from now. Who I am with youth ultimately determines whether my ministry points to Jesus Christ or to something else. All those Sunday night meetings, service projects, whitewater rafting trips, and spaghetti dinners matter *only* to the extent that they serve as occasions to live my faith in the presence of youth and to remind youth that they have a faith to live too.

Fatigue as a Spiritual Gift

After a few years of ministry—three, to be exact—the program I worked with began to seem weary. That's about how long it took to attend enough continuing education events in youth ministry before they all started sounding alike. If God made me gung-ho, God also made me *tired*—and not just because I needed more sleep. My soul was on empty; I was running on fumes, and the ministry entrusted to my care was too. The depressing truth was that youth were not the only ones who needed more substantial faith; *so did I.* The college students I met for lunch were not the only ones in spiritual jeopardy; *so was I.* What a humiliating revelation. Here I was supposed to be teaching them to pray, immersing them in scripture, involving them with the poor— and when was the last time I did any of that for the sake of my soul and not for the sake of my job? God knew I was faking it, and I knew I was faking it; but I didn't know how to stop faking it without "dropping out" altogether, an option with plenty of appeal but that was out of the question (just ask my spouse and my banker).

Often fatigue is the consequence—and the warning sign—not of too many roles but of too shallow roots. Recently I learned that giant sequoias, weighted by huge branches that by all rights should cause them to fall over, remain upright because their roots actually grow together in an intertwined system. The sequoias hold one another up because they are connected at the root. Despite the fact that our responsibilities to others forever seem to seduce us away from our souls, God intends us to live in community, connected by our roots in Jesus Christ, lest we topple over. "Remember," Paul wrote to the Romans who were growing in faith, "you aren't feeding the root; the root is feeding you" (Romans 11:18, THE MESSAGE).

No wonder people who pastor youth stress out, wear out, and burn out faster than people in almost any other form of ministry. Our root systems are in terrible shape. A Carnegie Council on Adolescent Development study identified a "lack of networking" as one of the most devastating problems facing religious youth workers. The absence of these networks reinforces the image of youth ministry as an alienated, isolated profession.[1] Most of us do not know what the church across the street (much less around the world) is doing with youth, so we reinvent the wheel every day. We are neither connected to Jesus Christ nor to each other in ways that adequately feed our souls or the souls of young people. These connections are not "skills" for more effective youth ministry. They shape who we are, called by God and sent out in the name of Jesus Christ to change the world. Our integrity as pastors depends upon these connections. So does our survival.

In the next few chapters, we will suggest that our connection to Christ and to one another—fundamental to the faith of young people but also to the faith of their leaders—comprises the backbone of authentic youth ministry in which adults as well as youth grow in faith. This kind of ministry requires a significant change not only in the way we approach youth ministry but in the way we imagine ourselves as pastors. Surprisingly, we get some help in this transition from the writer of Luke's Gospel, whose account of God's "youth ministry" provides a model for our own.

Becoming Godbearers: Youth Ministry as a Spiritual Discipline

In the sixth month of Elizabeth's pregnancy with John the Baptist, one of her young cousins named Mary is "touched by an angel." In Luke 1:26-38, the story begins this way:

> In the sixth month the angel Gabriel was sent by God to a town in Galilee called Nazareth, to a virgin engaged to a man whose name was Joseph, of the house of David. The virgin's name was Mary. And [the angel] came to her and said, "Greetings, favored one! The Lord is with you!" But [Mary] was much perplexed by [the angel's] words, and pondered what sort of greeting this might be.

Perplexed? Startled from stem to stern is more like it. *Angelos*, or angel, means "messenger" in Greek; an angel is one who bears God's message to others. Gabriel is having a busy, if not altogether smooth, season. Just six months ago he had made a similar visit to Zechariah, and we can hardly blame Zechariah for being suspicious. "How will I know that Elizabeth will have a son as you say?" Zechariah had demanded. "I am an old man, and my wife is way past the soccer mom years."

Maybe Gabriel did not expect to be challenged; maybe he thought his angelic appearance provided evidence enough. In any case, the

Annunciation had not gone as smoothly as he had hoped. "How will you know?" sputters Gabriel, groping perhaps for his photo ID. "Because I am Gabriel; I stand in the presence of God who has sent me to speak to you and bring you good news!" And then Gabriel pronounces the most prolonged case of laryngitis on biblical record: "Because you did not believe my words, which will be fulfilled in their time, you will become mute, unable to speak, until the day these things occur" (Luke 1:20).

So here is Gabriel again in verse 26, only the stakes are higher—and God has sent him to a teenager. She is young, probably thirteen or fourteen years old, and a "virgin." She is uncompromised: as whole and unbroken as the day she was born, uncompromised by the outside world. In short, she has integrity. God wants someone with integrity to bring God into the world; and so, as the Gospel writer tells us, Gabriel comes to a virgin named Mary.

Gabriel begins as he always begins, as God always begins (since this is God's message, not Gabriel's), with the affirmation of God's creation. "Greetings, favored one!" Gabriel proclaims to Mary. "The Lord is with you!" Before she hears anything else, God wants Mary to hear this: She is favored. Eugene H. Peterson paraphrases Gabriel's greeting this way:

> "Good morning!
> You're beautiful with God's beauty,
> Beautiful inside and out!
> God be with you" (Luke 1:28, THE MESSAGE).

Although a teenager, Mary need not "find" her self. Her identity is a gift, bestowed upon her by God alone. *Who am I?* Mary may wonder. And God replies, "You are my favored one, beloved and beautiful to me."

In truth, Mary does not stand much chance for an identity *apart* from God. She is too young to have had time to achieve much on which to base her identity. She is too poor to purchase her place in society. Add to this the fact that she is female, which means that even if she did have accomplishments or social stature to her credit, they likely would have gone unrecognized because of her gender. All of this makes Mary a most unlikely candidate for helping God save the world, which is precisely why God enlists her. Nothing about Mary suggests that she can be who she is apart from God's favor of her.

Developmental psychology has taught us that if we gain nothing else from adolescence, we must obtain a coherent sense of self, or "identity," to navigate future life stages successfully. Psychology also tells us that we form our identities through the eyes of other people. Mirrors matter to teenagers (just ask anyone who has had to share a bathroom with one) and not just because of adolescent egocentrism. Teenagers use mirrors to obtain clues of consistency amidst the sea of changes they see and feel in themselves. They are looking for a center that holds despite the seismic changes in their bodies and the proliferation of roles they now must play. The most important mirrors, of course, are the eyes of peers and respected adults who reflect a "self" that young people accept almost without question.

For this reason, relationships and peer groups (even church youth groups) play a pivotal part as youth navigate the "mirroring" process necessary to identity formation. In young adolescents, the undeveloped self is vulnerable to fusion with outside influences. As a result, the young adolescent's peer of choice is a "chum"—another individual who really serves as a projection of the young teenager's idealized self. Young adolescents do not distinguish between themselves and their "chums," which makes them more vulnerable to peer pressure than their older brothers and sisters and more prone to thinking alike, dressing alike, and wanting to be in the same clubs and sports as their peers.

By midadolescence the self has begun to take shape, so moderate differentiation between the adolescent and his or her peers begins to be possible. The need for relationship is still paramount, especially among girls; differentiation does not require separation, especially not at this point in the life cycle. The clique, a circle of similar others, replaces the chum, who primarily has been an extension of the self. Having many friends is important at this age because no one person offers a totally accurate reflection of the self. Multiple reflections serve as correctives to one another; the overly affirming reflection can counterbalance the overly critical one.

By the time youth reach college or young adulthood, identity formation is well under way (although not usually complete until the mid-to-late twenties or at whatever point the youth chooses and enters into enduring career and ideological commitments). An older adolescent can acknowledge others as truly "other" without jeopardizing his or her own sense of self. In "trying out" this new appreciation for otherness, older adolescents may develop friendships with persons wildly different from close friends of their past. The "clique" diminishes in importance as youth no longer need an endless stream of self-affirmation. In place of the clique arises the "significant other," someone the older adolescent acknowledges as "other" and still values in a relationship that often moves toward intimacy.

The adolescent need for relationships is so strong that teenagers will chart this course instinctively. But for the church to be missing from this process represents a serious, if not lethal, sin of omission. Significant relationships with Christians are crucial if we stand any chance of forming an identity that takes into account who we are in God's eyes. Only God's eyes reflect who we truly are; all others distort, even the loving eyes of peers, parents, and significant adults. Only through the church do we hear God's message to Mary: "Greetings, favored one!" And we hear it before we are old enough to "do" much of importance—whether we have noteworthy accomplishments or none at all, whether we are boys or girls or youth or adults. Of all the mirrors that help us establish identity, only the church allows us to see ourselves as God sees us: favored, beloved, blessed.

So the angel continues,

> "Do not be afraid, Mary, for you have found favor with God. And now, you will conceive in your womb and bear a son, and you will name him Jesus. He will be great, and will be called the Son of the Most High, and the Lord God will give to him the throne of his ancestor David. He will reign over the house of Jacob forever, and of his kingdom there will be no end" (Luke 1:30-33).

God's message to Mary and to us has two parts—affirmation and expectation. *Because* Mary is beloved by God, *because* she has found favor in God's eyes, God has a plan for her. It is an astonishing plan: never mind the angel in the living room, never mind the impossible conception, never mind the fact that this child will grow up to be king.

The child's name must have caught Mary's attention. *Jesus*, a derivation of the Hebrew name Joshua, means "YHWH will save." Something revolutionary is happening here: God has just asked a *teenager* to bring *salvation* into the world! Gabriel has never delivered a message like this before to an adult, much less to an adolescent! Frederick Buechner renders the scene from Gabriel's point of view:

> She struck the angel Gabriel as hardly old enough to have a child at all, let alone this child, but he'd been entrusted with a message to give her, and he gave it.
>
> He told her what the child was to be named, and who he was to be, and something about the mystery that was to come upon her. "You mustn't be afraid, Mary," [the angel] said.
>
> As he said it, he only hoped she wouldn't notice that beneath the great, golden wings he himself was trembling

with fear to think that the whole future of creation hung now
on the answer of a girl.[2]

How much do we ask of youth—ninety minutes on Sunday night? a
retreat or a car wash? "Come on," we say enticingly. "Worship only lasts
an hour." But God has no qualms about making the most profound request in human history of a teenager. Mary is not altogether naive to
the situation: "How can this be, since I am a virgin?" she wants to know.
We always read that question at Christmas with a mixture of awe and
wonder, although from the lips of most thirteen-year-olds (not to mention most of the rest of us) it would have sounded a lot more like
Zechariah: "Yeah, right—how can this be, since I'm a virgin?"

That is how most of us greet God's call to us. Impossible. Out of the
question. There is just no way. When God asks Moses to pack for Egypt:
"How can this be, since I am slow of speech and slow of tongue?" When
Sarah hears that she will bear a son: "How can this be, since I can't even
remember menopause?" When Zechariah learns that Elizabeth will
conceive: "How can this be, since we are older than the hills?"

Many people approach youth ministry this way too, and we still use
the same excuses. "How can this be, that you're asking me to teach Sunday school? I can't talk to kids." "How can this be, that I should spear-
head the mission trip? I'm too old for this!" "You want us to volunteer
with the youth? How can this be, since we are virgins?"

Gabriel replies with the obvious but overlooked answer to each of
us: This is God's miracle, not ours.

> "The Holy Spirit will come upon you, and the power of the
> Most High will overshadow you; therefore the child to be
> born will be holy; he will be called Son of God. And now,
> your relative Elizabeth in her old age has also conceived a son;
> and this is the sixth month for her who was said to be barren.
> For nothing will be impossible with God" (Luke 1:35-37).

The Holy Spirit is more than a pick-me-up in this story. According to
Gabriel, the Holy Spirit, the very power of God, will be sure that credit
for this wonder goes to God and no one else. As with every pregnant
woman, people gradually will turn their attention away from Mary and
toward the miracle within her. As with every new mother, passersby will
stop looking at Mary and focus on the child, a foreshadowing of events
to come. "He must increase, but I must decrease," observed John the
Baptist (John 3:30). "It is no longer I who live, but it is Christ who lives
in me," proclaimed Paul to the Galatians (2:20). The Holy Spirit will

overshadow you, Mary, so that God's salvation will take center stage. For nothing will be impossible with God.

And so Mary, after "pondering" for how long—minutes, days, weeks, we don't know how long—says, "Okay. Here am I, the servant of the Lord; let it be with me according to your word." We quibble over the strength of God's invitation in this story. Is God issuing an invitation or merely informing Mary of her destiny? God's salvation is coming with or without Mary's help. But God does not seize Mary and take her by force. God does not enter this girl, or any of us, without our consent. After all, we don't know how many stops Gabriel made before he got to Mary's house.

What sets Mary apart from the rest of us is quite simple: She says yes. Zechariah, defined by his adult commitments, had difficulty receiving God's surprising grace. Zechariah understood his identity as a faithful, childless husband and priest. Everything was settled as far as he could tell. God's ability to turn who he was upside down and inside out dumfounded Zechariah. But Mary, a poor, unmarried teenage girl, has no preconceived identity apart from that endowed by her Creator. While Zechariah's reluctance to believe led to silence, Mary's malleability before God erupts in song.

Developmentally, youth are capable of extraordinary commitment to someone who believes in them, of ridiculous fidelity to a cause worthy of their total commitment. God did not choose a teenager to bear salvation to the world by accident. Who else would agree to such a plan? While the coming of Jesus Christ in a virgin's womb is the unrepeatable mystery of God, God invites all of us to become Godbearers—persons who by the power of the Holy Spirit smuggle Jesus into the world through our own lives, who by virtue of our yes to God find ourselves forever and irrevocably changed.

God's yes always comes first: "Greetings, favored one!" Mary, however, meets God's affirmation with a yes of her own: "Let it be with me according to your word"—a yes that changes her life forever and, because of her, the world in which she lives. Mary is actively involved in this transformation, undergoing all of the metamorphoses that occur during pregnancy plus a few that undoubtedly go along with being the mother of God's son. From Mary's yes forward, she becomes "Godbearer," or as the Eastern Orthodox call her, *Theotokos*. Ministry does not end with Mary's transformation; it begins.

Implications for Youth Ministry

If we look closely at the Annunciation story, we can see a process taking place that wins this young girl over to the divine plan of salvation in which she plays a decisive part. First, God employs a third party to bear the good news, a Godbearer of sorts, an *angelos*, or messenger. We think of the Annunciation as a Christmas story, but it is also a courtship scene. God plays Cyrano de Bergerac, wooing Mary through a third party, but the desire for her is entirely God's. The message is organized carefully. First comes God's affirmation, followed immediately by God's invitation. Divine will follows divine love; Mary discovers identity and vocation in one spare text. Mary's experience of God mirrors our own. God's yes to us always comes first. Before we think to ask for divine mercy, God's grace and affirmation are at work in us, bringing us to repentance and holiness. Our true identity lies in the person God created each of us to be: favored, beloved, blessed, unbroken, and uncompromised by the world—virgins, all of us.

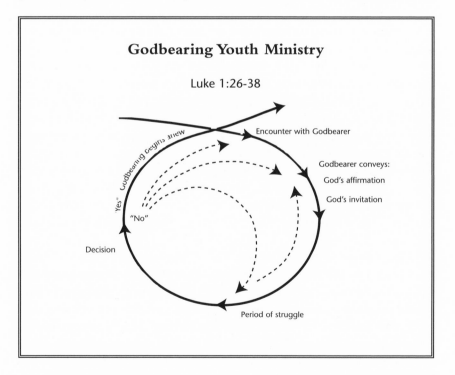

Godbearing Youth Ministry

Luke 1:26-38

Encounter with Godbearer

Godbearer conveys:
God's affirmation
God's invitation

Godbearing begins anew

"Yes"

"No"

Decision

Period of struggle

After Mary hears and understands God's affirmation, the divine *invitation* follows: God calls Mary to a vocation of her own. Mary struggles with this call; she "ponders," questions, wonders if the angel has the right address. The messenger responds with gentle persistence, repeating the divine affirmation and invitation. After all, God is courting Mary, not recruiting her. Recruiters drum up business; suitors invite freely offered affection. Coercion plays no part in a love scene; love is a choice. God wants Mary's willing hand, not her grudging acceptance. But at the same time, God is a skillful and a patient lover. Finally after some struggle, Mary makes her decision. She opens herself fully to God whose Spirit fills her, transforms her, and, by extension, the world she inhabits. Mary's decision is not the end of God's ministry through her but the beginning.

What is at stake in imagining ourselves Godbearers with youth is redefining ministry—youth ministry in particular—as a holy pursuit and not a service profession. Theologically (and we can never divorce authentic spirituality from theology), we must work out what it means to place sanctifying grace at the center of youth ministry. Sanctifying grace is the gift of the Holy Spirit who enters us, dwells among us and makes it possible for Christ to enter the world through us. Sanctifying grace allows us to burn without being consumed by ministry. We do not "win" sanctifying grace by avoiding sin or by doing good. Sanctifying grace is the gift of the Spirit that *enables* us to avoid sin and to do good. God makes human beings holy (Rom. 15:16) through this power. If ministry is possible at all, it is only because God dwells in our soul and works patiently and persistently to form Christ within us so that we can bear Christ into the world. God gives us grace in creation, long before we have sense enough to beg for it. This "prevenient" grace works patiently to ply our souls long before we wake up to the fact that the cross was meant for *us*. And yes, sometimes Jesus enters the world through angels unawares, through people who though they deny God's existence nonetheless bear Christ's love in ways that change us decisively.

Godbearing ministry, however, begins with a conscious yes to God, a decision that flings open the doors of our souls so that grace no longer needs to sneak in through the cracks. Now the Holy Spirit rushes in "like a mighty wind" and fills us, overshadows us, transforms us by forming Jesus within us, restoring us to the image in whose likeness we were created. Now our soul-wombs, already prepared by grace, can carry Jesus into the world. Now there is no denying that God is at work within us for creation's sake: a simple yes, and we find ourselves up to our necks in God's plan of salvation, participants in God's restoration of the *imago dei* in every human being. "Here am I, the servant of the Lord. Let it be with me according to your word." No phrase in human history has had more cataclysmic consequences.

Most of us can swallow the doctrine of sanctifying grace up to this point. It sounds sweeping and radical, and it is. But let us be blunt. The upshot of sanctifying grace is sanctification—the making of saints out of sinful people like you and me—a concept lost on many contemporary Christians but front and center to the history of our faith. Godbearing youth ministry stops at nothing short of holiness, perfect love, robust and unapologetic Christian maturity, the setting apart of persons in community for transparent witness to Jesus Christ.

At this point most of us turn tail and run for cover, scrambling for fig leaves and a speedy tailor. After all, on God's next stroll through the garden God will surely discover us naked. So to avoid lowering our eyes in embarrassment, we simply lower our sights in ministry. Holiness? Sanctified living? Perfect love? Maybe next year. This year we'll settle for some new members in the junior high group and a decent showing on Youth Sunday.

The word *sanctify* means "to set apart." It comes from the Hebrew word that means "to separate" or "consecrate." The Hebrews understood the term to mean separation from the profane, the manner by which people and places were set apart for God and therefore deemed "holy." God chose Israel not because Israel was a great nation—Israel was the least of all nations—but because God loved Israel and therefore expected Israel to be a holy nation (Exod. 19:6). The writer of First Peter believed the church was likewise "set apart" as a "holy nation, God's own people" (1 Pet. 2:9), and Paul went so far as to suggest that all Christians are called to be saints (Rom. 1:7), people "set apart" because their lives are windows through which we glimpse Jesus Christ.

Since we will discuss this concept further in chapter six, for now let us simply admit that we are advocating impossible ministry. We do so because impossible ministry is the only kind that matters to youth or anyone else. Godbearing youth ministry is impossible: Nothing you and I will ever do can transform a single adolescent, restore God's image to a single earnest eighth grader, or free a single well-meaning volunteer for perfect love. On the other hand, sanctifying grace makes impossible ministry happen every day. It is by grace that we engage in Godbearing ministry; by grace that somehow God uses us to "get through"; by grace that we dare to "be Christs" to young people; by grace that our lives gradually give us away as Jesus' followers. And this same grace by the power of the Holy Spirit overshadowed an unlikely teenage girl to bring Christ into the world.

Youth ministry is a womb, an incubation ward for potential God-bearers as they ponder and struggle with the news that God is crazy in love with them, would die for them and, in fact, has. What youth need more than gung-ho adults are Godbearing adults, people whose own yes to God has transformed them into messengers of the gospel. Youth ministry does not just make Godbearers out of adults for youth; Godbearers convey God's affirmation and invitation to youth so that *they* become Godbearers, carrying Christ into the culture that adolescents inhale daily. The moment we say yes to God, we become bearers of God's word. From the second we lower our defenses—"Here am I, the servant of the Lord; let it be with me according to your word"— the Holy Spirit enters us, fills us, takes us over, changes everything about us, and, through us, the world in which we live.

QUESTIONS AND EXERCISES

1. Dig out your calendar. Would you want God to judge the integrity of your ministry on the basis of your schedule? If God were evaluating your ministry on the basis of next week alone, what on your calendar would you want to keep? eliminate? reprioritize?

2. How would your ministry look different if you began to view yourself primarily as a Godbearer instead of as a youth pastor, Christian educator, parent, or volunteer leader? What would change? stay the same?

3. What is keeping God from entering you? How would your life change if you said, along with Mary, "Here am I, the servant of the Lord; let it be with me according to your word"?

IDEA FOR THE ROAD

Pass out diaper pins as reminders that Godbearers are "pregnant with the Holy Spirit." Fasten your diaper pin on a partner with the prayer, "You are a Godbearer, called by God to bring Christ into the world."

FARE FOR THE SOUL

Self-surrender, trust and faith, the universal means of accepting the state chosen by God's grace for each one is what I preach. To long to be the subject and instrument of divine action and to believe that it operates each moment and in all things in so far as it finds more or less good will—this is the faith I am preaching. Not a special state of grace or perfect love but a general state whereby each one of us may discover God....Love is the true way to this surrender. Love always prevails, is never denied. How can it be since it only asks for love in return for love? May not love long for what it gives? Divine action cares only for a willing heart and takes no account of any other faculty.[3]

—*Jean-Pierre de Caussade*

Notes

1. See Kenda Creasy Dean, "A Synthesis of the Research on, and a Descriptive Overview of, Protestant, Catholic, and Jewish Religious Youth Programs in the United States," working paper (Washington, D.C.: Carnegie Council on Adolescent Development, February 1991), 118.

2. Frederick Buechner, *Peculiar Treasures: A Biblical Who's Who* (San Francisco: HarperSanFrancisco, 1979), 39.

3. From *The Sacrament of the Present Moment,* trans. by Kitty Muggeridge (Glasgow: Collins, 1981), 31–32.

THREE
Heeding While Herding

It is a great thing to seize and improve the very now.
—*John Wesley, Letter to Mary Bishop*

THERE ARE those who argue that the term *pastor* fails to describe people engaged in postmodern Christian ministry. Few of us recognize the word's agricultural roots; and even if we do, not many of us know enough real livestock to appreciate the chutzpah actually required of Little Bo Peep. Many cultures routinely assign the job of shepherding to village youth who have two responsibilities: protect the herds as they graze, and lead them home come nightfall. Straightforward, yes; simple, no. For one thing, sheep and goats love to graze in open, unprotected spaces, a habit that places them perpetually "at risk." In addition, getting them home can be tricky since sheep possess no native sense of direction. In spite of this, the basic idea behind shepherding is not to lose anybody. Losing even one sheep, as Jesus pointedly reminded his followers, simply will not do. If you're going to be a shepherd, you must account for every last kid—double entendre intended.

We like the term *pastor* because it doesn't fit our postmodern expectations of excess. Consumer culture convinces us that losing one, two, maybe even three sheep or goats isn't such a big deal; we can always buy more. Humane societies across the U.S. braced themselves for an influx of dalmatians they expected to be dumped at their doors the summer following Disney's holiday release of the live-action film *One Hundred and One Dalmatians*. Local chapters were warned that once these cute Christmas puppies became gangly adolescent dogs, many people would no longer want them as pets. Little wonder that our culture simultaneously grapples with the problems of disposable income and throwaway youth.

Godbearing has none of this easy-come, easy-go mentality. Godbearing youth ministry takes the straightforward tasks of shepherding by conveying God's affirmation of, and invitation to, every single human being seriously. Whether youth or adult, pastors are charged with protecting a flock at risk and with leading them home to the persons they truly are: favored ones of God.

All major Protestant, Catholic, and Jewish youth programs report two primary objectives in religious youth work, whether part-time or full-time: (1) to help youth navigate safe passage into adulthood and (2) to offer youth a specific faith/cultural identity.[1] Programmatically, these goals suggest room for substantial cooperation, despite the fact that most churches plunge into ministry as though their congregation were humanity's last and only hope. In theory, society has many institutions charged with protecting the flock of young people. As Godbearers we are negligent when we fail to work cooperatively with and through our communities to improve the safety and quality of "grazing" therein.

Pastoral work with young people, then, includes protecting adolescents so that they can grow and thrive. In this task we are not alone. Though communities vary in intentional commitment to the well-being of adolescents, we all want youth to make it to adulthood as productive, healthy people. Protecting the flock becomes immeasurably easier with multiple persons (or institutions) on the look out for danger and with strong and resilient sheep. Furthermore, cooperation with other community institutions similarly invested in adolescent development actually gives us more time to be the church for these youth in ways we cannot when our energy is siphoned off in other directions. Godbearers must be outspoken and proactive about joining our communities in a mutual commitment to young people's health and well-being.

But Wait, There's More

However, Godbearing youth ministry is about more than protecting young people. The life of faith, like the life of sheep, takes place "in the field"; risk may be reduced but not eliminated. Although protecting the flock is a part of our job, that protection is for naught unless the flock follows the shepherd *home*. Godbearing youth ministry leads adolescents home by helping them claim and become who God created them to be: favored ones of God, human beings called to take part in God's plan to redeem creation.

By stating that youth ministry leads adolescents to their identity in Jesus Christ, we assume that youth ministry is first and foremost a theological endeavor, which social sciences such as adolescent psychology, sociology, and cultural analysis serve in important but secondary ways. Framing youth ministry theologically recognizes that God can and does break through the limitations of our cultural lenses and developmental stages. The Holy Spirit's presence in the church makes the Christian community a likely place for divine breakthrough to occur. Identity formation—the process of figuring out who we are and why we are here is a matter of discerning the gods that direct us. Consequently, ministry with adolescents naturally begins with the theological issues implicit in the life stage. Christian theology serves as a the homing device for youth ministry, because it explicitly acknowledges Jesus Christ as the "home" to which we will lead one another at the end of the day—and that destination makes our daily work ministry and not something else.

Barriers to Godbearing Youth Ministry

Of course, leading a flock home differs from chasing the sheep there. When my eight-year-old friend Justin banged out the front door to meet the bus recently, his new puppy slithered through the open door and took off like a shot. She narrowly missed being flattened by two cars (Justin didn't name her "Lucky" for nothing). Alarmed, Justin sped after her, which made the race even more fun from Lucky's point of view. Every time Justin got close to her, Lucky mustered cocker spaniel warp speed to run faster. Pretty soon, Justin's grandmother was out on the front lawn, wildly motioning Justin to get back home. Justin protested: Bus or no bus, he had to catch Lucky! His grandmother waved all the harder for him to come home. Thinking she was pulling rank, Justin finally turned around and ran toward home—with Lucky hot on his heels until both returned safely to the garage.

The pastor in this picture is not Justin but his grandmother—the one who never lost sight of home. Instead of chasing Justin chasing Lucky around the neighborhood, Justin's grandmother stood in the front yard as a visible reminder that the important point was not to catch Lucky but to get Lucky home. To get Lucky home required that Justin come home first. For many youth, the idea of "coming home" is practically an alien concept. Sociologist Wade Clark Roof describes the millennial generation as "questers," young people who understand themselves as travelers on a spiritual journey but who describe this journey in terms of process, not destination.

Godbearing youth ministry affirms youth on this journey, but it does more than that: It reminds these earnest "questers" that the journey has a destination in the cross. In the life, death, and resurrection of Christ, God is waving us home. Ultimately the gospel calls youth not to affirmation but to ministry. The journey is not without cost. God wants to enlist young people in a love-crazed plan to save the world. However, leading youth back to their identity in the cross of Jesus Christ will never happen as long as we are chasing Lucky. The sad fact is that youth ministry resources, curricula, and training are far more likely to teach us how to chase youth in order to "catch" them for the church, than how to lead them home to God.

Shepherds do not shoo sheep from behind (sheep hate this and will not cooperate). Shepherds go ahead of them and get to the fold first, standing at the gate to count and bandage every wounded, woolly head. If Godbearing ministry is to lead youth home to their identity as favored ones of God, then as Godbearers we have to get home to our identity in the cross of Christ first.

The reminder that God calls me to a cross and not to recognition (or at least acknowledgment) of the thankless hours, fruitless phone calls, and meaningless meetings I endure for the sake of loving teenagers in the name of Jesus Christ makes me a tad itchy. Do I really want to invite teenagers to youth group so they can get nailed by society? On one level I want them to take up their crosses and follow Jesus; but I am far more likely to preach to them—and to myself—Christ's promise of abundant life, conveniently omitting the fact that this abundance comes as the result of excruciating suffering.

The Godbearing life stands in the tension of these two gospel themes. Giving birth is excruciatingly painful, but the new life on the other end of delivery abundantly makes up for the suffering. If I am honest, I know that my return home depends on returning to the cross with the help of holy disciplines that remind me of who (and whose) I am. I also know that returning to these holy disciplines will demand a major reallocation of the energy I currently expend dashing madly around the neighborhood chasing young people in the name of abundant life.

The truth is, my commitment to abundant life without my commitment to practices and relationships that lead to the cross is wearing me to a frazzle. I can see Christ beckoning to me from the front lawn, wanting me to turn around and come back. Yet somehow, a huge chasm has grown between me and the practices and friendships that ignite faith, a chasm filled with newsletters and football games and the quicksand of meetings, volunteer recruitment, and my own need to schedule a trip to the dentist.

I can see home from here. But in all the busyness, the barriers be-tween here and there seem insurmountable. I remember my own "turn-ing around" as a young person and how completely I abandoned myself to Jesus Christ to pursue the call to serve him. I could get home to Christ then; why can I not turn around now? *How do I get back to the rhythms and relationships that will remind me of my identity in Jesus Christ?* I start ticking off all the ways I know to build a bridge across the morass, for-getting that nothing I do can ever traverse the space between myself and God. With the best of intentions, I start chasing Lucky around the neigh-borhood, pursuing youth, trying to be needed, trying to be efficient, try-ing to be liked. Little wonder that these barriers to coming home to Christ paralyze me as I try to do for God what only God can do for me.

Me Tarzan, You Jane: The Need to Be Needed

The first barrier to Godbearing ministry is our need to be needed, the belief that there are youth to be had for the church; and they need us to fetch them. That pithy dialogue from the early ape-man movies summa-rizes the issue here: "Me Tarzan, you Jane." Me pastor, you not; me trained, you rookie. This attitude stems from a shrink-wrapped definition of pastoral ministry, and unfortunately we often learn it from people who go to seminary. Theologian Edward Farley called the ordained ver-sion of this pitfall the "clerical paradigm,"[2] an outmoded but trenchant model of ministry in which pastoring begins—and ends—with the clergy, who "dispense" ministry like Pez to people in "their" parishes. Today, despite the proliferation of worship bulletins that claim the min-isters to be "all members of the congregation," we still deploy our the-ologically trained personnel to churches with the expectation that the "pastors" will solve the problems of ministry.

Theologically, of course, this approach doesn't have a leg to stand on. The nature of Godbearing ministry asks youth and adults to become Godbearers in their own right, theological pedigrees notwithstanding. A "me Tarzan, you Jane" attitude points straight down the road to a Messiah complex with or without ordination. We come by our desire to save people naturally enough; most of us enter ministry as volunteers or as professionals because we like to be needed. We thrive on "making a difference." We are perceptive and sensitive; we try to bind the wounds of our fellow human beings wherever we see blood. We are gifted heal-ers who sincerely want to honor God by using our good gifts on behalf of Christ and the church. But "me Tarzan, you Jane" can also subtly say, "me better, you worse," "me stronger, you weaker." In our earnest desire to meet the needs of our fellow human beings, we become smug surrogate saviors stealing center stage when we are called instead to be John the Baptists, opening acts for the One who is greater still.

Godbearing is about following a trail, not blazing it. The alternative to "me Tarzan, you Jane" ministry is *entrainment*, or drawing oneself alongside another, adopting one another's rhythms. Godbearers adeptly "tune in" to the rhythms of others, resonate on the same wavelength, travel the same frequency—not because we can "fix" people, but because we sing the same song. Nature practices entrainment so gracefully we barely notice. Crickets in a field chirp in one chorus. Clocks ticking on a wall find the same rhythm. Communication scholars point out that subconsciously we adopt each other's body positions when we face each other in conversation. Women will tell you that living with female roommates means everybody inevitably winds up on the same menstrual cycle. People sleeping within earshot of one another naturally adjust their breathing to that of the person beside them—which is why snoring annoys us. Snoring impedes our ability to adopt another's rhythms.

Entrainment is also an apt metaphor for the spiritual life. When we draw ourselves alongside God, when we stop and listen to the breath of the Holy Spirit—God breathing in us—our rhythms align with God's. The Hebrew word for "spirit" (*ruach*) means "breath," the life force God breathed into Adam at creation. We listen to God breathing in us so that our spirit becomes completely entrained to God's. Unfettered by ideological commitments, youth easily attune themselves to others in ways we have long forgotten—a fact that partially accounts for high degrees of altruism found among adolescents, particularly younger teens.[3]

Youth are not problems in need of repair but God's beloved in need of repentance and conversion. The "problems" of adolescents may well be our own problems, acutely rendered in persons too young to have erected defense mechanisms against them and who are therefore extremely pliable. Like a native basket, woven double so that its "inner reality" conforms perfectly to the basket's outer contours, entrainment allows us to conform to God's will for us, the divine design for our lives discerned through the practices and friendships of faith.

McFaith: The Need to Be Efficient

A second barrier obscuring the way home is our need to be efficient. The need to be needed may be the most insidious barrier to Godbearing ministry, but McFaith—the need to be all things to all people by addressing admirably every conceivable want and desire—is the most seductive. At every turn we are tempted by the drive-through spirituality summed up on the bumper sticker: "Jesus is coming—look busy!"

McFaith usually grows out of our desire to secure a quick fix for long-term spiritual neglect. Because we want to become closer to God, we do copious market analysis and develop ministries with "curb appeal." These appealing and lifestyle-friendly ministries give temporary satiation. McFaith has thousands of menu items, several worship services and styles to choose from, small groups for every conceivable interest in the church, an impressive range of opportunities for "fringe" youth as well as "die-hards," local as well as international outreach efforts, a cadre of volunteers guaranteed to win even the most stubborn eighth grader for weekend activities, all cheerfully packaged. What our efficiency lacks in depth it makes up for in scope, and it has tremendous growth potential. The shareholders—uh, parishioners—are tremendously pleased with our work.

McFaith represents a Disneyland approach to youth ministry. Our schedule assumes a comfortable kind of "chaos," which is really a studied attempt to keep thousands of balls in the air. Disney has taught us a lot both about the blessings and the perils of such ministry. For example, Walt Disney never forgot the day he took his daughters to a park and noticed that all the children clamored for the horses on the carousel's outer ring. He soon realized why: only the outside horses jumped. The horses on the inside had peeling paint and moved forward, not up and down. Years later, Disney issued this dictate to the designers of his theme parks: "All horses jump, no chipped paint." In other words, every single child is special enough to get the best horse at Disneyland—just as every youth is important enough to receive the best of what the church has to offer.

But Disney also learned to orchestrate our enjoyment through illusion. Another Disney philosophy says, "All lines keep moving." No one stands still while waiting for a ride at Disneyland; the line keeps moving, no matter what. Of course, the lines have elaborate twists and turns and extra complications to preserve the illusion of forward movement, but as long as the line keeps moving no one complains too loudly. Furthermore, every Disney character roaming a Disney theme park makes a personal contact with at least sixty guests each day. These characters are more familiar to children than the lady next door, and to encounter Tigger in all his seven-foot splendor is like meeting up with an old friend. The catch is that this Tigger is *not* an old friend; he is a virtual friend. A "contact" is not a relationship. Disneyland is a "virtual" reality that creates the illusion of action, adventure, and caring relationships. No wonder we love it. But Disney knew fact from fiction. He himself once wryly observed: "I only hope that we never lose sight of one thing—that it was all started by a mouse."

I wonder if those of us in the church are as clearheaded as Walt Disney about trafficking in make-believe. Walt Disney was a genius as an entertainer and a businessman, but he harbored no illusions about being a pastor. Godbearing youth ministry must weigh carefully what it borrows from the entertainment industry in order to reach youth. In a world increasingly defined by virtual reality, the church remains a harbinger of authentic relationships and primary experience. In a world saturated by fantastic special effects, the church claims direct access to the sacred. While the church may benefit from an "all horses jump, no chipped paint" atmosphere, the elaborate effort it takes to preserve illusion—lines that move but go nowhere, "contacts" that substitute for real caring relationships—are danger signals. Forward movement for the sake of forward movement may be a virtue in the Magic Kingdom but not in the kingdom of God, and coming into personal contact with a few familiar faces is a far cry from pastoring them. Pastors know the hearts, as well as the costumes and masks, of those they serve. And vice versa.

The danger of McFaith is that we become managers instead of ministers. We discern promise in young people; we want to be their guarantors, to help them spread their wings and develop leadership. But when we manage ministries rather than pastor people, we ever so subtly fuse our sense of faithfulness with the success of these ministries, confusing who we are with what we do. When this happens, the most important aspect of Godbearing youth ministry—who it is for—gets lost in the din of what we must accomplish to achieve the next marketing coup.

The alternative to McFaith in Godbearing ministry is *to wait*. Godbearing youth ministry recognizes that patience is essential to the spiritual life. I remember exasperating my piano teacher(s) as a child by flying through Chopin at breakneck speed, ignoring rests and fermatas in furious pursuit of *fini*. I knew the notes, but they never sounded very musical when I finished with them. I learned later from a maestro counseling his orchestra, "The music is *in between* the notes." Faith, like music, needs rest. After all, it started in a womb, and there is no such thing as instant incubation. Americans have pronounced a pox on waiting. Yet Sabbaths punctuate the Godbearing life. Godbearers live through Advents and dark nights of the soul in which Jesus tells us: "Sit here while I pray. Sit here while I do for you what you cannot do for yourself. Wait, and let me be the savior. Let me be God for you. Let me pray in your stead."

Godbearing requires a safe place where embryonic faith can abide and grow until it is mature enough to be born. "Abide in me," Jesus enigmatically told his followers. "Be patient. Hang in there. Incubate. I am your womb, the safe and fertile place where your soul can germinate until you are ready to become who you really are. The music is in between the notes. Wait—not *on* me but *in* me."

Called but Clueless: The Need to Be Liked

The third barrier to Godbearing ministry stems from our natural ability to affirm others and our natural aversion to expecting the impossible of them. When this happens, it is easy to be "called but clueless." If we fall into the "me Tarzan, you Jane" trap because we like to be needed, we become "called but clueless" because we need to be liked. Were it up to us, we would never have entrusted God's salvation to the womb of a teenager. We are much better at appreciating young people than at challenging them for God's sake. We boost their self-esteem immeasurably by the fact that they know we like them, even if we do not like (at all) some of the things they do. We have the gift of loving teenagers "where they are." We know how to construct opportunities for them to succeed, and we convey God's unconditional love for them unconditionally. We have no trouble viewing youth as "favored ones" of God.

The danger comes when we stop with Gabriel's opening line and fail to deliver God's message in full. Right on the heels of God's affirmation comes God's invitation and expectation. Despite all the positive messages we send to our youth, affirmation without invitation or expectation subtly tells teenagers, "We don't really expect much of you or ourselves because God loves us no matter what." Affirmation in the absence of expectation, as the self-esteem movement has discovered, does nothing to enhance our self-image. In fact, the self-esteem movement has fallen on hard times precisely because it fails to come to terms with hard times. In the face of abject rejection, anonymity, and powerlessness, our words "You're great!" "You're special!" "You can do anything!" ring hollow to suffering youth who simply conclude, "Grownups lie." The constant attention to "me" that the self-esteem movement in the 1980s required has been punctured already on college campuses, where 70 percent of college freshman in 1996 reported volunteering their time to help others.[4]

Godbearing ministry assumes that youth have a mission. God has utmost confidence in young people's ability to change the world, not to mention the church, and not only invites them but expects them to do so. "And now, you will conceive in your womb and bear a son," Gabriel tells Mary. God plunges ahead with the details while Mary is still figuring out what hit her. It simply never crosses God's mind to doubt Mary's ability to see this mission through. She might have qualms; she might say no; she might try to head for Tarshish instead of Nineveh. But we can't chalk up any hesitation on her part to a lack of confidence on God's part. God is recklessly sure of the difference this young girl can make and promises that the Holy Spirit can bring about through her a miracle she cannot pull off on her own. Godbearing ministry recognizes that the miracle of faith is not only that we believe in Jesus Christ but that Jesus Christ believes in *us*.

If we were more sensible of conditions—if we had a clue—we would not hesitate to send youth out to carry God's salvation into the world, and to be unashamedly and unapologetically Christian about it. Instead, we are cautious evangelists. We respect pluralism. We recoil from cramming our faith down someone's throat. We believe in human freedom. We want to be liked. Because we hope youth will chart their own course (to a degree, often, that would never occur to us were the subject algebra instead of religion), we allude to faith more often than we proclaim it.

Yet behind these honorable reasons for Christian reticence lurks a more dastardly one: Our reputations as reasonable people are on the line. Parents would never want their children in the tutelage of some religious nut. "You are one of the twelve!" someone might say to us. "Your accent gives you away!" And because we do not want to lie (perish the thought that we repeat Peter's blasphemy), we tiptoe over the dangers of faith as youth leave the church with a colossal shrug.

Our tendency to affirm youth without expecting world-changing ministry fails to grasp the power God has placed at our disposal. It's an age-old problem. Jesus didn't call his disciples "duh"-sciples for nothing.[5] Like the disciples, nothing short of a resurrection will convince us that Jesus is who he says he is (Luke 9:44-45; 18:15-16, 31-34; John 13:6-10) or that the invitation he extends is real. Separating God's affirmation of young people from God's invitation to them to participate in the divine transformation of the world is like separating sodium and chloride. Together, sodium and chloride make life-giving salt; apart, they are unstable and toxic. Likewise, affirming adolescents while expecting little of them spells "duh-saster," both for youth and the church.

The Godbearing alternative to such cluelessness is *discernment*, the double responsibility of paying attention and calling attention to God. We shy away from our theological language with young people, assuming that it is an alien tongue, when in truth theology is their daily struggle:

■ "The only way they will respect me is if I have a gun." (*Fear not, for I am with you always.*)

■ "I am working so hard just to fit in." (*Behold, I go to prepare a place for you.*)

■ "There is no way I can talk to my friends about God." (*You did not choose me, I chose you.*)

■ "My parents will kill me." (*Christ has set you free from sin and death.*)

■ "Who am I, anyway?" (*Greetings, favored one! The Lord is with you!*)

Theology is not an "added ingredient" that we adults are called to layer over the experience of youth like so many croutons. Young people see the entire fabric of their existence as a theological tapestry, the dramatic story of their desire for a God who cares enough for them to ask something of them. It is a search not only for a God to believe in but also for a God who believes in *them*.

Barriers to Godbearing Youth Ministry

Barrier	*Danger*	*Godbearing Alternative*
Me Tarzan, You Jane	Messiah complex	Entrainment
McFaith	Manager complex	Waiting
Called but Clueless	"Duh" complex	Discernment

Godbearing youth ministry teases out theology from the day-to-day work of being young and raises it to the surface, making God's affirmation and invitation to youth explicit. Discernment requires us to name God's work in the world and to claim youth as holy participants in God's transformation of our lives and culture. But calling attention to

God requires that *we* first pay attention to God; otherwise discernment disintegrates into garden-variety projection. Paying attention to God is a way of being, not a way of behaving—a way of heeding while herding, a way of tending the soul while tending the sheep.

QUESTIONS AND EXERCISES

1. With a partner, sit close to each other and close your eyes in silence. Listen attentively to the breathing of the other. Continue listening for a minute or so. Did your partner's nearness affect your own breathing? How is this experience of "entrainment" like or unlike your walk with God?

2. To what extent has your church bought into an "all lines keep moving" mentality for youth ministry? In what areas could you and your ministry stand to "wait"?

3. Raise your congregation's expectations of young people. Identify three places where expectations of youth could be higher, and make specific suggestions that will challenge youth to meet God's expectations for them.

IDEA FOR THE ROAD

Pass out brightly colored house keys to each youth leader. Ask them to place their key on a key chain alongside the keys they use most as a reminder to "come home" to the cross whenever they find themselves chasing in another direction.

FARE FOR THE SOUL

"Take care that you do not despise one of these little ones; for, I tell you, in heaven their angels continually see the face of my Father in heaven. What do you think? If a shepherd has a hundred sheep, and one of them has gone astray, does he not leave the ninety-nine on the mountains and go in search of the one that went astray? And if he finds it, truly I tell you, he rejoices over it more than over the ninety-nine that never went astray. So it is not the will of your Father in heaven that one of these little ones should be lost" (Matt. 18:10-14).

A sheep found a hole in the fence
and crept through it.
He wandered far
and lost his way back.
Then he realized that he was
being followed by a wolf. He ran
and ran, but the wolf kept chasing
him, until the shepherd came
and rescued him and carried him
lovingly back to the fold.
In spite of everyone's urgings
to the contrary, the shepherd refused
to nail up the hole in the fence.[6]

—Anthony de Mello

Notes

1. Kenda Creasy Dean, "A Synthesis of the Research on, and a Descriptive Overview of, Protestant, Catholic, and Jewish Religious Youth Programs in the United States," working paper (Washington, D.C.: Carnegie Council on Adolescent Development, February 1991).

2. Edward Farley, *Theologia: The Fragmentation and Unity of Theological Education* (Philadelphia: Fortress Press, 1983).

3. *A Matter of Time: Risk and Opportunity in the Nonschool Hours* (New York: Carnegie Corporation, 1992), 26, 35; also Peter L. Benson, Dorothy L. Williams, and Arthur L. Johnson, *The Quicksilver Years: The Hopes and Fears of Early Adolescence* (San Francisco: Harper and Row, 1987), 128.

4. "The American Freshman: National Norms for Fall 1996," report of the Higher Education Research Institute, University of California, Los Angeles.

5. I once heard "clued-in" Ed Trimmer, professor of Christian education at the The Methodist Theological School in Ohio, refer to the "duh"-sciples in a sermon, which inspired this exegetical nugget.

6. Anthony de Mello, "The Lost Sheep," *The Song of the Bird* (New York: Image /Doubleday, 1984), 156.

Section 2

 Soul Tending on
Holy Ground

FOUR
Tending the Fire
Finding Holy Grounds for Youth Ministry

Earth's crammed with heaven,
And every common bush afire with God:
But only [those] who see, take off [their] shoes;
The rest sit round it, and pluck blackberries.
— Elizabeth Barrett Browning, "Afire"

OUTSIDE OF cookie sales, the most marketable skill I learned from eight years of Girl Scouts was how to build and tend a campfire. You can start a campfire in dozens of ways, but unless you resort to canned lighter fluid or prefabricated "logettes," every fire begins with tinder. Tinder is made up of the tiniest sticks, smaller even than kindling, that ignite at the touch of a match. As fuel goes, tinder is fussy. It can't be green or wet or big. Only seasoned, dry, diminutive brush will do. Once lit, the tinder fire must be carefully stoked with more challenging kindling and logs, or it will die for lack of substance.

Lack of substance threatens faith as well as campfires. When we are spiritually malnourished, we are more likely to fuel our faith with gasoline than with God. The growth of spiritual renewal movements like Walk to Emmaus and Cursillo testifies to our desire to catch fire, but whether or not we have adequate fuel to keep the fire going under our faith remains an open question. We mean to tend our souls, to stay alert to God's presence, and to be open to God's direction for our lives. But in practice, instead of seeking the brush that provides soul tinder, we find ourselves trying to light sequoias with a match. We look for burning bushes after the fact—which is something like getting the AAA Triptik *after* going on the trip—to see if we have traveled God's route. What we need to learn is how to conduct youth ministry on holy grounds in the first place, to develop a ministry with young people that takes place where God is in the bushes, and where we can risk being vulnerable enough to let God set us on fire.

Godbearing youth ministry requires energy to burn, or the very young people we love will consume us. The Byzantine liturgy of the Eastern Church also praises Mary—the "Godbearer"—as "the burning bush that is not consumed."[1] Through her, God's deliverance comes a second time. Deliverance, as the Israelites discovered in their trek across the desert, requires holy fire: the gift of energy that will never use us up, an inexhaustible fuel supply, an alertness to shrubbery that ignites our souls and lights our paths with the unquenchable fire of the Holy Spirit.

Most of us are more than ready to tap into this kind of energy. We find an underrated fragment of the Exodus 3 account of Moses and the burning bush tucked away in verse 2: "The bush was blazing, yet it was not consumed." We tell the story as though the first part of the sentence contains the miracle, when in reality the second clause reveals God's vast and mysterious wonder. God is most evident in our ministries not when we are "on fire for Jesus" but when we burn without being consumed. This verse implies that if Yahweh is going to use us to get youth's attention, if the Lord is going to ignite our lives and our ministries in such a way that youth "turn aside" to look, then God is not calling us to identify with Moses. God is calling us to identify with the bush.

The challenge is that all fires, even fires of the soul, need tending. The word *tend* has two roots. The first goes back to a Middle English word for *attend* and originally meant "to give ear" or "to listen." When we tend the soul by watching over it the way a servant pays attention to a master or the way a gardener cultivates a flower bed, then tending implies a kind of caretaking in which we actively participate. This kind of tending suggests an attunement with someone else who guides us. When we "give ear" to God, pay attention to God's call, and oversee others on God's behalf, we tend the soul in the sense of attending or cultivating it.

But the verb "to tend" also comes from the French word *tendre* meaning "to stretch," from which we get the word *tendon*. In this case, tending means to move or direct, to develop one's course in a particular direction. Tending a fire also requires throwing on logs, poking and prodding wayward sticks in the direction of the heat, making sure sparks don't go astray and coals don't burn out. In this sense of the word *tend*, the soul tender acts only as a steward who creates the conditions for likely combustion. We can prod the wood near the heat, poke a twig into the center of the flames—but we cannot make it ignite. The source of our transformation is elsewhere. The best we can do is stay near the flames and remain receptive to its heat.

In this sense of the word, the real job of soul tending belongs to God. Not that I don't promise myself that I will be a better soul tender, starting this week, starting right now, starting with my own soul. I have a list of five hundred ways to help my faith catch fire, and I promise myself (for the five thousandth time) that I will do them. No wonder we give up. When God is the Soul Tender, our main responsibility is to be soul "tinder." We simply render ourselves flammable, submitting to Christ hearts ready to receive the unremitting passion of God. Only if we are seasoned and dry and small, only if we remain close to the Flame, only if we allow room for the Holy Spirit to fan the sacred sparks that have come to rest in us do we create the conditions for flammable faith. Holiness allows these requirements to develop a way of life in us that does not use us up, a way of life in which God sets us on fire and, through us, ignites others.

Godbearing youth ministry requires vulnerable leaders, leaders who serve as God's tinder and are ready to catch fire. They are not green or wet, big or self-important. Vulnerable leaders' outstanding virtue is combustibility. By sheer proximity to God's word, vulnerable leaders perceive God's purposes and burst into flame because they allow God to prod them into the center of the fire. Vulnerable leaders notice burning bushes—people, events, circumstances—that remind us who we are and why God needs us to do what we do. These moments call us to, and keep us in, ministry. And if we are going to stay in ministry, we must find holy ground for daily shepherding and notice and heed the bushes burning there.

Barefoot Youth Ministry: Coming Clean before God

Holy ground seems quaint to us postmoderns. We think God no longer speaks to us in such ways; burning bushes are banned inside the city limits. In the Bible, we easily recognize holy ground: Shrubs burn without turning to ash; donkeys speak; big fish spit up prophets on the beach. But twenty-one centuries later, we are a pretty hard crowd to impress, even by celestial standards. Our closets overflow with shoes that protect us from gravel (and God). We can no longer tell when we stand on holy ground and when we don't, much less discern what God would have us do—which is the point of the story of God's encounter with Moses in the fields of Midian.

In retrospect, we know that when Moses takes his father-in-law's sheep "beyond the wilderness," past Horeb, the mountain of God

(Exodus 3:1), the experience serves as a dry run for the next flock Moses will shepherd down the same route. Maybe Moses should expect holy smoke on the mountain of God—and maybe we should expect holy fire in the sanctuary at church too—but we don't, and neither apparently does Moses. The text nonchalantly describes Moses' journey with Jethro's sheep the way we describe a trip to the mall. This is familiar territory. Never mind the fact that Moses knows Horeb is "the mountain of God" (just as we know the church as "God's house"). The fact of the matter is that we have been here hundreds of times and so has Moses, and nothing very earth shattering has happened so far. Why should today be different? On the surface, holy ground looks like all other ground, until suddenly God speaks up.

When I'm honest, it irks me that God called Moses through a burning bush, and God has sent nothing of the sort in my direction as far as I can tell. How hard can it be to refuse the great I AM when you hear God in the hedges? Surely if a burning bush told me what God needed me to do, I would do it, wouldn't I? The voice asked Moses to remove his sandals on this holy ground in deference to God's presence. But today things are so much muddier. I need my shoes so much more than Moses did. In fact, I am so covered with clothing, so knee-deep in vanity, so buried in my disguises and defense mechanisms, that it is nearly impossible to hear—much less heed—God's call to me from the flames.

We don't know how long God has been trying to get Moses' attention. Maybe God had been burning shrubbery for decades to no avail. Maybe God had tried more traditional means to attract a worthy candidate for the position, but no one applied. Or maybe one day God just decided that the person for the job was the one who noticed Yahweh's presence on Horeb, and so God ignited a bush for minutes or millennia until a miracle occurred: Somebody finally paid attention. Moses turns around long enough to wonder why the bush is not burning up, and that impresses God: "When the Lord saw that he had turned aside to see, God called to him out of the bush." God, glad to be noticed, calls, "Moses! Moses!" Moses has no time to reply before he hears the bush's bizarre self-disclosure: "Come no closer! Remove the sandals from your feet, for the place on which you are standing is holy ground....I am the God of your father, the God of Abraham, the God of Isaac, and the God of Jacob" (Exod. 3:5-6).

Maybe God wants to see the look on Moses' face. Will Moses give in to this wonder, or is he just like all the others God has tried to flag down throughout history, others who were simply too busy or too careful or too sane to pay attention? "Remove your sandals!" God commands Moses. Show me that you will serve me, that you will not run away, implores the great I AM, and I will reveal what I have in store for you.

This, of course, is exactly what Moses fears. The text does not tell us whether Moses removes his sandals or not. What it does say is that Moses hides his face in fear, for the ancients believed that to look upon the face of God was to die. Anyway Moses has plenty to hide: the murder back in Egypt, the out-of-control temper, the life of cowardice here in Midian—all has come back to haunt him. What Moses is slow to realize is that God has not come to destroy him; God has come to transform him into a bearer of God's salvation.

When it comes down to it, none of us wants to stand barefoot before the blazing glory of God. Chalk it up to shyness, or maybe our desire to pretend that we are just an inch or two taller than we really are. Maybe we don't like to have the dirt between our toes remind us that we too are creatures of the dust. Maybe (as numerous adults complain whenever I invite them to a foot washing) "our feet are just so personal." I never really buy this excuse; we go to the beach barefoot, and nobody thinks a thing about it. We really are just plain scared stiff to stand naked before God, to remove our neat protection from all of life's manure. Like Moses, we find that the evidence of the waste in our lives cakes our feet. Now, brought up short by the cauterizing fire of truth, God says to each of us: "Remove your sandals! Leave all that behind. I am not out to destroy you; I am out to *change* you. Take off those smelly shoes—this is holy ground, the place where you leave your old ways behind and start over as the person I made you to be."

This, then, is the fire that engulfs but does not consume us, the grace by which the Soul Tender converts our soul's "tinder" into blazing faith. Sometimes God speaks to us from the foliage, and sometimes God sets us on fire to get through to someone else. In both the Old and the New Testaments, fire connotes holiness, the Holy Spirit's empowering presence that transforms us for ministry. Fire proves, purifies, adds durability—and not only for clay pots. The surprise of Exodus 3 is not what God does with Moses—Moses' transformation happens later—but what God does with the bush. Bushes catch fire: big ones, scrawny ones, robust ones, sick ones—given the proper conditions, all will go up in flames. But this fire is sacred and eternal, welling up out of the endless fuel supply that is God.

Four Flammable Assumptions about
Soul Tending in Youth Ministry

1. Soul tending understands youth ministry as a holy pursuit, not a service profession.

2. Soul tending relies on the historic practices of Christian community as the decisive vehicles for ministry.

3. Soul tending fuels faith in young people, adults, and congregations simultaneously.

4. Soul tending offers a paradigm for being the church, not just for being in youth ministry.

Burning without Being Consumed: Godbearing on Holy Ground

Perhaps the structure of this passage about Moses sounds familiar. The burning bush serves as a Godbearer of sorts, employed by God to get Moses' attention. Moses first hears God's affirmation in the sound of a voice calling him by name, followed in short order by God's invitation and expectation. "Come," the Lord tells Moses. "I will send you to bring my people out of Egypt." Next comes the period of struggle for Moses (reminiscent of Mary's, but Moses proves a far more stubborn candidate for ministry). Moses does more than ponder this moment; he raises glorious doubts. "No one will believe me! I can't speak! Send (oh, please send) my little brother!" But finally Moses decides; he consents to God's plan for his life. He asks Jethro's permission to leave the safety net of the family business in order to rescue the Israelites. Reluctantly but with God's total confidence (and Jethro's unqualified blessing), Moses heads for Egypt. In following God's lead, Moses the murderous coward is transformed into Moses, Godbearer for the people of Israel.

What are the holy grounds for youth ministry? Where do we find the conditions for flammable faith, burning bushes that speak to us—and to youth—by name? We think of holy ground in youth ministry as those mystical mountaintop experiences at camps, on mission trips, during rites of passage programs and confirmation ceremonies—the "big stuff" that over the years has brought God to our humble attention. Even in the middle of these unrepeatable moments we somehow know that we must savor the holiness of "now."

Statistically, however, the bushes most likely to convey God's forgiving confidence in us grow closer to home. After all, Moses did not discover the burning bush on a pilgrimage; it discovered him in the middle of a workday. The places most likely to fuel our faith include the familiar terrain of families, congregations, and significant relationships with Christian adults who bring us face to face with the God who wants to transform us, not destroy us. On these holy grounds for youth ministry, faith catches fire, and life directions change with or without regularly scheduled trips to the mountaintop.

Families: Little Congregations

Research overwhelmingly identifies the family as the most important faith field in a young person's life. We are more likely to attend church as adults if we participated in church and Sunday school as children—but congregational influence pales beside the influence of families on developing faith. In the words of sociologist of religion Robert Wuthnow, "It is religious training in the home that appears to [best predict adult church attendance]: family devotions as a child are the best predictor of adult attendance, followed by seeing one's parents read the Bible at home, and after that, by parents having read the Bible to the child." Wuthnow concludes that religious leaders interested in preserving their own institutions must attend to the religious upbringing of children. Two out of three regular churchgoers come from families in which religion was very important. Wuthnow warns, "Such statistics give urgency to the question of youth ministry."[2]

These statistics also suggest that youth ministry must address the religious life of families in order to take soul tending seriously. Wuthnow's findings support the conclusions of Search Institute's "Effective Christian Education" study (1990), which identified "family religiousness" as the best predictor of faith maturity in adults as well as adolescents. The frequency with which adolescents talked with their parents about faith, the frequency of family devotions, and the frequency with which parents and children worked together to help other people were of particular importance.[3] Yet, with few notable exceptions, Protestant youth ministry resources are designed to strengthen youth ministry through congregations, not through families.

Ironically, our Protestant ancestors viewed families as the *primary* congregations of their lives. John Calvin believed families made monasteries unnecessary, since in his view Christian formation properly took place in the "religious community" of the home. Jonathan Edwards considered the Christian family "a little church" and family religious education "some of the chief means of grace."[4] John Wesley—himself a product of intense religious nurture at home—preached explicitly on the family's duty to children, exhorting parents to attend diligently to the religious education of their youngsters from the time they could speak until they married and left home. As Gayle Carlton Felton points out, "Wesley realized that the home influenced the lives of children even before the church, and that parents were, for good or evil, the first religious teachers of their children."[5]

Sadly, some people do not experience their families as "holy ground," for families have the power to crush the soul as well as tend it. Still, on the whole we are more likely to hear God call us by name in our families than anywhere else. Family kinship occurs between blood relatives as well as unrelated persons in both official and unofficial family arrangements. Regardless of our family configuration, most of us "go barefoot" at home: We are more likely to expose our psyches in the protected space of families than anywhere else, a fact that opens us both to the good and the bad that families have to offer. In their landmark study of adolescent time use, Mihaly Csikszentmihalyi and Reed Larson found that although youth would rather spend time with their friends, they are most self-conscious when with their peers and least self-conscious when with their families.[6] While teenagers spend only about one-fifth of their waking hours with their families—about two and three-quarter hours a day—the unguarded psychological state common to family life makes these hours extraordinarily potent ones.[7] Any effort families make to increase the amount of time they share together or to tap into the time teens already spend at home intensifies the impact of these hours.

Godbearing youth ministry focuses on the holy ground of family as a context in which faith catches fire. This focus includes both the families of youth and the families of the people who pastor them. Sometimes youth leaders who are parents—functionally or legally—need permission to act as a pastoral presence to their own children. We forget that coaching our stepdaughter's soccer team can have as much pastoral integrity as attending a teenage parishioner's band concert, or that sacrificing a junior-high trip in order to have "down time" with a surrogate family of friends may not be a vocational loss. In fact, youth notice the priority we place or do not place on pastoring those most dear to us—and they judge our authenticity accordingly. This is not to say that adult leaders' families must be perfect (a stereotype pastors' children have been trying to live down, sometimes with remarkable effectiveness, for centuries). In a world marred by social fragmentation of every possible sort, a model of family caretaking is a ministry of extraordinary power. Youth are skilled eavesdroppers; they listen to our lives far more carefully than to our words.

Like many of us, I have had to learn this lesson over and over again. Several years ago, thanks to an ongoing, unalterable Friday evening commitment with my own family, I missed meeting with the college students who gathered at our church late on Friday nights, despite the fact that I was the resident campus minister. I found being with my two-year-old and my husband on those evenings enjoyable, but I would rather have spent at least some of those Fridays with college students (who, after all, were refreshingly far removed from potty training). I was torn with guilt until finally, at the end of the year, an undergraduate unwittingly absolved me with these words: "You know, it would have been fun to have you come on Friday nights. But I think it's cool that you'd rather be with your family. I've never met anyone who would rather be with her family." *If only he knew*, I remember thinking ashamedly but humbled to realize that God could use me for ministry even by removing me from ministry a few nights a year.

It is a sad commentary on youth ministry—and on ministry in general—that we often pastor other people's families better than we tend to the soulful needs of our own. Single pastors find this as true as married ones. We wrongly divorce family life from ministry when we forget that family life is a calling as well, a place for people we love to pastor us as well as the other way around. Families are religious communities whether we recognize the "family religion" taught there or not.[8] Well-meaning, church-going families often worship different gods at home than they do on Sunday morning. Yet families, flawed as they may be, remain the most important congregations most of us ever have. Either we learn to worship the God of Jesus Christ there, or we learn to worship something else.

While Christian worship expresses itself in the gathered community of Christ, the family is also a gathered community of faith. Family devotions in no way replace worship with the larger Christian community any more than kindness to friends and relatives substitutes for justice in the broader society. But mainstream Christians, by and large, have forgotten the family's role as a "little church," and today's parents often bring their children to church to have "professionals" (meaning the Christian education staff) teach them what it means to be Christian.

For youth ministry to offer substantive fuel for faith instead of wholesome entertainment or muted family therapy, we must remind spiritually impoverished families that every household of believers is a witnessing, worshiping, teaching, serving, praying, and playing community of faith. And we must support the practice of these holy disciplines in our families as well as in our congregations. Mark DeVries argues persuasively that teenagers' developmental need to distance themselves from the family of origin is a mandate for youth ministry to pay special attention to families. For DeVries, youth ministry must help families become communities of Christian practice, while helping congregations become "extended families" for adolescents—surrogate aunts, uncles, and grandparents who affirm youth's sense of belonging even as they pull away from their parents. Congregations can offer youth a community of secondary adults whose wisdom can guide them, protect them, and help them take flight into the public spheres of adulthood.[9]

Such an approach to ministry energizes (and maybe revolutionizes) congregations as well as youth ministries. Of course, departing from the norms of program-based youth ministry has cost more than one youth pastor his or her position and has sent legions of church volunteers into civic work. Models of the church resist change; and when ministry with young people seems to threaten a congregation's self-understanding, the casualty is often the offending youth ministry.[10]

Congregations: Extended Families

DeVries's thesis that families serve as the primary location for youth ministry deserves careful attention for another reason. Although secondary to families, local congregations do exert a profound influence on the formation of the soul. At their best, Christian education programs, youth groups, and even entire congregations provide teenagers ongoing communities of care and not simply catechetical content. These communities serve as extended families for adolescents who are beginning to distance themselves from their families of origin. They often serve as surrogate families as well, complete with "extra" aunts, uncles, and grandparents for youth whose own family structure is fractured or absent.

Faith communities can become "holding" environments for teenagers, emotional safe havens as youth experiment with various selves that—put bluntly—drive their families crazy. The congregation as secondary family becomes a vital link in helping youth mediate the transition from their place in their family of origin to their place in the broader society.

Youth instinctively seek such communities as they pull away from traditional authority figures. In the absence of a sanctioned extended family like a congregation, youth will adopt a substitute—and it's worth remembering that the surrogate families of gangs, peer groups, cults, and "virtual" communities over the Internet often welcome adolescents more readily than the church.

Like families, congregations fuel faith in subtle ways. Lisa was a regular in our youth fellowship; Lisa's mother had been carting her to Sunday school and worship since birth. During her freshman year in high school, Lisa returned from a Young Life weekend and announced that at the Young Life retreat she had "heard about Jesus for the very first time." Her mother was furious that a parachurch youth group could usurp a lifetime of intentional Christian upbringing. I confess that I too gulped back my first reaction ("Just where have you been all this time you've been coming to church?"). But Lisa guilelessly confessed what she perceived to be true; the Young Life weekend focused fourteen years of religious preparation into a commitment she could count as her own. Moreover, she shared her experience with us because she believed the congregation that had loved and nurtured her would rejoice over her newfound identity in Jesus Christ.

One of the ironies of parachurch youth movements like Young Life and Youth for Christ is that, while originally conceived to reach unchurched youth, they inevitably appeal to churched youth who have historically comprised the bulk of their membership.[11] For good reason: The measured, weekly ritual of participating in a community of faith gives us a grammar with which to interpret our religious experience, and the security of belonging to a caring community gives us confidence to make a genuine commitment at a developmentally appropriate point in time. For adolescents, developmentally appropriate behavior includes making decisions outside the reach of traditional authority figures like moms and youth pastors. Had Lisa been unchurched, her Young Life experience may have been so much gasoline on a fire—a dramatic flare-up. Without solid fuel to follow (which many parachurch youth ministries offer), Lisa's spiritual high would have amounted to no more than a brief and showy flirtation with faith.

But Lisa's participation in a congregation meant that she came to the Young Life event with fuel in hand. She had a context for faith lived out in the believing community back home, and her Christian upbringing gave her a latent language of faith that could "fill in" the truncated gospel inevitably presented by a single weekend event. Furthermore, she returned to a congregation that invited her further participation in Christian practices like service, tithing, and confirmation, which continued to shape and define her. These practices added more substantive kindling to her newly owned faith that had burst into flames on that one decisive weekend.

For Lisa, the Young Life speaker was a burning bush, a person through whom God's call to her became clear. But the Young Life weekend was also part of a field of burning bushes she encountered Sunday after Sunday. Perhaps these burning bushes were less intense than the Young Life speaker, but they were also more constant. They mediated Christ's presence and confidence to Lisa through a caring congregation, where faith was punctuated by the periodic epiphanies available in congregational worship, mission projects, and celebration.

Congregations constitute the practice fields of Christianity. Involving youth in the total life of the congregation allows teenagers to experience Christian community in its fullness and to become agents of ministry, not merely objects of ministry. We often confuse integration with "addition." Whenever I realize that I need to beef up the practices that nourish my own faith and mark me as a follower of Christ, I invariably "add" them to my current pastoral responsibilities. I am forever trying to add prayer time to my ministry, to add a covenant group to my schedule, to add music and holy friendships and personal retreats into my life. And then I wonder why I'm exhausted and crabby. If we wait until we finish tending other people's souls, we are too tired to care about (much less for) our own. I forget that the practices of faith *comprise* my ministry with young people, and my primary responsibility with teenagers rests in inviting them into the practices of faith with me. My job as a soul tender is to create soul tinder in youth, to help them become combustible before God.

A youth pastor I know demonstrated this integration dramatically when he suddenly found himself the solo clergyperson for a medium-sized congregation. By the time our paths crossed, Jerry was struggling mightily with his vocation. He loved youth ministry dearly, but the responsibilities of being the sole pastor of the congregation left almost no time for ministry specifically geared to youth. Finally he hit upon an experiment: What if the youth helped him pastor the congregation?

Instead of developing separate activities for youth, Jerry began treating the teens in his congregation as lay ministers. He trained some middle highs to accompany him on hospital visits. He invited high school youth to form a lectionary study group that helped him get a head start on his sermons. He asked youth to take part in worship leadership, inviting their own creative offerings from time to time. A few programs—the youth mission trip, weekday basketball—remained intact because Jerry found so much personal renewal in them. He attended a few school events during the year, in part to support the youth and families involved, and in part to meet youth outside of his own congregation. The Sunday evening fellowship group became the responsibility of two parents who (truth be told) had argued with Jerry for years over the nature of the program, preferring a recreational format to Jerry's spiritual formation model. Needing to let something go, Jerry opted for spiritual formation elsewhere; Sunday evening became an explicitly recreational gathering under parental supervision. The upshot of this integration was tremendous validation of youth as bearers of ministry, while giving Jerry the opportunity to pastor up close more youth than the fellowship group had provided.

Significant Christian Adults: Faithful Mentors

Among the gifts that families and congregations offer are significant relationships between teenagers and mature Christian adults. Developmental theorists have long noted the importance of an "adult guarantor"—an adult who somehow believes in us before there is any good reason to do so—to the process of adolescent identity formation. Several studies have noted the decisive role mentors play in a young person's future success.[12] The presence of significant adult-youth relationships critically affects faith identity as well; a 1991 report of the Carnegie Council on Adolescent Development found that significant adult-youth relationships forged in religious youth work had more positive impact on youth development than any other youth ministry delivery system.[13] These adults may present themselves in the form of parents, but the presence of an adult guarantor outside the immediate family is especially important for adolescents, who take these friendships as signs of society's acceptance and appreciation of them and of the gifts they have to offer.

Significant friendships between youth and mature Christian adults constitute another kind of holy ground for youth ministry. Given the shift in the location of youth ministry away from programs toward relationships, we can hardly overestimate the importance of adult-youth relationships as burning bushes for adolescent faith. Increasingly, secular agencies are recognizing churches as communities capable of fostering such relationships, so much so that mentoring organizations now offer training to help congregations mentor young people.[14] Such relationships provide emotional spaces that bring teenagers face to face with Godbearers who communicate God's affirmation and invitation to them and who make it safe to shed protective footwear to stand barefoot before God. Most of us have a keen awareness that our relationship with young people is one place God wants to set us on fire in hopes that youth will turn aside to listen to God speak to them through us.

Relationship-centered youth ministry also comes equipped with irony. One irony is the potential for parental jealousy of other adults' relationships with their children. Significant Christian adult mentors often do get more of a response from teenagers than parents do. Parental jealousy may be a clue that something within the family system needs pastoral attention, but often it is a parent's way of telling pastors: "Hey, I need to learn how to pastor my child too," or "Help! My child has grown beyond me." These responses summon us to return youth ministry to the holy ground of family and to help parents understand that families as well as congregations are contexts where significant adult-youth relationships can incarnate Jesus Christ.

Perhaps the most profound irony of relationship-centered youth ministry is that it can isolate adult leadership. Youth leaders consistently identify personal and professional isolation as a key reason they quit youth ministry. In the absence of professional networks and personal support systems, brokering relationships between youth and significant adults is simply not enough to stave off burnout of adult leaders. Healthy human development requires different kinds of mentors at different points in the life cycle. Even as Christian adults we need people of faith who believe in us and what we are doing every bit as much as youth need us in this role. For pastors to burn without being consumed, we need holy companionship for the journey, people who continue to stoke our faith with ever more challenging fuel.

Holy Ground Is for Leaders Too

Missing from this list of "holy grounds" for youth ministry are the two most common delivery systems in youth ministry: the youth group and the so-called "mountaintop experience," those special events where Christian conversions often take place, whether for a lifetime or a weekend. We omit these two settings not because they lack importance—we wouldn't want to do youth ministry without them—but because by themselves they do not offer adequate fuel to stoke lasting fires of faith.

Often youth groups are too far removed from the center of congregational heat (namely, from participation in the practices of faith that echo the life, death, and resurrection of Jesus Christ) to have much bearing on faith maturity, although they consistently contribute to positive youth development. Mountaintop experiences represent needed kerosene thrown onto sluggish faith, but kerosene alone cannot keep a fire alive. Youth groups and mountaintop experiences most often serve as entry points that lead to other kinds of holy ground—relationships with significant adults, for instance—and do their best work in faith environments populated by many burning bushes of varied shapes and sizes. These environments offer young faith different kinds of fuel, all necessary at different points in the life of faith.

Holy ground offers youth ministry "flammable ecologies," contexts that surround adolescent faith with God-sparks. Given the proper tending, the sparks can be fanned into full-blown Christian faith. Our job is to help youth attend to the burning bushes in these ecologies and to encourage them to shed their shoes accordingly. The irony, of course, is that we often forget to take off our own. We overlook the fact that families, congregations, and significant relationships with other Christian adults are the holy ground for *our* faith as well. Instead of pastoring on neutral soil, God calls us to invite youth to join us in the fiery fields of ministry, where God may send up a flare with our name on it.

QUESTIONS AND EXERCISES

1. What image best describes the faith of the young people you know —brushfire, bonfire, or hearth fire? What about your own faith? What kind of fuel is missing from your ministry right now: tinder, kindling, sticks, logs?

2. How have your family, your congregation, and important Christian friendships influenced your faith and your ministry? What persons or events have been the most important "burning bushes" in your life?

3. What would your youth ministry look like if families, congregational life, and significant friendships between youth and Christian adults became "holy ground" for your ministry? What would change? stay the same?

IDEA FOR THE ROAD

Build a campfire. Try it first just with logs; then ask everyone to add tinder and kindling and watch as it catches fire. Go around the circle and offer thanks for "flammable people" in your lives, people aflame with the Holy Spirit who have helped make you good "tinder" for God's love. Then ask each person to add a stick to the fire. The stick is a reminder of the part of ourselves we are still protecting from God. Giving thanks to God as the Soul Tender, invite each person to stoke the fire with his or her stick and to share what it represents. Prod each stick into the middle of the fire until it ignites.

FARE FOR THE SOUL

My whole heart I lay upon the altar of thy praise, an whole burnt-offering of praise I offer to thee....Let the flame of thy love...set on fire my whole heart, let nought in me be left to myself, nought wherein I may look to myself, but may I wholly burn towards thee, wholly be on fire toward thee, wholly love thee, as though set on fire by thee.[15]

—*Saint Augustine*

Notes

1. "Star Illumined by the Sun," taken from the Byzantine Liturgy, in Richard J. Beyer, *Blessed Art Thou: A Treasury of Marian Prayers and Devotions/With Summaries of Current Apparitions* (Notre Dame: Ave Maria Press, 1996), 61.

2. Robert Wuthnow, "Religious Upbringing: Does It Matter and If So, What Matters?" in *Christ and the Adolescent: A Theological Approach to Youth Ministry* (Princeton: Princeton Theological Seminary, 1996), 79.

3. Peter L. Benson and Carolyn H. Eklin, *Effective Christian Education: A National Study of Protestant Congregations—A Summary Report on Faith, Loyalty, and Congregational Life* (Minneapolis: Search Institute, 1990), 38.

4. Quoted in Clyde A. Holbrook, *The Ethics of Jonathan Edwards: Morality and Aesthetics* (Ann Arbor: University of Michigan Press, 1973), 83.

5. Gayle Carlton Felton, "John Wesley and the Teaching Ministry," in *Religious Education* 92 (Winter 1997): 96.

6. Mihaly Csikszentmihalyi and Reed Larson, *Being Adolescent: Conflict and Growth in the Teenage Years* (New York: Basic Books, 1984); 137, 159.

7. Ibid., 71.

8. Robert Kegan, *In over Our Heads: The Mental Demands of Modern Life* (Cambridge: Harvard University Press, 1994), 268.

9. Mark DeVries, *Family-Based Youth Ministry: Reaching the Been-There, Done-That Generation* (Downers Grove, Ill.: InterVarsity Press, 1994).

10. For examples of theologically based approaches to youth ministry that have threatened the broader congregation's self-understanding, see William R. Myers's analysis of St. Andrew's Church in *Black and White Styles of Youth Ministry: Two Congregations in America* (New York: Pilgrim Press, 1991); and Michael Warren, *Youth, Gospel, Liberation* (San Francisco: Harper and Row, 1987), 98–106.

11. Mark H. Senter III, *The Coming Revolution in Youth Ministry* (Wheaton, Ill.: Victor Books, 1992), 130.

12. A Proctor and Gamble study on mentoring programs in Cincinnati schools showed that young people with mentors were more likely to stay in school, achieve and aspire to better grades, and go on to college. A Public/Private Ventures study of Big Brothers/Big Sisters' one-to-one mentoring found that Little Brothers and Sisters who met with their "Bigs" regularly for a year were far less likely than their peers to start using illegal drugs or alcohol, far less likely to skip school, and had higher levels of trust and self-regard than their peers. A Prison Fellowship study maintains that mentoring reduces recidivism up to 80 percent. Researchers Arthur Levine and Jana Nidiffer conclude in *Beating the Odds: How the Poor Get to College*: "Those who overcome poverty to reach college often share a common bond: a mentor, or perhaps several, who shepherds students across unfamiliar terrain." All statistics and quotations cited by One to One, "Mentoring Works" (New York: One to One, 1997).

13. Kenda Creasy Dean, "A Synthesis of the Research on, and a Descriptive Overview of, Protestant, Catholic, and Jewish Religious Youth Programs in the United States," working paper (Washington, D.C.: Carnegie Council on Adolescent Development, February 1991), 51.

14. For example, the mentoring organization One-to-One sponsors a church-based initiative with the help of the Ford Foundation to offer training and support to mentors primarily in African-American congregations.

15. Augustine of Hippo, *Expositions on the Book of Psalms* (LF VI, 178).

FIVE
Sharing the Mantle
A Community of Colaborers

*A team is a team is a team. Shakespeare said
that many times.*
— *Dan Devine, football coach*

At some point in your ministry, you've probably been there: the
Desert of Whining. Trapped in a car on a road trip with bad music blaring, cheese curls flying, and constant complaining; surrounded by a
horde of griping middle-high youth on a service project ("But I don't
want to do that raking thing—I'll get my new $175 running shoes
dirty"); trying every way you know to hold the attention of a gaggle of
fourteen-year-olds more intent on side conversation than on your thoroughly prepared and, you once thought, creative lesson on stewardship;
spending eight solid hours with the youth on your shift at work who
do not want to cooperate with you or anyone else. Sometimes immediately, sometimes later when we have the luxury of solitude, we wring
our hands and cry aloud (or mumble under our breath): "Why again was
it, God, that you picked me for this? If this is what ministry with youth
is like, God, then you can have them back."

From Burning Bush to Burning Out

If the burning bush story in Exodus 3 describes the call that motivates
Moses (and us) for ministry, then the less well-known but equally significant eleventh chapter of Numbers is where Moses learns to live out that
call by sharing authority. In Numbers 11 we see Moses move from
burnout to team leadership and ultimately to freedom and renewal. The
scene is the wilderness. Moses has helped lead the rag-tag people of God
out of Egypt only to be stuck with a bunch of grumblers and gripers
who take exception to God's current provisions for them. They have
been delivered from Pharaoh's hand, seen mighty miracles performed on
their behalf, and now they have a bone to pick with God about the daily

menu. They've had it with all the manna and want something more substantial. In a fit of anger and frustration, Moses cries out to God,

> "Why have you treated your servant so badly? Why have I not
> found favor in your sight, that you lay the burden of all this
> people on me? Did I conceive all this people? Did I give birth
> to them, that you should say to me, 'Carry them in your
> bosom, as a nurse carries a sucking child,' to the land that you
> promised on oath to their ancestors?'" (Num. 11:11-12)

Moses goes on to complain that he has no idea where to get meat (their
latest demand) and that "if this is the way you are going to treat me, put
me to death at once…and do not let me see my misery" (Num. 11:15).

This opening diatribe reveals a man on the edge of burnout. These
words bear witness to a leader with a heart for God and for God's people who has tried faithfully to do it all on his own and who discovers
(surprise, surprise) that "I am not able to carry all this people alone, for
they are too heavy for me" (Num. 11:14). Moses cries out for a different kind of ministry. Quitting is still a live option for him at this junc-
ture, but God rarely lets any of us off the hook that easily.

God responds with a compelling suggestion. Instead of giving Moses
the ax and starting the headhunt for an alternate leader, God has a plan:

> "Gather for me seventy of the elders of Israel, whom you know
> to be the elders of the people and officers over them; bring
> them to the tent of meeting, and have them take their place
> there with you. I will come down and talk with you there; and
> I will take some of the spirit that is on you and put it on them;
> and they shall bear the burden of the people along with you so
> that you will not bear it all by yourself" (Num. 11:16-17).

The solution for the burned-out Moses consists neither of letting go of
the people nor of abdicating his position of leadership. God instructs
him to gather the elders *for God*—not for himself, not for the sake of
easing his schedule or relieving his weekend responsibilities, although
the upshot of Moses' obedience may indeed lighten his pastoral load.
Moses is to gather a cadre of volunteers for *God's* sake, and God will
spread the spirit given to Moses throughout the community for the
good of all Israel.

Gathering the Elders for God

We've heard it so often that it has become a truism of contemporary
ministry: Pastors who operate as "lone rangers" tempt professional frus-

tration and vocational infidelity, not to mention the real possibility of failure. We know teamwork is often the missing link of ministry and that capable volunteers can sustain our work and maintain our viability over the long haul. So why do we get tired even thinking about recruiting these crucial "elders," people who could help us with our work? Why does ferreting out these all-important coleaders often seem impossible? Sure, we can find plenty of moral support for our efforts, but where is a young people's choir director when we really need one?

What we overlook is the fact that God does not ask Moses to recruit volunteers for Moses' ministry. These volunteers share *God's* workload, not ours. "Gather for *me* seventy of the elders of Israel," God instructs Moses, "and they shall bear the burden of the people along with you so that you will not bear it all by yourself" (emphasis added). We hear the last part of God's instructions loud and clear: Finally, the cavalry is on the way! Then, just as they gallop onto the horizon, we gather these precious volunteers for ourselves, farming out responsibilities that do not use our gifts, tasks that have been diverting us from "real" ministry. Of course, these tasks often divert the elders from "real" ministry as well, and soon we have drained dry the original energy and enthusiasm that brought these willing souls to our attention in the first place. Instead of inviting our coleaders to the meeting tent where God "will come down and talk with" them, spreading God's spirit among them, we invite volunteers into a ministry moving too fast to allow time to hear God talk at all.

Numbers 11 calls us back to a form of ministry in which we gather people for God so that God can give them what we cannot: a share of God's spirit, the spirit that empowers ministry. God admonishes us as leaders to bring not just youth but one another to the meeting tent. The most underresourced people in youth ministry are volunteers, people who—despite their best efforts—often lack time, means, or inclination to read books on youth ministry, attend leadership training events, or enroll in continuing education courses. In our best moments, we become one another's primary resources for ministry, bringing our collective learnings to the table where we cheerfully pilfer one another's best ideas and swap survival stories from the latest youth mission trip.

Yet by itself this approach to team ministry cannot develop leaders capable of surviving untold trials in the wilderness, nor is that what Numbers 11 describes. God doesn't ask Moses to gather volunteers to hone their leadership skills. God asks him to gather the "elders of the people and officers over them"—in other words, those to whom the community looks for guidance—so that God may address them, be among them, and baptize their gifts for the sake of getting the people of Israel to the Promised Land. God not only seeks the trust of the rank-and-file Israelites wandering through the desert; God wants a specific relationship with their leaders. Such a passage implies an embrace for Godbearing youth ministry that includes adults who need to hear God's affirmation and invitation to participate in God's saving action. Godbearing youth ministry addresses the company of "elders" who gather for one another for God to receive a portion the Lord's spirit.

Godbearing youth ministry gives volunteers sacred space, "meeting tents" where God calls their myriad talents into service for the sake of all Israel. This form of leadership development represents a significant shift in our usual thinking about volunteers. I confess that the phone calls I usually make when I haven't thought things through carefully go something like this: "The junior highs are desperate for a Sunday school teacher. I know you work with adolescents; wouldn't you consider teaching for a year?" In my more enlightened moments, I remember to add something about prayer, so the would-be volunteer will better discern that what I have already decided is true; namely, that it is indeed God's will that he or she teach the junior-high Sunday school class (otherwise we would have found somebody by now).

But what if we approached potential elders on the basis of God's invitation instead of ours? What if we called them and said, "We've noticed that you have gifts for teaching; and because of that, we'd like to offer you some sacred space in your life. We want to give you room to listen to God's word to you and to experience God's nearness and what that might mean for you. That's why we're gathering people to a 'meeting tent' [or retreat, small group, class meeting, or spiritual direction session with a qualified director], where we will listen to what God has to say to us, remain open to God's presence, and consider how God seems to be equipping us for ministry."

The first time I intentionally tried to cultivate coleaders along these lines instead of out of sheer desperation, the response was as different as the phone calls. The first type of call elicited responses ranging from "no, thanks" to grudging "oh well, why not?" acceptance. The second call yielded a group of leaders who came to their various ministries only after a conscious, collective effort to act upon the share of God's spirit each person felt was his or hers. Not all of them said yes to being youth counselors, but every single one said yes to ministry. The first approach "stuck" someone with the chore of ministry. The second saw ministry as a gift someone was blessed to receive.

We hasten to point out that the "meeting tent approach" to team-building in youth ministry is about more than recruitment. It provides sustenance, meeting tents where leaders can beg for and receive the manna and quail that nourish our journey through the desert. The premise underlying this form of leadership is that spiritually mature leaders are more likely to bear spiritually mature youth and that every Godbearer requires a Godbearer on his or her behalf. Godbearing youth ministry calls leaders to gather one another for God and to bring one another to the place where God's spirit is spread throughout the entire community—for the sake of delivering all people and not just the youth in the fellowship hall.

From Deliverer to Delegator

How then do we gather one another for God? What might a "meeting tent approach" to team-building for youth ministry entail? God did not advise the burned-out Moses to withdraw or to flee further into the wilderness (though at times that may be God's healing plan for us). God responds: "Build a community for me,"—and more particularly, a community of coleaders. Most of us discover quite painfully—and often quite late—that our overstretched schedules prove not that we are living into God's will for us but that we are living outside of it. We naturally equate busyness with business. The more appointments and tasks we have scheduled, the more "faithful" we feel. After all, isn't showing up for the wedding feast without a full daily planner like wearing the wrong clothes (Matt. 22:11-14)? Like Moses, we try to address the bottomless pit of human need out of our own resources without realizing that we are in bondage, not ministry, at least until we have finally accumulated enough frustration and resentment to explode or quit or both.

When God frees Moses from the unbearable weight of trying to carry the people all by himself, a second Exodus occurs—Moses' personal deliverance. God releases Moses from a self-destructive paradigm of solo, self-focused ministry into the mosh pit of community where people may discern Yahweh's voice and where others help carry out the Lord's purposes. As it turns out, holy ground is never private turf but always communal space. Likewise, when we learn to set aside "meeting tents" for leaders to become a community for God, we learn to share ministry with others. Our shoulders sag less. Our faces glow again with holy fire. Our own faith becomes rekindled in the presence of friends.

Doing God's Work Together

The appointing of the seventy elders is not only a revolutionary event for Moses; it transforms Israel as well. No longer free to ride on the coattails of their great leader as spectators to the holy drama, Israel's elders step up and assume their rightful place in the formation of a holy people. In so doing, they relieve Moses of the burden of being the lone soul tender for the people of Israel. In sharing the mantle at the tent meeting, God calls Moses to step back and others to step forward. Notice what God is *not* doing in this passage as well. When God instructs Moses to choose seventy partners in ministry, God does not say, "Grab that new young couple who just came through the tent door," or "Make an announcement during worship to see if there are any volunteers out there." God clearly instructs Moses to look for people who already command the people's respect. God seeks the cream of the crop, a clue as to how we might approach building our formal and informal ministry teams.

In practice, this means that our usual approach to shared leadership in youth ministry is largely out the window. No more "here's the curriculum, good luck" approaches to teacher training. No more handing over the reins to willing but immature adults, who graciously volunteer their time in a ministry for which they lack emotional preparation. No more bribing and wheedling: "There is a group of nice young people who are meeting on Sunday nights, and they would love to meet you," and "It really won't demand too much of you; just a couple of hours a week and an annual retreat." Occasionally by the grace of God we stumble upon some incredible people for ministry this way. However, as a method for discovering and developing leadership, this approach fails to gather the elders for God and to bring them to a place where they can hear God's word, experience God's presence, and receive God's spirit.

Notice also that God chooses to share God's spirit *through* Moses. In other words, Moses has to learn to share what Yahweh has given him, including his status in the community. We are in ministry because someone somewhere has shared the mantle with us. Mantle sharing means freely offering our gifts and willingly removing ourselves from the role of youth ministry expert. Gathering the elders for God means that we will bear Christ to them and get out of God's way so that they may become Godbearers in their own right.

Who Are the Elders, and Where Is the Meeting Tent?

Godbearing youth ministry asks two questions in developing a team of leaders: 1) Who might be an elder? and 2) Where is the sacred space that can avail God's spirit to them? In ancient Israel, the "elders" were the people to whom the community turned for guidance, not because of their individual talents (divinity degrees, guitar playing, and teaching ability were completely optional) but because of their *wisdom*, the practical knowledge that comes from intentional reflection on a body of experience. Because the community valued both experience and considered reflection upon that experience, *elders*—as the term implies—were often (but not always) old. Sometimes the community accorded elders official status as "officers" over the people; elders could simply be those whose opinions mattered greatly. Elders were people whose character and gifts were established and respected in the community. Their trustworthy views grew out of the openness that comes with trial and error. They knew both triumphs and failures, and they feared neither risk nor tradition.

Historically, youth ministry has not typically turned to the community's "elders" (chronological or otherwise) for leadership. Thanks to churches' widespread assumption that anyone under thirty possesses the innate ability to "relate" to teenagers, youth leaders are overwhelmingly young themselves, and churches routinely farm out youth ministry to the least experienced person on their professional staff. Thankfully, scores of inexperienced youth leaders become "elders" much as Moses did, *en route*. Most of us come to value the community's collective wisdom after shooting ourselves in the foot a few times with reckless innovation. What is at stake in gathering the elders for God is not their age but their wisdom. The meeting tent represents a pooling of the community's experience that God calls into service for God's purposes instead of ours. So despite God's track record for calling unexpected prophets, in Numbers 11 God specifically chooses the elders to bear the weight of leadership. While Moses came equipped with God's spirit but lacking a leadership portfolio, the elders have plenty of wisdom but need God's spirit to transform their expertise into ministry.

God calls people of all ages who have a heart for Jesus Christ and for God's people, even if they have never led in youth ministry before. For some people, baptism "by fire"—or burning bush—is an apt depiction of their journey into ministry. Just as often, God calls people into youth ministry who *already* possess substantial leadership ability, whose gifts are respected but whose faith is dusty, whose appreciation for young people has gone undetected but whose wisdom is desperately needed by them. God does not suggest that these gifted individuals be thrown into ministry straightaway. On the contrary, God has in mind an intentional formation process in which they are brought to a "meeting tent" where together they may hear God's word, experience God's presence, and receive God's spirit. Then they will be ready to bear the people's burdens alongside Moses or you or me. In these cases, God asks us to cultivate potential for leadership—not because it will help us out but because this cultivation is part of the divine plan to gather the people for God.

Partnering with Youth

Where do we look for elders with gifts worthy of cultivation for youth ministry? One often overlooked source is adolescents themselves— some of whom make exceptionally good "elders," despite their years. Godbearing ministry is never a one-way proposition. Many youth have reflected deeply on what it means to be young and faithful, wisdom worth sharing in the meeting tent. By and large, adolescence provides a gold mine of leaders waiting to be asked, waiting to be gathered for God and to share the load in God's plan of deliverance. Not only does their inclusion freshen our perspectives and inject vital energy in our under-takings, but it also creates an atmosphere of mutuality in ministry. God-bearing youth ministry does not abandon its responsibility "to" youth and "for" youth, but it is always conscious that ministry exists "with" youth as well. We are Godbearers to youth so that they may become Godbearers in their own right.

Inviting youth to assume significant leadership (rather than being elected to nice-sounding offices) powerfully affirms their gifts. Encour-aging and supporting their Godbearing presence with peers at school, coleading meetings with teenagers, integrating youth into the overall leadership of a congregation, entrusting a project to a group of adoles-cents for completion: All of these measures communicate trust and accep-tance and send the message that youth are part of the kingdom of God *now*, not just when they grow up to become "real" Christians. We do not abdicate our roles as adult guides in this process. Here is one help-ful model for sharing the mantle of ministry with young people:

1. I do it.
2. I do it, and you help.
3. You do it, and I help.
4. You do it, and I move on to something else.

Any method of partnering with youth should include a process for equipping and transferring authority to youth themselves if youth are to genuinely receive a share of God's spirit alongside their adult workers.

Garrison Keillor frames this concept in terms of his story about a group of Lutheran ministers aboard a pontoon boat. When they are out in the middle of the lake with a barbecue grill going full tilt, it becomes apparent that they have overloaded the vessel. The boat begins to sink, little by little, until twenty-some Lutheran pastors in hush puppies find themselves chest-deep in lake water, immobilized despite their years of theological training and accumulated experience. They stand there, lock-kneed, faces searching heaven for divine intervention, which finally comes in the form of a twelve-year-old boy who points them back safely to shore.[1]

The metaphor is worth tucking away: Sometimes the youth teach the elders in the temple, point the way home despite dozens of adults who ought to know better. Godbearing congregations willingly view youth as prophets in their midst, voices and lives of witness capable of passing the faith up the generational divide just as the adults are capable of receiving a faith handed down to them.

Partnering with Parents

Whether single or paired, parents sometimes feel like the odd people out when it comes to ministry with youth. In many subtle and not so subtle ways their teenagers are telling them that they are already auxiliary to the real action: Don't kiss me in public. Can't you just drop me off here (where none of my friends can see us)? As a normal consequence of growing up, adolescents intentionally pull away from adult authority, creating space to differentiate themselves from their forebears. Parents can expect and celebrate their adolescent's emerging independence and identity. Still, the process often leaves parents feeling marginalized or out of the loop entirely.

We have already discussed the primacy of the family in young people's spiritual development. Because families are holy grounds for ministry, parents make natural partners with us when it comes to tending the souls of adolescents. Unfortunately, the church often unwittingly confirms parents' sense of being expendable. We put out "all-points-bulletins" for parents to serve as drivers, to send snacks, or occasionally to chaperone an event. Rarely do we cultivate them as "elders" in the community, persons concerned with the deliverance of the people—including their sons and daughters. At a national gathering of youth workers, we heard one youth minister remark, "Parents are like gnats. They're not harmful, just annoying." How sad when the church perpetuates parents' deepest fear in raising adolescents: that they will be swatted away as their children grow up. In that scenario, it is all too easy to give parents what they sometimes think they want (a spiritual baby-sitting service) and not help them become what God needs them to be (elders in the community of faith).

Parenting adolescents is closer to experiencing life through the eyes of a housefly. Flies view the world as a pastiche of dozens of images gathered from optical facets looking in different directions all at the same time. Out of one eye we watch our own work and community responsibilities, out of another the household and health maintenance of our families, out of another eye our teenager's weekend and after-school job schedule, out of yet another eye her school performance and her afterschool commitments. We keep an eye on the friends our teen-ager chooses and another on the friends we wish she would choose, one eye on her future and one eye on our own—not to mention all the eyes watching other family members at the same time. Amid such fragmen-tation, we often lose any sense of what it means to be an "elder" in the lives of our own adolescents.

Bringing these multiple images into focus requires time and reflec-tion. An invitation to the meeting tent is often a surprising and wel-come gift for parents, who experience it as an act of tending to their own souls as well as to the souls of teenagers. Offering "sacred space" to parents helps them realize God's gift to them of a portion of the spirit given to Moses. In the meeting tent, parents can begin to see themselves as Godbearers by design rather than by default—for one another, for one another's children, and for their own.

Unlikely Partners: It Takes a Whole Church to Make a Christian

We have all witnessed the power of the unlikely youth pastor. At eighty-five, "Sully" (as our senior highs called him) was invited by youth to teach their Sunday school class, and he accepted. Last summer a group of middle-high youth, carefully mentored by a local seminarian, pro-vided some of the most effective Bible school leadership I have ever witnessed, while their own faith was stretched by a Bible study specifi-cally geared to teen Bible school "helpers." A Christian businessman in our county makes a point of giving unemployed youngsters "a break" in his construction company. Ed Augsburger, a senior citizen in the congregation where I grew up, never held a recognized position in youth ministry but made it his personal business to "keep track" of teenagers, watching the newspaper for mention of familiar names, noting school activities, paying attention to hobbies and football scores, showing up for high school graduations "just because."

All of these people, and dozens like them from your own experience, are elders to be gathered for God in the meeting tent for youth ministry. Godbearing youth ministry means helping the entire congregation recognize its role in raising up a child in faith—a vow we make at an infant's baptism, and one we take rather seriously in the case of young children but routinely abandon to "youth leaders" come adolescence. Godbearing youth ministry embraces all the formal (Sunday school, confirmation, worship, youth group) and informal (worship, casual mentoring, participation in community rituals) ways of passing on faith. Godbearing youth ministry helps church members and governing boards own that it takes an entire church to raise a Christian and not simply the youth pastor or Sunday school teacher. When the leaders come complaining to Moses about the unauthorized prophets among them, Moses dreams of a community of witnesses: "Would that all of the Lord's people were prophets, and the Lord would put his spirit on them" (Num. 11:29).

Smaller congregations, which tend to be more intergenerational in character, can lead the way in this area. The more defined segmentation characteristic of large congregations, especially Euro-American congregations organized on a corporate model, can work against a view of youth ministry that includes the entire congregation. Even the presence of paid staff can create the impression that youth ministry is separate from, and not integrated within, the total ministry of the church. We forget that God wanted Moses to gather the elders, not for the benefit of Moses but for the benefit of Israel. When congregations claim their roles in the formation of youthful disciples, the body of Christ is the real beneficiary.[2]

Be Ready to Be Out of Control

Return with us to the account in Numbers 11. One of the unsettling results of God's revised standard of leadership is that it generates spiritual chaos. Others (beyond the officially sanctioned select seventy) get into the act and exert their own brand of leadership (Num. 11:26 and following). The real trek through the desert doesn't look as neat as it did on the original organizational chart, and this made some people anxious, even jealous. The same problem is inherent when we genuinely begin to share ministry with the "elders" in our own ministries.

What happens when *other* people lead the singing or sponsor successful Christian outreach into the community or teach the lesson or develop a relationship with your favorite senior-high youth? And when we entrust a program to two thirteen-year-olds, what happens if they forget to show up, or if they remember to show up but have planned something that lasts only seven minutes? The temptation is to step in and take control. But Godbearing youth ministry allows room for the trial and error of others, celebrates new faces in the spotlight, and derives genuine satisfaction from watching coleaders blossom as pastors. Godbearers learn to factor in a little more chaos and a little less personal recognition in favor of sharing the mantle. Love, after all, is messy.

Moses' initial question ("Did I conceive [them]?"—Num. 11:12) is precisely what we groan when our youth do incredibly dumb things, and the implicit answer ought to humble all of us who work with youth. When we find ourselves drifting toward messianic pretensions, we do well to pause and remember to whom these youth ultimately belong. They are not and never were "ours" to begin with. They are gathered for God. It is God who has birthed them, God who is forming them, God who will go with them long after they leave our care. At best God calls us to be colaborers, to help bring Christ to life in one another.

A Litany of Thanks

Heather was eighteen when she preached the sermon one Sunday this past spring. Her delivery was casual, her words simple and not particularly eloquent. She moved the microphone around a lot and played with her hair. She repeated herself a few times, but none of that seemed to matter or detract. For the twelve or so minutes that she spoke, Heather simply said thank you, in a variety of ways to a variety of people. On behalf of an extraordinarily faith-grounded group of graduating seniors, she thanked the Sunday school teachers who cared about them. She thanked youth counselors—volunteers and staff—who shared their lives and leadership with them. She thanked individuals in the congregation who made them feel welcome, important, accepted. She even thanked her pastors for talking about matters of faith with her and with others who had questions. She said thank you, thank you, thank you.

I cannot think of a more affirming message a church could receive about youth ministry than the one Heather brought us that morning. Her energy, her sincerity, and the breadth of her gratitude spoke volumes. I was incredibly proud of her, her peers, the youth ministry volunteers, and the whole church. In so many words, what Heather said was that maybe, just maybe, we are starting to share the mantle.

One of the abiding principles of business/organizational guru Stephen Covey is to "begin with the end in mind."[3] This principle bears repeating for ministry as well. Please do not misunderstand: We are not suggesting that one pursues youth ministry in order to receive plaudits. No single formula or procedure will replicate the scenario described above in your own ministry. But what would happen if you were to imagine your own Heather standing before your congregation or agency or denomination issuing a similar litany of thanks—not just to you personally (though we hope your name at least makes the list) but to the whole church? As we share the mantle of God's spirit, a mental image of the end—a meeting tent full of mature, faith-grounded leaders gathered for God, and not for ourselves—might just help get us there.

QUESTIONS AND EXERCISES

1. Does viewing potential leaders as "elders" change the way you would cultivate leadership for youth ministry? In your ministry, are these people gathered for God, for youth, or to ease the existing leaders' responsibilities in some way?

2. Do you bring potential leaders to a "meeting tent," a place of collective discernment where they can hear God's word, experience God's presence in their midst, and receive a portion of God's spirit that was given to you? What does that "meeting tent" look like in your ministry? Do you use it primarily for recruiting or do you return to it for sustenance of leaders already involved in ministry?

3. Which partners do you need to bring on board in your ministry? On a scale of 1–10 (with 10 being total involvement), how much a part of your youth ministry leadership team are
    *   youth?
    *   parents?
    *   volunteer leaders/counselors?
    *   members of the congregation at large?
    *   church staff members?

IDEA FOR THE ROAD

Plan a pizza get-together with two youth, two parents, two youth counselors, and two members of your congregation at large. Invite your pastor to come. Spend some time talking about the concept of sharing the mantle in youth ministry. Ask them to describe the "sacred space" that would equip them for ministry by allowing them to hear God's word, experience God's presence, and receive a share of God's spirit. In what ways is God sharing the spirit given to the youth minister with others in the faith community? Be open to hear something new.

FARE FOR THE SOUL

In the feeding of the five thousand, Jesus...did not act alone—and that is the key to his "miracle." He acted in concert with others and evoked the abundance of community. Ultimately the body of Christ, so central to incarnational theology, is not the physical body of Jesus but the corporate body of those who gather around the Spirit, wherever it is found...Jesus exercises the only kind of leadership that can evoke authentic community—a leadership that risks failure (and even crucifixion) by making space for other people to act. When a leader takes up all the space and preempts all the action, he or she may make something happen, but that something is not community. Nor is it abundance, because the leader is only one person and one person's resources invariably run out. But when a leader is willing to trust the abundance that people have and can generate together, willing to take the risk of inviting people to share from that abundance, then and only then may true community emerge.[4]

—*Parker J. Palmer*

Notes

1. Garrison Keillor, "Faith," *More News from Lake Wobegon,* audiotape © Garrison Keillor, 1989.

2. For an example of how congregations can develop congregational ownership in youth ministry, see Roland Martinson, *Effective Youth Ministry: A Congregational Approach* (Minneapolis: Augsburg Press, 1988).

3. Stephen R. Covey, *The Seven Habits of Highly Effective People: Restoring the Character Ethic* (New York: Simon and Schuster, 1989), 99.

4. Parker J. Palmer, *The Active Life: Wisdom for Work, Creativity, and Caring* (San Francisco: HarperSanFrancisco, 1990); 136, 138.

Section 3

Ingredients of the Godbearing Life

SIX
A Rhythm of Life
Practices That Shape the Soul

Can't act, can't sing, slightly bald.
Can dance a little.
—Hollywood talent judge's comments on
Fred Astaire's first screen test

M ost of us grow up under the misleading impression that "practice" is temporary. Playing scales, shooting hoops, rehearsing plays, jumping into a double jump rope: We think that if we stick with it, one of these days we'll get it right. "Practice makes perfect," we are reminded—implying that, once we perfect the activity, we can quit. We will own it. It will be ours forever.

Of course, anybody who has tried to hit a golf ball after a year off the course knows this isn't the case. Practice has to become a habit, or the activity falls into disrepair. The world's Fred Astaires, Marilyn Hornes, and Tiger Woodses have pursued their crafts with such faithful discipline—a faithfulness made possible only by sheer love of the activity, not by innate fondness for rigor—that their practice becomes part of who they are. To reduce these people to their practices, to equate Fred Astaire with dancing or Marilyn Horne with singing or Tiger Woods with golfing, obviously fails to render faithfully who God calls them to be as human beings. Yet the fact that they have persisted faithfully in practice has formed these gifted individuals into particular kinds of human beings, people whose identities have been carved out amid a specific set of disciplines that have helped make them into who they are.

Christian practices form us in similar ways. In Christian tradition, "perfection"—Christian maturity, perfect love, sanctity, or holiness as different branches of the Christian family tree refer to it—is a way of life empowered by the Holy Spirit that enables us to love and serve God and neighbor as we were intended.[1] We *practice* this way of life. It is not something we achieve; it is a faithful pursuit. Holiness is what we mean when we talk about mature Christian faith, the kind of faith that makes us capable of giving ourselves to others. Kathleen Norris compares the pursuit of holiness to life in a rock tumbler: Perfection is the kind of inner peace and polish that comes from having been hard-scrubbed by the rough and tumble of life in the Christian community.[2]

Jesus calls his followers to practice faith until our contours are defined by our conformity to God. "Be perfect, therefore, as your heavenly Father is perfect," Jesus tells his listeners in the Sermon on the Mount (Matt. 5:48). In other words, live toward God in the way God lives toward us. Jesus did not expect we would always get it right. But he did expect his followers to practice perfection, to develop the "habits" of holiness. If we are not shaped by practices that point to the God who is perfect, then we will be shaped by practices that point to imperfect gods instead. What all great artists, athletes, and mystics eventually discover is this: We do not master practices; practices master us.

So practices have extraordinary power. When the historic practices of the Christian community become our primary curriculum for youth ministry, we risk transformation—not only in adolescents but in ourselves. Practices are things that both give us away as Jesus' followers and that shape and mold us into people conformed to God. The saints of the early church taught that this transforming way of life, the way of "perfection," is a path all Christians are called to travel. Yet nothing makes achievement-oriented, postmodern people more nervous than being called to "perfection." As a species, we have pretty much learned to control our environment from carpools to gene pools. We are accomplished, persuasive, and savvy. But we are not perfect, nor do we want to be. That injunction from Jesus about being "perfect"—maybe it was a medieval copywriter's typo.

Part of our skittishness about Christian perfection is linguistic confusion. The English word *perfect* has absorbed the Greek notion of *teleos*. When the Greeks looked at a building's blueprint, they pictured the building whole and complete. They envisioned the blueprint finished down to the bathroom tile and announced, "Ah, this is perfect." The problem is that *teleos* suggests that perfection is something we can build or achieve. The Hebrews looked at the same blueprint more practically. They envisioned the *process* of building from hard hats to hammers, from scaffolding to skylights. "Ah," the Hebrews said. "This is perfect." The Hebrews and the early Christians understood perfection as a process, not a product. Our identity as Christians depends upon life lived in relationship with God, not upon the quality of our achievements.

However, this process-centered understanding of perfection has its own drawbacks. One is the sheer magnitude of the task. Perfecting a skill is one thing; perfecting a way of life is another. We may be capable of a holy act or two but a whole life? At this point the practices of faith help. When we break down the holy life into its constituent practices, it seems less overwhelming. Tiger Woods did not start golfing with holes in one. He started to golf when his father put a club in his hand and showed him where to place his feet. Only grace enables the practices of Christian life; nobody comes to them all at once. The faithful pursuit, like walking, begins awkwardly with one practice at a time.

Examples of Christian Practices

Baptism	Fasting	Simplicity
Eucharist	Forgiveness	Speaking truth in love
Almsgiving	Healing	Spiritual direction
Catechesis	Hospitality and care	Spiritual friendship
Chastity	Intercession	Spiritual resistance
Christian conference	Justice	Stewardship
Christian marriage	Keeping Sabbath	Stillness
Confession	Ordination	Supplication
Confirmation	Praise	Testimony
Contemplation	Preaching	Thanksgiving
Covenanting	Reconciliation	
Discernment	Repentance	
Dying well	Searching scripture	
Evangelization	Self-denial	

What Is a "Practice"?

We use the term *practice* in the way scholars use it rather than soccer coaches' definition, although similarities exist. Practices are the constitutive acts of a community that both identify us as, and form us into, people who belong to that community. Christian practices mark us as and make us into Jesus' followers. Our salvation comes by grace through faith, not through practice—but Christian practices are means of grace by which God strengthens individuals and the church to live faithfully.

Together, these practices form a river of holy water that washes over us day in and day out, shaping and smoothing us into people recognizable as Christians.

The ordinariness of Christian practices makes them easy to overlook. Practices are much like the back and forth, give and take rituals that happen around a family dinner table, ongoing activities that subtly shape us into people who bear a family resemblance beyond the nose on our faces. Practices constitute the daily rhythm of our life together. Through them God shapes us and uses us as a point of entry into the world. They align our steps with God's and, in so doing, create holy vibrations that radiate far beyond the church.

What characterizes a practice? First, *a practice requires doing.* We might study prayer, think about prayer, talk about prayer—but the practice of prayer does not happen until we pray. We may weigh the value of living simply, but we don't really make the connection between faith and economics until we practice living with less. We might appreciate what goes on in the sanctuary on Sunday morning—the quality of the music, the clarity of the preaching, the robust voice of the congregation, the beguiling presence of children—but we don't recognize God's overwhelming grace there until we worship. "Doing" our faith teaches us things about God that we simply cannot learn any other way.

Second, *a practice "does" things* as well. God uses practices (and through them, us) to heal, teach, shape communities, celebrate. Yet we don't participate in Christian practices for their results. We participate in them because they are themselves good. If someone spurns my offer to help, should I stop offering to help people? Obviously not. Compassion's value does not lie in the fact that it "works." Youth go on countless mission trips, not because they see "results" from their labors but because serving others transforms them in ways teenagers readily recognize. The good of compassion comes from being compassionate.

Third, *a practice involves others* who "do" faith with us. All of the ways we practice faith, live it out, make it a habit, and maybe even become more proficient at it are deeply intertwined with a community of others. Even though we may pray by ourselves, we never pray alone. The communion of saints, perhaps others in our immediate congregation or circle of friends, and above all the Holy Spirit pray with us.

Fourth, *a practice is ongoing.* God uses Christian practices to enter the world again and again, so they take place over time. People didn't sit around after church one Sunday and decide almsgiving would be a Christian practice, nor will they vote at next week's presbytery meeting to have almsgiving discontinued. Almsgiving is a practice we learned from generations of Christians before us, and we will teach it to our children to pass on to theirs. Christian practices reach back to the origins of our faith. They recall Jesus' life, death, and resurrection and usher them into the present in easily overlooked but often life-shaking ways.

Fifth, *a practice possesses standards of excellence.* Just because Christian practices have been around for centuries doesn't mean that we necessarily do them well. Some ways of practicing our faith provide windows to Jesus Christ, and some do not. We know the difference between good preaching and poor preaching, between a strong spiritual friendship and a weak one. Still, because practices echo God's saving work in Jesus Christ, God works in and through them them even though we may pray poorly, serve sadly, and preach pitifully despite two thousand years of rehearsal. There is no learning curve. "You join by jumping in where you are," write Dorothy Bass and Craig Dykstra in *Practicing Our Faith.* "Once in, you find that a practice has a certain internal feel and momentum. [The practice] is ancient, and larger than you are; it weaves you together with other people in doing things none of us could do alone."[3]

One final word about practices: *Christian practices are means of grace* that God uses to strengthen us for the otherwise impossible task of living faithfully. While most practices are not "sacraments" of the church, all practices are sacramental in the sense that they invite us to take on Christ's life as our own. They are the community's way of enabling every generation to "put on Christ" (Gal. 3:27, KJV) and to participate in God's saving work in the world. Congregations as well as individuals take on new identities when immersed in Christian practices. The grace God leaves with us in these practices is sacred mortar that strengthens people and communities to risk reaching beyond themselves.

Because Christian practices shape our identity in Jesus Christ, they are basic to ministry with adolescents. When our curriculum for young people focuses on the practices of faith, these practices shape their souls so they can bear Christ into the world. But soul shaping takes a lifetime—not an adolescence—to complete. It is essential that the community of faith, and not adolescents alone, participate in the practices that compose the Godbearing life. We all need to see ourselves through one another's eyes if we want to sharpen our sense of who God has called us to be. And adults, as well as youth, need to participate in the practices of faith if we want God to shape us and enter the world through us. Every Christian practice is a means of grace in which the Holy Spirit transforms us into Godbearers for youth as well as for one another.

Wholesomeness or Holiness? Christian Practices and Identity Formation

Think about how you spent your pastoral energy last week. Imagine a line: At one end of the spectrum stand Christian practices (like those listed on page 107), and at the other end stand wholesome activities, valuable ways you and your youth spend time with one another (like picnics, cleanup projects, and fundraisers). Youth ministry and church life as a whole necessitate such activities, and some activities look very much like Christian practices without the "Christian" brand name. Still, we cannot experience these activities as *Christian* practices without an interpreter who can point out the cross in the middle of the moment and explicitly connect the activity with our life in Jesus Christ.

Now ask yourself, "Which end of this continuum occupies most of my time? Where do I spend most of my energy with youth?" Don't despair if your scale tips toward wholesome activities. Flip through most youth ministry resources, and you will find reams of advice on planning wholesome activities with young people but far less guidance on integrating youth into the practices of faith. Wholesome activity keeps youth busy, often in productive ways that benefit both youth and community. But Christian practice shapes lives and forges identity in youth as people who belong to Christ.

If youth ministry is going to foster identity, then we must do more than involve youth in wholesome activities. The practices of faith invite us into the life, death, and resurrection of Jesus Christ every time we participate in them. The One who stands at the center of our faith also stands at the center of every Christian practice. If Christian identity is a goal of ministry (and it is), then ministry with adolescents immersed in the search for self must take seriously practices that transform youth, not merely occupy them, for Christ's sake.

The Curriculum of Christian Practice

The question, then, is how do we invite youth more deeply into the practices of faith? The answer is deceptively simple: *We* become more deeply involved in the practices of faith. Our submission to this curriculum of Christian practice and our invitation to youth to do the same forms the heart of Godbearing youth ministry. As we participate in the soul-shaping practices of faith, our life begins to look like Jesus' life, increasingly defined by a love so enormous that it even suffers willingly on behalf of the beloved. Youth ministry as a spiritual discipline implies submitting who we think we are to the merciful shaping of God's hand. Often we view our job as youth pastors as providing God with raw material for the holy art studio. We gather young, malleable souls and present them to God for completion. "But not so fast," God reminds us. "You are my child too. Let me see what I can do with you first."

And so we practice. Participating in the practices of faith defines our shape and our calling as Christians and as people who pastor youth. Deepening our involvement in Christian practices does not mean we become busier. On the contrary, to enter deeply into a practice of faith may mean eliminating distractions caused by other surface commitments. Nor does deepening our involvement in Christian practice mean that we plan a year's worth of new youth activities around these practices. The curriculum is already in place in every church, in every community of Christians in every region in the world. A workshop on reconciliation is all to the good, but transformation comes only in the *practice* of reconciling.

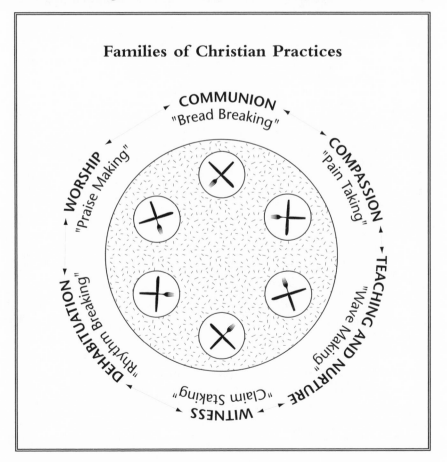

Families of Christian Practices

COMMUNION
"Bread Breaking"

WORSHIP
"Praise Making"

COMPASSION
"Pain Taking"

TEACHING AND NURTURE
"Wave Making"

DEHABITUATION
"Rhythm Breaking"

WITNESS
"Claim Staking"

So what holy disciplines compose a Godbearing life? To describe these practices is to render them tidier than they actually are. Practices have persisted through the centuries in "families," loose categories with enduring significance for Christian identity. Admittedly, delineating "families" of practices is an artificial exercise, since practices overlap, interweave, evolve and intersect over time. So what might a snapshot of Christians seated around the table reveal about who we are?

Bread Breaking: Practices of Communion

The most obvious thing we do at the dinner table is dine; we offer one another sustenance in the form of life-giving calories and companionship—literally, *com-panos*, people with whom we break bread. Christian tradition understands "breaking bread" as the most basic way Jesus reveals himself to his followers. The life of God begins in communion, in the oneness of the Father, Son, and Holy Spirit. Therefore, the life of Godbearers, as persons created in God's image, also begins in a life of communion with God and other human beings. This oneness is only possible through the body and blood of Jesus Christ, which is why we call the Eucharist "Holy Communion."

Most groups of Christian youth are *communities*, not communions. A community's identity depends on common characteristics, interests, and history. *Communions*, however, strive for more than having things in common. While communities can exist without intimacy, communions cannot. In communities we are generally nice to one another; and while this is true of communions, in communions we also take on the lives of one another—we participate in a common life, united by Jesus Christ, not by mutual interests or similar personalities, and experience the joys and pains of others as though they were our own. This is far more difficult than being nice. Communions require repentance and forgiveness, speaking the truth in love, hospitality and reconciliation, the tender trust of knowing and being known, the assurance that our friends would lay down their lives for us. Not surprisingly, as sociologist Robert Wuthnow demonstrated in his massive study of American small groups, "communities" in the U. S. (including those sponsored by churches) rarely go this far.[4]

All of the practices of communion, especially the sacraments of baptism and the Eucharist, unite us with Christ, and through Christ, with one another. In youth ministry, the practice of holy friendship, or *koinonia*, is one of our most explicit goals both for youth and adults. The temptation with practices of communion, of course, is to reduce them to "group-building." Often we undertake youth activities in the name of "communion," when they actually serve "community," a collective governed by hospitality with little or no thought given to accountability to our shared lives in Jesus Christ. For adolescents wrestling with issues of identity, practices of communion incarnate one of the building blocks of self: fidelity. These practices enact God's utter fidelity to us, made real in the steadfastness of faithful friends.

Pain Taking: Practices of Compassion

The family table also lends itself to the bearing of one another's burdens. We share the ups and the downs of our days, bemoan our troubles, and lay out our concerns. We do not share our distress because we think others at the table can get us out of our pain; we share because we know they will love us *through* our pain. People who pastor youth often find themselves deeply involved in practices of compassion as well as practices of justice, care, and kindness—all of which share another's load.

Historically youth ministry has stood at the vanguard of social reform. From the social gospel movement to the civil rights movement, churches organized student groups who, in many cases, led the charge for bettering the human condition. Even before volunteerism had the sanction of a Presidential summit, service was a viable part of youth ministry. In 1991, the Carnegie Council on Adolescent Development identified "other-directedness" as one of the primary benefits adolescents reap through their involvement in religious youth organizations.[5] Four out of five teenagers in a recent Gallup poll said that serving the needs of others appeals to them. Twenty percent said they were currently involved in church-sponsored activities to help less fortunate people, and 68 percent of teenagers who "have not been attracted to attend church recently" said they would like to be involved in church-sponsored service activities.[6]

But the increased popularity of service to others does not in itself measure participation in practices of compassion. Practices of compassion involve acts of *servants* more than acts of service. In practicing compassion, persons willingly suffer beside others in acts undertaken in the shadow of the cross. While practices of compassion include both the serving and the healing arts, these practices do not "fix." Fixing is a form of judgment; and all judgment creates distance, disconnection, an experience of difference. "In fixing," writes Rachel Naomi Remen, "there is an inequality of expertise that can easily become a moral distance."[7]

Compassion, on the other hand, means "to suffer alongside"—and being alongside someone requires the elimination of distance. It involves the possibility of touch. Remen sums up Mother Teresa's basic message in these words: "We serve life not because it is broken, but because it is holy."[8]

We distort practices of compassion when we use them to "fix" things. Sometimes distortion comes from confusing social activism that points to society with Christian practice that points to Christ. Sometimes distortion occurs when we marshal youth in order to fulfill adults' political agendas, what Robin Maas has called the "Pied Piper" syndrome of youth ministry.[9] Sometimes distortion results from translating caring into therapeutic rather than pastoral practice. In the current cultural climate that focuses on "inner" experience (*my* feelings, *my* spirituality, *my* struggle), self-absorption tempts us to treat sin as a matter between "me and my psyche" rather than as a concern of the community of faith.

Sometimes grace intervenes. Sometimes God redirects our impulse to "fix" in spite of ourselves. A pastor we know near Philadelphia took teenagers from her church into the city with sandwiches for some homeless men. The youth distributed the sandwiches, but no one ate. After an awkward moment of staring at one another, one of the men asked, "Well, isn't anyone going to say grace?" Taken aback, the youth looked from one to another wondering what to do next. Finally the homeless man returned thanks for the food, and everyone enjoyed dinner together. The simple practice of giving thanks transformed a wholesome service activity into a holy practice of faith. A service project became a *servant* project, reminding everyone that God calls homeless men as well as affluent youth to pastor one another and that Christ was the One served that evening.

Wave Making: Practices of Teaching and Nurture

The dinner table is also a place where families teach one another what it means to be a member of the family. Although Martin Luther advised hanging the Ten Commandments on the dining room wall so that fathers could teach their children the catechism during meals, most table talk takes the form of informally trying out new vistas with trusted others who allow us to question, dispute, and entertain new ideas.

Historically the practices most closely associated with youth ministry are teaching and nurture. Catechesis, sacred reading and study of scripture, and confirmation are classic disciplines of faith that have involved young people from time immemorial. These practices expand the boundaries of our faith toward the expansiveness of God. Faith development is not a linear progression (the Holy Spirit cares nothing for sequence). Instead, like ripples around a rock plunked in a pond, faith grows like an expanding series of concentric circles emanating from a central point, the cross of Christ.

Despite our substantial experience involving young people in practices of teaching and nurture, evidence suggests that we have not effectively used these practices to help young people mature in their faith. About two youth in five participate in Christian education programs, and 45 percent of American adolescents say religion is less important to them than to their parents.[10] Confirmation, the rite of passage adopted by many mainline traditions as an entry into the adult Christian community, has more often been treated as graduation out of it. In a study of five hundred people confirmed in the Presbyterian Church as teenagers, nearly half (48 percent) were unchurched by the time they reached their mid-thirties.[11]

Although we mean to hand on a living tradition, often what we actually offer youth are bleacher seats to the holy life. The term *curriculum* (from the French word *courir*, "to run") means "the course we run." Yet our paper-laden youth "curricula"—a misnomer if ever there was one—often teach youth about the baton of faith we intend to pass on to them without ever actually letting them run the relay. We often limit practices of teaching and nurture, which certainly include cognitive dimensions, to acts in which we tutor one another. Yet these practices also include activities that invite God's tutelage through prayerful discernment, the searching of sacred texts, and reflective participation in any of the practices of faith. Practices of teaching and nurture allow youth to "practice" practices within the protected space of peer groups that explore what it means to be a Christian.

Claim Staking: Practices of Witness

My father spent his life in politics, and among the more lively dimensions of dinner time at our house were "discussions" (which, in retrospect, were pretty one-sided) over current events, community issues, school policies, church decisions, and family brouhahas. These dinner discussions were seldom reasoned, intellectual treatises. They inevitably grew out of our "reports of the day"—what we had seen, heard, and experienced since breakfast. We offered our reports as evidence as we weighed in on whether punishment served as a deterrent in either classroom or capital offenses, whether abortion was a legitimate option for a pregnant friend at school, whether Uncle Martin qualified as a religious extremist even if he did think the rest of us were going straight to hell.

In the practices of witness, we take a stand for our faith. Practices of witness are those acts that send us racing breathlessly from the empty tomb to *tell*. They report to those who have heard and those who haven't that we have seen the Lord, that he is risen and among us. For most of America's history, many of the practices of witness—preaching, interpretation of scripture, prophecy—have fallen within the realm of the professional clergy, rather than within youth ministry repertoires. We have left some practices, like testimony and evangelism, to conservative evangelical traditions to the point that other Christians use them somewhat nervously. Both of these factors have the effect of shielding youth from the practices of witness except when they are on the receiving end of them (being preached *at*, interpreted *for*, prophesied *to*).

In practices of witness, we stake our claim on Jesus Christ because of what we have seen God do in him. Youth are especially suited to some practices of witness that have traditionally excluded their participation. Speaking the truth in love, for example, is an important way teenagers minister to the church. Undeveloped ideological filters—the kind that help you and me screen out certain emotional stimuli—contribute to the emotional roller coaster of adolescence. Teenagers have trouble sorting through lesser emotional claims in favor of primary ones; every emotion is primary to a teenager. This emotional openness has an up side: It helps teenagers "tune in" both to God and to other human beings in ways adults have long since forgotten. Consequently, youth can be prophetic voices in the wilderness who call us to respond on God's behalf to people we would otherwise overlook.

The down side of this openness is that young people also "tune in" to countless other claims on their identity as well. Because youth are unencumbered by ideological commitments and because they are still developing their powers of cognition, youth lead with their hearts— every time. Adolescents are quick crusaders, zealots as often as prophets. Church history is peppered with young people playing all of these roles at once (Joan of Arc, Francis of Assisi, Martin Luther, Dwight Moody, all come to mind). While emotional attunement opens us to God and other people, feelings provide notoriously fickle standards of judgment. Inviting youth into the practices of witness requires appropriate role modeling as well as affirmation of youth themselves in these roles. Most adolescents possess neither the cognitive tools nor the ethical experience to evaluate competing claims on the self thoroughly. Discernment requires thoughtful, critical reason as well as emotional engagement, and adolescents need guidance as they learn to combine the two.

Rhythm Breaking: Practices of Dehabituation

Sometimes we need to break out of our usual dinner routine to develop a true appreciation of those with whom we dine. We have a picnic; we set the table with good china and candles; we try a new recipe. These interruptions in our usual daily flow cause us to experience dinner anew and attune us to aspects of the meal and one another that we normally take for granted.

Dehabituating or "ascetic" practices are not usually compared to a picnic, but they recreate us in similar ways. The practices of asceticism are among "the currently least understood and most universally rejected features of historical Christianity."[12] We seldom incorporate these practices into our ministry with adolescents—at least not intentionally. We think of Robert DeNiro in the movie *The Mission* doing penance by dragging iron weights up steep cliffs, hunger strikes with dubious spiritual or political consequences, religious orders that require strict silence and bare feet even in January. We harbor justifiable suspicion of ascetic practices; we know them for their excesses and abuses, not for their potential in forming the self. Painfully aware of the adolescent penchant for excess, we fear connections between ascetic practice and self-mutilation or even self-hatred. We admire our ascetic forebears like John the Baptist, Julian of Norwich and Thomas Merton, but we also think they were a little bit nuts.

But look more closely. Though we seldom consciously involve youth in practices of dehabituation, these practices show up regularly in youth ministry, and resources abound for their use. These practices break us out of habitual rhythms and introduce God's cadence instead. Ascetic practices, designed "to awaken the soul from its inertia, to break destructive emotional and physical habits, and to renew energy and insight"[13] by removing us from the context and habits of daily living, serve as means to renewed and intensified religious experience. Modern-day youth make pilgrimages to summer camp, mission trips, retreats. Twelve-step programs, designed to eliminate addictive behavior, and wilderness education are programs of asceticism; and they have endured much of the same kind of criticism as their historical antecedents.

In our church, the senior pastor takes youth out to a "dress up restaurant" every fifth Sunday, just to remind them that—despite the snack menu usually served at youth meetings—they are worthy of God's excellent fare. Countercultural moral practices like chastity and nonviolent resistance, liturgical practices like stillness or (at the other end of the spectrum) "speaking in tongues" are "dehabituating." They reorganize our understanding of who we are around God instead of ourselves.

Askesis, the Greek root of ascetic, simply means "exercise." We might say that practices of dehabituation are the NordicTraks™ of our faith. They jolt us out of spiritual complacency, stretch us until we notice muscles we didn't know we had, push our endurance beyond what we thought possible for the sake of strengthening the body—not only the body of the believer, but the body of Christ. The danger that lurks within dehabituating practice in youth ministry, like the danger of asceticism generally, comes from interpreting such practices as sources of individual rather than communal strength. Fasting, for instance, has a time-honored place in Christian tradition. But when fasting becomes understood as an individual pursuit that "plays into" cultural norms of sexism and perfectionism, we confuse fasting with dieting, which can lead to self-destructive pathologies like anorexia.

We have chosen the term *dehabituating* instead of *ascetic* practices to remind all of us who pastor youth that these practices do not necessarily involve bodily self-denial. In the words of Catholic theologian M. Shawn Copeland, "Christian asceticism is not spiritual boot camp."[14] She calls ascetic practices the companion disciplines of faithfully "saying yes and saying no." Saying yes to God inevitably means developing spiritual resistance or the ability to say no to other demands that compete for our attention and compromise our openness to the Spirit. "Learning when and how, to what, and to whom to give our yes or our no," concludes Copeland, "is a lifelong project. It is learning to live not merely in dull balance or tedious moderation but in passionate, disciplined choice and action."[15] Practices of dehabituation make us alert to Christ both by attuning us to God's signals in our lives and by tuning out a lot of spiritual static.

Praise Making: Practices of Worship

Dinner at our house begins with grace, both the kind we say and the kind we receive. It is welcome "down time" in our tangle of daily commitments, a time when we come face-to-face with friends and family to give thanks for the blessings of life. Not to mislead you, dinner is seldom a culinary adventure with us. We have been known to have "cereal suppers" composed entirely of Cocoa Puffs when we are too tired either to cook or to care what we eat. Even these dinners are reason for praise, since on these nights we have chosen one another over the food pyramid, grateful to live in a part of the world where we will undoubtedly eat a more nutritious menu tomorrow.

The practices of worship—whether the elaborate spread of a full-blown Sunday morning service or the brief respite of a short prayer of thanksgiving—are actually "distilled" from all the families of practices. They restore us to unity with the risen Christ and with other people through his body, the church. They enable us to fall in love, stay in love, and express our love to the God smitten with us. Because worship involves a spectrum of practices (administered "full strength"), worship serves as an "immersion experience" in the Christian way of life. Someone has said that worship is to daily life

> as consomme is to broth. In liturgy at its best—in the common work of the people assembled to hear the Word of God and celebrate the sacraments—the meaning of all the practices appears in a form that is thick and tasty, darker and richer than what we get in most everyday situations....A Christian community at worship is a community gathered for rehearsal. It is "practicing" the practices in the same way a child practices catching a ball or playing scales.[16]

This rehearsal for Christian community is basic to the Christian life. The practices of worship alter our relationship to God and to one another and radically impact who we are.

Since worship is the signature practice of Christian community, practices of worship seem like obvious components of youth ministry. Unfortunately we often "tame" their transcendence to avoid scaring off teenagers. Most of us involve youth in these practices—but hesitantly. The last thing we want to do is to "preach" at the youth (a youth talk, maybe, but not a sermon). We cram reflection time with "active learning," despite the power of stillness to dislodge youth from their embeddedness in media culture. We have devotions, not prayers. Except for the Lord's Prayer (which fewer and fewer of them know), we hesitate to ask teenagers to voice their fears and desires before God. We are sensitive. We don't want to embarrass anybody.

The irony is that, developmentally, adolescents *need* a transcendent God worthy of their fidelity, a God who can transport them beyond the limitations of self. Millennial youth have cut their teeth on special effects and simulations of transcendence and are in search of the life-shaking, real article. Domesticating these practices succeeds only in dimming their wattage at a time when adolescents seek high-voltage (which is not the same as fever-pitched) encounters with the sacred. Rather than "taming" practices of worship that bring us into God's presence, implying that youth cannot handle direct sacred experience, we are called to create welcoming, undiluted worship that embraces the creative contributions and honors the critiques of adolescents who know real transcendence when they see it.

Ringing in Our Ears: Practices and Identity in the Community of Faith

For many centuries in Europe, the sound of a bell defined community life. By the bell, you knew the hour of worship, the performance of sacraments, and the tolling of death, not to mention the festivity of community celebrations. Both Lutheran and Reformed German immigrants in eighteenth-century Pennsylvania begged their congregations back home to send bells. The sound of the ringing bell defined a settlement. Bells provided the parameters by which people knew they were still within the confines of the parish. By keeping track of the liturgical hours, bells defined communities' sense of time as well as their sense of space.

Like bells, practices help define the community of faith. They order our life together, and they shape a certain lifestyle that responds to Jesus Christ. When we remain within earshot of the practices of faith, they remind us of who we are and how we are called to live. We share these daily rhythms with others who hear and respond to the same bell. Godbearing youth ministry does not merely "incorporate" spiritual disciplines into a curriculum for youth. It is a spiritually disciplined way of life through which Christians of all ages draw sustenance from the deep wells of historic Christian practice. By the grace of God, we practice the "way of perfection"—not because practice helps us get it right, but because practice helps us "get it," period.

QUESTIONS AND EXERCISES

1. How and when have you tried to deepen your faith on your own? What happened?

2. What are some of the "bells" or Christian practices in your own

faith life that have been especially important in calling you back to God? What makes these practices so powerful?

3. Look at the table, "Families of Christian Practices," on page 111. Which ones are prominent in your ministry with youth? Which ones are missing? What difference would it make if Christian practices became your primary curriculum or focus with young people?

IDEA FOR THE ROAD

Form two groups. Instruct Group A to choose an "aerobics instructor" and lead the group in calisthenics (either seated or standing) to some rhythmic music. Have each person in Group B apply a water-based temporary tattoo on a partner. After everyone in Group B is tattooed, switch tasks (Group A tattoos; Group B does aerobics.) How do these activities illustrate the way Christian practices function in the community of faith?

FARE FOR THE SOUL

"What message have you for young people?" asked Carl Stern of NBC in concluding a television interview with Rabbi Abraham Joshua Heschel shortly before his death.

Rabbi Heschel replied: "...Let them remember that there is a meaning beyond absurdity. Let them be sure that every deed counts, that every word has power, and that we all can do our share to redeem the world in spite of all absurdities and all frustrations and all disappointments.

"And, above all, [let them] remember...to build a life as if it were a work of art."

> Just to be is a blessing.
> Just to live is holy.[17]

> —*Abraham Joshua Heschel*

Notes

1. See John B. Cobb Jr., *Grace and Responsibility: A Wesleyan Theology for Today* (Nashville: Abingdon, 1995); 139–140, 142.

2. Kathleen Norris, *Amazing Grace: A Vocabulary of Faith* (New York: Riverhead Books, 1998), 57.

3. Craig Dykstra and Dorothy C. Bass, "Times of Yearning, Practices of Faith," in *Practicing Our Faith: A Way of Life for a Searching People*, ed. Dorothy C. Bass (San Francisco: Jossey-Bass, 1997), 7.

4. Robert Wuthnow found that while most groups succeeded in being "nice" to one another and "supportive" in terms of offering moral support, few small group members made sacrifices for one another (including financial ones). Conflict within a group usually resulted in leaving the group rather than disrupting it with resolution. See Robert Wuthnow, *Sharing the Journey: Support Groups and America's New Quest for Community* (New York: Free Press, 1994).

5. Kenda Creasy Dean, "A Synthesis of the Research on, and a Descriptive Overview of, Protestant, Catholic, and Jewish Religious Youth Programs in the United States," working paper (Washington, D.C.: Carnegie Council on Adolescent Development, February 1991), vi–vii.

6. "Helping Others Is the Way to Fill Church with Youth, Poll Finds," *Ecumenical News International* (January 16, 1997), E-mail.

7. Rachel Naomi Remen, "In the Service of Life," *Noetic Services Review* (Spring 1996), E-mail.

8. Ibid.

9. Robin Maas, "Christ and the Adolescent: Piper or Prophet?" *Christ and the Adolescent: A Theological Approach to Youth Ministry* (Princeton: Princeton Theological Seminary, 1996), 38–39.

10. Statistics vary on adolescent participation in Christian education. Search Institute's massive study of Christian education in five mainline Protestant congregations and the Southern Baptist Convention (whose youth exhibited the highest levels of faith maturity) reported three youth in ten were involved in intentional Christian education programs for youth (including Sunday school, youth groups, etc.) (Peter L. Benson and Carolyn H. Eklin, *Effective Christian Education: A National Study of Protestant Congregations* [Minneapolis: Search Institute, 1990], 4). George H. Gallup and Robert Bezilla report 41 percent of American teenagers randomly surveyed said they attended Sunday school or Bible study classes, and 36 percent said they were active in a church youth group (the sample allows for overlap between these two categories) (*The Religious Life of Young Americans* [Princeton: George H. Gallup International Institute, 1992], 32). The last statistic mentioned above is from Gallup and Bezilla, 64.

11. Richard R. Osmer, *Confirmation: Presbyterian Practices in Ecumenical Perspective* (Louisville: Geneva Press, 1996), xii. The 1989 study is cited in *Vanishing Boundaries* by sociologists Dean Hoge, Benton Johnson and Donald Luidens, and included people born between 1947–56. At the time of the study, these people were between 33 and 42 years old.

12. Margaret R. Miles, *Practicing Christianity: Critical Perspectives for an Embodied Spirituality* (New York: Crossroad, 1988), 94.

13. Margaret R. Miles, "The Recovery of Asceticism," *Commonweal* 110, no. 2 (28 January 1983): 41.

14. M. Shawn Copeland, "Saying Yes and Saying No," in *Practicing Our Faith*, Bass, 64–65.

15. Ibid., 67.

16. Dykstra and Bass, "Times of Yearning, Practices of Faith," in *Practicing Our Faith*, Bass, 9.

17. Abraham Joshua Heschel, *I Asked for Wonder*, ed. Samuel H. Dresner (New York: Crossroad, 1984); 63, 65.

SEVEN
A Circle of Friends
Inviting Spiritual Friendship

*What is almost unbelievably remarkable is that
God chooses friendship, available to everyone, as
the means of changing the world, its people, and
societies.*
—*Michael Williams, "The Midwives' Story"*

ON OUR DECK against a backdrop of oak, tulip poplar, and birch
trees sits a bluish-gray, maroon, and beige clay figurine, no taller than
eight or nine inches. Yet its full stature can't be measured so simply or
quickly. My family purchased the figurine on a trip to the West Coast
as much for its symbolic as aesthetic value. While simple and tasteful, the
piece of art is most certainly mass produced. It depicts a group of people, each person with both arms wrapped around his or her neighbor.
The figures stand facing one another, and the small space in the center
of this human ring houses a votive candle.

The woman who sold us the piece explained that part of its appeal
is the unique effect that a lighted candle has on the people in the circle. Though at first glance they are seemingly indistinguishable—the
sculpture is intentionally crude, more suggestive than detailed—these
people take on more individual personalities as the glow of the candle
lights up their faces. She was right. The friendship circle has graced our
table at many meals, and we have witnessed this remarkable transformation firsthand.

My attraction to the friendship circle is mostly theological. In its
current location, the figurine's dimensions are about right; the trees
dwarf this little clay piece. Against the overwhelming presence of a wild
and unpredictable world, this tiny band of seven cling to one another for
dear life. And as long as the flame is lit in the center, they actually appear
to have a chance. The Beatles may have said it best in the 1960s, but the
church has been proclaiming it for twenty centuries: In the Christian

123

community the only way we get by is with a little help from our friends.

None of us on the Christian path is ever a lone traveler. We always journey with companions at our side, before us, and trailing behind us. A great cloud of witnesses (Heb. 12:1), a communion of saints both living and departed, surrounds us. There is no such thing as a solitary Christian, which is both a descriptive reality and a great grace. To be a Christian means we are part of the body of Christ. The local communities in which we live out our faith give faces and names to our companions on the journey.

Authentic Christianity is an intensely personal matter, for the living Christ invades us at the core of our beings. But it is never a private affair just between us and God. The broader Christian community provides the means of support to stay on the road and the corrective against going down our own paths of self-obsession and sometimes self-destruction. H. Richard Niebuhr asserted that our individual revelation of God, or conversion—what he called the decision of self—must stay in balance with the revelation available through the Christian community of faith. This communion includes all those "who occupy the same standpoint and look in the same direction toward the same reality to which we look as individuals....Assurance grows out of immediate perception plus social corroboration and out of neither one of these alone."[1]

The practice of spiritual friendship warrants the special attention of people involved in youth ministry. Often spiritual friendship is the practice of faith that we instinctively place at the center of ministry with adolescents. In truth, however, *no* ministry can survive without a lively practice of spiritual friendship. Created for friendship with God, we humans require friendship to stay alive. Along with a rhythm of life rooted in the practices of faith, a circle of spiritual friends comprises one of the basic ingredients of Godbearing ministry.

Friendship and the Faith Community

The concept of friendship has ambivalent roots in Christian history. On the one hand, the early church borrowed notions of friendship from the Greeks and Romans who, influenced by philosophers like Plato, Aristotle, and Cicero, believed friends were preferential relationships between people with similar character, virtue, and worldviews. Like their pagan counterparts, the early Christians considered friendship a public affair. Friendship supported the communal good, occurring in the context of a larger community that supported and nourished bonds between like-minded people. Cicero, for instance, viewed friendship as "nothing else than an accord in all things, human and divine, conjoined with mutual good will and affection."[2] Luke's description of the early Christians strikes a similar chord: "The whole group of those who believed were of one heart and soul, and no one claimed private ownership of any possessions, but everything they owned was held in common" (Acts 4:32).

In contrast to their pagan neighbors, Christians believed that friendship's primary virtue lay in its ability to nurture discipleship. This belief made it possible for Christians to befriend persons unlike themselves as well. The point of Christian friendship was not mutual confirmation as much as mutual empowerment to follow Jesus. Christian friendship sought unity in the body of Christ, and any love that undermined that unity (however noble) impeded the faith. In the Eastern monasteries, the "desert fathers and mothers" discouraged friendship among monks (except with a spiritual mentor), fearing that the preference of one person over another violated a Christian's duty to love all people equally.[3] More optimistic Western theologians viewed friendship "as a metaphor for life together in community, and as a metaphor for life with God."[4] While significant friendships between religious men and women did exist (the soulful friendship between Francis and Clare of Assisi is perhaps the most famous), society generally viewed male-female friendships as impossible. After all, true friendship implied equality—and cultures that maintained inequality between the sexes believed friendship was possible only among persons of the same gender.

Modern individualism removed friendship from the communal assumptions of the ancient and medieval worlds. Today we consider friendships private, intimate bonds between consenting adults. These bonds shift amidst a kaleidoscope of cultural patterns. Contemporary Christianity has inherited a fairly undifferentiated view of friendship, allowing us to apply the term willy-nilly to relationships ranging from casual acquaintances to romantic lovers.

Spiritual friends are people who pull us toward God. The unity of souls found among Christian friends stems not from attraction (although we may be attracted to one another) but from the union Jesus seeks with each of us. Some theologians warn against confusing friendship, which often stresses common values and worldviews, with *koinonia*, the Christian fellowship that "reaches across all earthly barriers and distinctions."[5] Although we consider Christian fellowship a form of friendship, we agree that Christian friendship is unique. Christians are lashed not to one another but to the cross of Jesus Christ. Consequently, the intensity and passion basic to Christian friendship lies in the fact that we suffer love—not merely profess love—for the God-given "others" in our lives.

A Place Where Everyone Knows Your Name

For the past decade or so I have been waging a rather low-key, one-person crusade to have a television theme song included in our denomination's hymnal. I am speaking of the theme song to *Cheers*, the long-running sitcom set in a Boston bar with a motley gathering of regulars. I have always based my contention on a theological as well as historical precedent. If Charles and John Wesley could raid the pubs and rewrite the drinking songs of their day with Christian lyrics, then certainly we ought to be able to borrow a bar song with overt Christian overtones and baptize it for the church.

Week after week this band of friends return to their familiar haunt where everybody knows their name to share their lives and to offer one another the gifts of companionship. By standing with one another in mutual support and vulnerability, they create a strong and appealing sense of community in which many viewers shared vicariously.

Historically youth ministry has offered the gift of community more effectively to adolescents than to the adults who pastor them. The main draw in many youth programs continues to be the bonds of friendship, the sense of belonging that comes from being part of a group. That sense of belonging is the appeal of small groups in general: Someone notices when we aren't there and makes us feel welcome when we are. For adolescents who need to be looked at more than looked up to, this is a powerful dynamic. Even in churches with little else going on in youth ministry in terms of teaching, worship, or structured program, chances are good that if youth group is happening at all, it is surviving on the strength of relationship and community.

However, those of us in ministry with youth miss the point if all we provide adolescents is a Christianized *Cheers* gathering. We should provide nothing less—acceptance, vulnerability, and a place "where everybody knows your name" are good things and honorable goals. But we need to strive intentionally for a kind of community that offers something more, something deeper, something God-centered. Ask almost any youthworker about the core elements of his or her youth ministry, and almost without exception creating a sense of community will rank high on the list.[6] But community for community's sake is not enough.

Godbearers seek *communion* as well as community, a circle of friends rooted in God's friendship with us.

Over the past several years, I have had the privilege of watching such a Christ-centered community form among some of our youth. The bonds of friendship this particular class of graduating seniors has established with one another are clearly grounded in Christ. These seniors pray together in school before classes begin; they self-lead a Bible study; they go to Young Life together; they go on mission trips together; they lead and participate in our youth group meetings; they actively participate in many ways at church; they hang out together on a regular basis. Something more than typical high-school friendship is going on here, more than a loyalty to a particular group (Young Life, our church, their school), more than a Christianized *Cheers*. They come together on a regular basis to spark one another's growth toward God, and their communion feeds a spiritual hunger that isn't fed anywhere else. They are experiencing the joys and depths of spiritual friendship.

Godbearers seek to foster these types of spiritual friendships—for youth, absolutely—but also for ourselves. We must not be content to admire such community when it evidences itself among our youth. One of the ironies of our vocation is that while many of us help create community among adolescents, professional isolation is a tremendous problem in the field of youth ministry. In a worst case scenario, our youth become our only group of spiritual friends (bad idea) and/or we quit because we lack supportive companions for our own spiritual journeys. Godbearers seek to develop their own circle of friends who make the way of Christ more visible and less lonely.

Is Your Circle Complete?

Spiritual friendship, one of the neglected disciplines of community, nurtures our attentiveness to God. Such friendships give life to leaders in youth ministry, or any form of ministry for that matter, and when they are absent from our lives, we wither, we die. What is true for our youth is equally true for those who minister with and to them: We need a company of friends to keep us on the path of salvation. Kent Ira Groff writes, "Spiritual friendship is an ancient form of communal guidance and prayer support. It may take the form of finding another person as a *spiritual companion* with whom you can listen for the promptings of the Spirit, formally or informally; and it may also take the form of family prayer and sharing or a small support group."[7]

Spiritual friendships are really love triangles whose three angles include the other, the self, and—always—God. Spiritual friendships are a means of grace that serve as avenues for truer and deeper communion with God. What sets these relationships apart from other sorts of friendships is their intentional verticality, the self-conscious referencing of the relationship to God. When we grow closer to God, the gap lessens between us and our friend, and we find ourselves experiencing deeper intimacy. (See "Spiritual Friendships" below.) Since we grow at different rates, one of the wonderful effects of a spiritual friendship is the Godward pull of another. If my friend deepens his or her communion with God, and I am open to and invested in that friendship, I may find myself almost magnetically drawn closer to God as well.

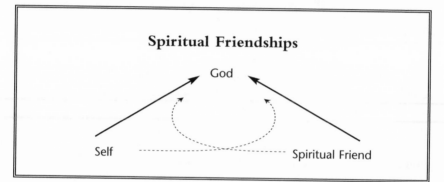

Spiritual Friendships

Spiritual friends can nurture our ability to listen for God, offer us company and direction as we seek God's will, and strengthen us for the long road of faithfulness. Spiritual friendships come in many shapes and sizes. We need an assortment of friends who gather around the flame of Christ with us. In our circle of friends we may find companions, mentors, invisible friends, soul friends, and outsiders (who are really insiders).

Companions

Companions are usually the most plentiful of our spiritual friends. These people share faith with us in many settings: church, work, school, study group, neighborhood. Their mere presence in our lives helps light the path of faith for us and combats loneliness along the Christian way. We can ask these people to pray for us (and they will). We can call them to watch our children. We trust and respect them. We need no intimate connection for someone to function as a companion in our circle. Sometimes they are just there, traveling a parallel path, and we acknowledge one another's presence from a distance with a knowing smile.

Here we can take a page from the meerkat. Meerkats are among the most sociable creatures on earth. Because of their size, these small mammals must band together in order to survive the harsh conditions of the Kalahari Desert. From baby-sitting and grooming to hunting and defending, they do nearly everything together. Remarkably cooperative, they display a high degree of selflessness. They find strength in numbers against enemies that could easily wipe them out one by one.

Christians need companions on the faith journey much in the way that meerkats need one another: for survival. The fellowship of companions in Christ strengthens us to face the world faithfully, enabling us to do together what we cannot do alone. Spiritual companions make us more than we can ever be on our own because God's love binds us together. The presence of friends makes God's love more real to us. Noting this indispensable link between faith and friendship, W. Paul Jones writes that "faith, by its very nature, is a weaving on the loom of friendship, a weaving patterned by the warp and woof of promise-making and promise-keeping."[8]

Mentors

Another member of our circle of friends is a mentor or sponsor, someone who possesses more experience, spiritual maturity, accumulated wisdom, or a combination of all three than we do. Typically a mentor fuels our faith journey in intentional and direct ways and helps us discern a faithful life course. A mentor may be someone who helped us sort out our call and entry into ministry. A mentor may be the person we touch base with once or twice a year just to check our bearings. When a mentor (or "sponsor") effectively performs this role,

> there is a whole new dimension of reality for the one who is being sponsored. Sponsors help generate spiritual passion and vision. They often convey the sense of possibility....Very few things would be more effective in the raising up of a powerful and passionate people to expand Christ's kingdom than the choice by mature Christians to become special-friend sponsors to younger Christians in need of models and cheerleaders.[9]

Mentors do not use their spiritual maturity as a weapon or as license to create a relationship of superiority. Instead, mentors graciously see their role as fellow travelers and offer appropriate support and guidance

Broadly speaking, Godbearing ministry is more akin to mentor-friendship than any other type within the circle we have drawn here. Godbearers are called to help pass on to youth a passion for God. That does not mean that all Godbearers will be mentors to the youth in their care. In many cases, they will not. But the real possibility exists that youth may claim us as a mentor for a period of time in their lives. That privilege comes with profound responsibility, along with the joy of watching a young life grow in commitment toward Christ.

Soul Friends

Soul friends, or *anmchara* as the Irish refer to them, are those intimate few in our circle of relationships who take an avid interest in our soulful self, just as we do in theirs. These are one or two special fellow travelers who help us attend to the state of our spiritual lives. Soul friends ask questions like these: What have you been praying about lately? Are you making time for God in your schedule? What do you hear God calling you to do or to be in your vocation? Do your priorities need some shifting? What is preventing you from letting go of that bad habit? Soul friends don't advise as often as they listen and sift through our life experience with us. In this respect, they act as informal spiritual directors who intentionally partner with us in the quest for deeper communion with God.

Soul friends come to us as a gift from God when we discover another heart that beats in a similar cadence with ours. We don't set out to create a soul friend, though the relationship does require a certain attentiveness. Sometimes soul friendships evolve out of a relationship with a spiritual companion. At other times, a person drops into our lives at the right time and place, immediately creating a unique bond, a special kinship. All spiritual friendships are a means of grace, but none to the degree that a soul friend is. With a soul friend we share our deepest doubts, joys, longings, fears, dreams, confusion, searching. Soul friends know how hard to push and when gently to give us space.

Thomas Moore writes, "Friends interested in each other at the soul level do not simply look at each other's lives and listen to each other's explanations. They look together at this third thing...and in that mutual gaze they find and sustain their friendship."[10] For Moore, the third thing is the soul itself; in a Christian context, the third thing is nothing less than God.

Invisible Friends

Also prominent in our circle of friends are those whom we refer to as invisible friends or unknowing friends. These friends remain at a distance, unaware of any relationship with us, though we keenly sense a relationship with them. The people in this category include saints (official and unofficial) of the church or prominent role models of the faith for us, who may or may not be prominent to others. For example, Mother Teresa, Desmond Tutu, Oscar Romero, or Martin Luther King Jr. might be some contemporary witnesses with whom we enjoy an invisible yet quite influential relationship.

Equally possible is an invisible friendship with someone whose faith we have admired in our community, our professional networks, or our family trees. Since invisible friends need not be famous, a former pastor, a teacher, a youth counselor from our teenage years may all fit the bill in varying measure. The point is that God uses these people to grace our lives, even from a distance. Though somewhat one-sided, the spiritual kinship we experience with our invisible friends is nonetheless real; and depending upon the degree to which their story, their writings, and/or their witness have influenced our own faith journeys, they may be good friends indeed.

Perhaps the most obvious group of invisible friends (and in my case, the most influential) are writers, both secular and sacred. Many of us develop friendships with a particular writer or a select few authors who nourish our souls in deep ways. For me that author and spiritual friend has been Eugene Peterson. I first became acquainted with Peterson after reading his book *Working the Angles* a number of years ago. Ever since then, Peterson's delicately carved images and soul-piercing passages about maintaining pastoral integrity in a market church always call me back to my core identity as person and pastor. When I lose my bearings and find myself drifting, I read Peterson to regain my focus.

Now, I've never met Eugene Peterson. I spoke with him by phone once when I invited him to lead a clergy retreat (he was otherwise engaged). Aside from that, I have had no personal contact with him. Yet I sense a spiritual bond with this man who seems to understand me and ministry in a way that few people in my life do. His invisible friendship has graced my vocation, and his writing has influenced my spiritual journey profoundly. Other writers have had lesser but still an important influence upon me, including Annie Dillard, Frederick Buechner, and Garrison Keillor, to name a few.

You probably have discovered certain authors (or teachers or neighbors or others) who challenge and deepen your faith in extraordinary ways. Our list of invisible friends may vary widely because friendships, even invisible ones, are an intensely personal matter. What matters is that we seek out those friends who sing our heartsong, who replenish our wells, who draw us into deeper communion with God and that we claim them as part of our sacred circle of friends.

Outsiders Inside the Circle

By outsiders, we mean people who may be self-avowedly outside the Christian community or at least those for whom religion is not a core commitment. These outsiders include friends of other faith traditions or people who have no defined tradition of faith at all. While we need to surround ourselves with Christian friends, we will suffocate if we only breathe "Christian air" at all times. Jesus, after all, did not impose theological criteria on his associates. When we interact only with brothers and sisters in Christ, we miss out on the rich diversity of all God's people as well as the opportunity to invite others in. Leonard Sweet says it pointedly: "[Christians] are called to be in the world. Not of it. But not out of it, either."[11]

Sweet argues for a faith that remains in dialogue with contemporary philosophies, worldviews, scientific discoveries, and sociological trends. What he advocates on a global and theological level, we advocate on a relational level as well. Since many of us travel most naturally in Christian circles, we may have to seek out these "outside" friendships intentionally. Our relationships with outsiders work in at least two directions. First, outsiders keep us honest in our faith journeys: rooted in reality, challenged by difficult questions, and broadened by other perspectives. We need friends with whom we can share recreational interests, social similarities, and provocative dialogue though not necessarily theological common ground.

Second, these friendships may be the bridge that extends the hand and invites a seeker to faith. We want to be clear: Godbearers do not use friendships (or friends) as tools for evangelism. Friends are never objects. Communion is always and ultimately a mutual relationship wrought by God. Yet we recognize that sometimes God works through friendship to extend greater communion to our "outsider" friends. By invitation and example (as opposed to confrontation and argument), genuine friendship may be a means of grace for the other who is searching openly or quietly for a way home. For our sake and for theirs, we need outsiders inside our circle of friends.

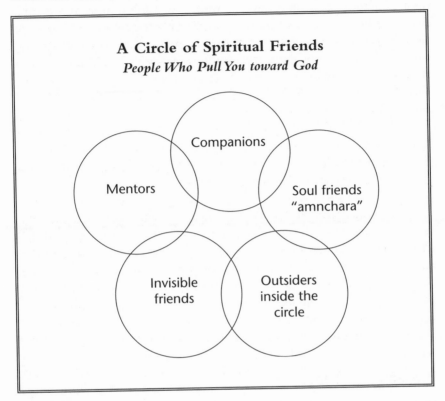

A Circle of Spiritual Friends
People Who Pull You toward God

Companions

Mentors

Soul friends "amnchara"

Invisible friends

Outsiders inside the circle

Accountable Friendship

We need to speak briefly about the unique dynamics of the relationship when our spiritual friends are persons of the opposite sex. Spiritual friendships with youth or with other adults have the potential for intimacy. For that reason, Godbearers need a clear and healthy sense of boundaries. God created us to desire relationship with God and with others. Our desire for God is rooted in our desire for "other-ness," a desire that also manifests itself in our desire for other people. Both prayer and sex, as expressions of deep intimacy, are holy expressions of this thirst for communion. A fine line exists between emotional/spiritual intimacy and sexual intimacy. In male-female spiritual friendships some lines clearly should not be crossed. Godbearers do not deny their own sexuality, nor do they abuse the sacred trust of another and act out their sexuality in inappropriate ways.

Refraining from sexual intimacy is always appropriate in relationships involving adolescents and almost always appropriate for adult spiritual friendships as well. If our soul mate is not our spouse or romantic partner, we need to be honest with ourselves and with our spiritual friends about the psychosexual dynamics in the relationship. What may begin innocently as a genuine spiritual friendship, a true brother-sister relationship grounded in and pointing to Christ, can easily become distorted in ways that take advantage (sometimes mutually) of the other's vulnerability. Keeping spiritual friendships honest and accountable may mean being very public (that is, out in the open) in the time spent together, involving others in the relationship, naming the psychosexual dynamics as they arise, and even being willing to lose a spiritual friendship for the sake of continuing a marriage.

We intend these words as a caution, not a prohibition against male-female spiritual friendships. Because of the complementary nature of men and women—we see and experience faith and the world quite differently—a person of the opposite sex may be the most appropriate candidate to help us stretch our spiritual horizons. A man may help a woman relate to the masculine imagery for God laced throughout scripture; a woman may open up new forms of relationship and nurture in the Christian life to a male friend. Male-female spiritual friendships are indeed a grace but a grace to be honestly and openly handled with care.

Becoming Theophilus

In the circle of spiritual friendship, among the community of believers, we find our truest selves. Just as the candle illumines the individual faces of the people in our clay figurine, so too does the light of Christ cause our faces to glow with a holy fire. We see that light reflected in the lives of those special friends who, arm in arm, keep us gathered around the fire and whose presence in our lives draws us closer to the center of the ring. As we grow in grace, our circle of friends will abound with companions, mentors, soul friends, invisible friends, and outsiders (who are really insiders)—all of whom make it possible for us to offer the gift of spiritual friendship to others in equal measure.

The writer addresses The Gospel according to Luke and its sequel, The Acts of the Apostles, to Theophilus. Scholars have long debated whether Theophilus was an actual person or a code name for those who might read the book in later years. We favor the latter interpretation; the invitation is for all of us to become Theophilus, a lover of God. Jesus told his disciples and reminds each of us as directly: "I do not call you servants any longer...but I have called you friends" (John 15:15). Ultimately, the true goal of spiritual friendship is to be known and counted as a lover of God, a friend of God—to mediate communion with God through a circle of friends.

QUESTIONS AND EXERCISES

1. Look at the chart on page 133. Who would you include in your circle of spiritual friends, and what are their roles (mentor, companion, soul friend, invisible friend, outsider/insider)?

2. Do you see yourself as a spiritual mentor to anyone in particular right now? How comfortable do you feel in that role? What intentional steps are you taking to nurture this person in his or her spiritual journey?

3. What person(s) would you like to add to your circle? Which relationships would you like to seek out or nurture for your own or another's spiritual growth?

IDEA FOR THE ROAD

On a small slip of paper, take the friends you've listed above and write one name next to a different day of the week. Carry the paper with you in your wallet or purse and pray for them/give thanks for them daily.

FARE FOR THE SOUL

Being a spiritual friend is being the physician of a wounded soul. And what does a physician do when someone comes with a bleeding wound?

Three things: He or she cleanses the wound, aligns the sundered parts, and gives it rest. That's all. The physician does *not* heal. He or she provides an *environment* for the dominant natural process of healing to take its course....an environment for the birthing and nourishing of a whole soul.[12]

—Tilden H. Edwards

Notes

1. H. Richard Niebuhr, *The Meaning of Revelation* (New York: MacMillan, 1941), 103.

2. Cicero, *De Amicitia,* VI, 20, *De Senectute, De Amicitia, De Divinatione,* trans. William

Armistead Falconer, Loeb Classical Library, ed. E. Capps, T. E. Page, and W. H. D. Rouse (London: William Heinemann, 1923), 131.

3. Elizabeth Zarelli Turner, "Love, Marriage and Friendship," in *Men and Women: Sexual Ethics in Turbulent Times*, ed. Philip Turner (Cambridge, Mass.: Cowley Publications, 1989), 161.

4. Ibid., 162.

5. See Diogenes Allen, *Love: Christian Romance, Marriage, Friendship* (Princeton: Cowley Publications, 1987), 56–59.

6. Peter Scales et al., *The Attitudes and Needs of Religious Youth Workers: Perspectives from the Field* (Minneapolis: Search Institute, November 1995).

7. Kent Ira Groff, *Active Spirituality: A Guide for Seekers and Ministers* (Bethesda: Alban Institute, 1993), 63.

8. W. Paul Jones, "Friendship and Circles of Commitment," *Weavings* 7, no. 3 (1992): 38.

9. Gordon MacDonald, *Restoring Your Spiritual Passion* (Nashville: Thomas Nelson, 1986), 182–84.

10. Thomas Moore, *Soul Mates: Honoring the Mysteries of Love and Relationship* (San Francisco: HarperCollins, 1994), 99.

11. Leonard I. Sweet, *Quantum Spirituality: A Postmodern Apologetic* (Dayton: Whaleprints, 1991), 1.

12. Tilden H. Edwards, *Spiritual Friend: Reclaiming the Gift of Spiritual Direction* (New York: Paulist, 1980), 125.

Section 4

Godbearing Practices for Youth Ministry

EIGHT

Hand-holding and Finger-pointing

Practices of Communion

Hold my hand, just hold my hand…
Because I want to love you, the best that,
the best that I can.
— Hootie and the Blowfish, "Hold My Hand".

J SAT ON a park bench one summer day, eating my lunch and soaking in my surroundings. I felt a hint of a breeze as teenage boys traipsed leisurely through the area. A woman walked her dogs, and a worker from a nearby store grabbed fifteen minutes of solace on a break from his shift. Just as I was about to leave, two more people crossed the threshold from parking lot to park, and their journey caught both my gaze and my imagination.

A young mother, laden with two blue plastic grocery bags in one hand, gently held the fingers of her toddler daughter with her other hand as they meandered across the grass. The two-year-old methodically and somewhat awkwardly navigated the grassy terrain. They were heading in a general direction but in no particular hurry to get there as the mother allowed the little girl the freedom of a controlled wandering.

From time to time, the mother would point to a tree, a bird, a flower. The little girl would stop, giggle, point, and sound out a word and then move on once more on her self-made path. Eventually they got to the other side of the park, and I presume they headed to their home in the neighborhood bordering the park's far entrance. I had watched them for no more than two or three minutes, but their brief crossing became a living metaphor for me.

I had witnessed an enacted parable that contained the core elements of spiritual direction with youth. Spiritual direction often is considered one of the practices of communion, since the ultimate objective is not

139

to offer moral instruction or pastoral care. The goal of spiritual direction is reaching toward oneness with God by discerning God's direction for our daily lives. As the young people entrusted to our care make their way across the threshold of adolescence and chart their paths into adulthood, they too stand in need of hand-holding and finger-pointing.

Hand-Holding: the Ministry of Presence

Sitting up with a teenager as she pours out her heart over a love relationship that seemed so right and turned out to be so wrong. Hanging out with a couple of youth at Pizza Hut and talking about lots of things, nothing in particular. Listening to a sixteen-year-old boy hesitantly begin to tell the story about his parents' divorce. Playing video games and hearing the bits and pieces of a middle-high boy's story of trying to be accepted. Praying with a sobbing young woman who doesn't feel that anyone likes her any more. Sitting quietly as a young man tries to figure out what God wants him to do with his life.

What these scenarios have in common is hand-holding, or the ministry of presence. Spiritual hand-holding is more than just a set of refined counseling skills. It means listening attentively to the lives and the stories of youth with a particular ear for the God-strands woven into the narrative. Spiritual direction is not about the right techniques. Godbearers with youth are called to listen for the whispers of grace in the gaps and in the cracks, to filter out the background noise as much as possible, and to help youth tune in to God's voice. Hand-holding means offering a supportive, caring presence that helps draw youth into the presence of God. In many instances hand-holding is the best gift (and sometimes the only gift) that we have to offer in the name of Christ to the youth with whom we are in ministry. Hand-holding reflects *being* rather than *doing*, *presence* more than *activity*. However, certain skills prove extremely useful as we learn the proper grip.

Good listeners are not passive hearers. Familiarity with the basics of active listening techniques will serve every youth pastor well. Empathic listening—deep listening, soul listening—requires an attentiveness and energy that seeks to get below the surface. Asking clarifying questions, paraphrasing, pausing to process, eye contact, withholding judgment, intently listening to what the other is saying without simultaneously formulating your response: All of these things combine to make someone feel heard and accepted.

This is no small thing. The need to be heard and understood runs deep in all of us, and we can sense when someone has done it well. To listen well is an act of love and acceptance. When our caring presence gives others permission to drop their guard and venture cautiously into the depths of their souls, we are involved in a powerful form of ministry. We may not feel that we are doing anything of value; our compulsive sides may tempt us to be more productive in our ministries than just sitting and listening and talking. The expectations of parents, church boards, and other staff members feed this tendency toward frenzied activity: the fuller the youth calendar, the more successful our ministry appears to others.

Godbearers need to resist the temptation toward numbers and constant motion and take the time to be with youth one on one, simply to be present with them, knowing that it is enough—maybe even more than enough. Douglas Steere describes the art of active listening by transforming the word itself into a transitive verb: "To 'listen' another's soul into a condition of disclosure and discovery may be almost the greatest service that any human being ever performs for another."[1]

Spiritual hand-holding is a ministry in its own right—the ministry of presence—that also opens the door for its complement, the ministry of guidance. The practice of spiritual direction binds the two inseparably. But hand-holding lays the groundwork for finger-pointing, the necessary prerequisite for the ministry of direction. Hand-holding assures youth that they are not alone on their life/spiritual journey and offers them the confidence to take the next steps of faith. Only when youth view us as a trustworthy presence will our ministries of finger-pointing have any real impact.

Finger-pointing: the Ministry of Direction

As a tourist traveling in unfamiliar territory, you may opt to go it alone and to chart your own path by trial and error. A better plan might include consulting a map and defining the roads and side streets with more precision. With a map you'll arrive at your destination but perhaps not in the most direct way, or you may have to overlook some of the more fascinating sights that (unknown to you) are just blocks away. A third course of action is to hook up with a guide who knows the terrain, one who can point out the interesting diversions and steer you away from some common wrong turns. Your guide can do this precisely because he or she has been there and is familiar with the route.

Christians need people in their faith journey who can help point the way. This is especially true for young Christians: the thirteen-year-old who makes a first-time, personal commitment to follow Christ, the eighteen-year-old sorting through vocational confusion, the fifteen-year-old who is asking the hard questions and ready to pack in this whole God thing. All of these people stand in need of some serious spiritual finger-pointing. What they all need (though few would name it as such) are spiritual guides, caring individuals who have been there or who are at least just a little further down the road and able to point the way.

We use the term *finger-pointing* as a positive behavior. Sometimes this phrase evokes images of blame and guilt: We point a finger at someone to pick out flaws and offer critique. While a measure of accountability accompanies spiritual direction, Godbearers do not wag condemning fingers. We don't point at people as much as we point people toward something or Someone else, namely to the cross of Jesus Christ.

Finger-pointing is always in a Godward direction. Godbearers point youth to the scriptures, helping open up the word of God so that it speaks to them in compelling and accessible ways. Godbearers point to the tradition of the church and the lives of faithful men and women to offer models and heroes from whom we learn. Finger-pointers help youthful travelers know that those who make the journey for the long haul fill the backpack with prayer and meditation, worship and service, study and compassion, solitude and community; in short, the spiritual disciplines of the church.[2]

Spiritual Direction: Not Just for Experts

Sometimes we are reluctant to claim the authority inherent in the role of spiritual guide or director. After all, spiritual direction belongs to the province of people with specialized training and special callings, or so we have been told. And to a certain degree, our hesitation is well founded. Spiritual direction is not an area to be entered into lightly or casually. Spiritual Directors (with a capital *S*, capital *D*) are people with a unique blend of compassion, discernment, wisdom, and (increasingly) training through organizations such as the Alban Institute or The Academy for Spiritual Formation. Spiritual Directors also have accumulated a wealth of firsthand experience in the ways of God on their own spiritual journeys. Not everyone feels called to become a formal Spiritual Director or to be under the direction of such a person, although pastors often benefit from such a relationship. However, few would dispute that youth need spiritual guides (even if not formal Spiritual Directors), and we are often those most suited to fill that role for them. Godbearers remain aware of the fact that our authority, vested by God, is a sacred trust. We neither abuse it or flaunt it. We do not become the spiritual authority in someone's life as much as a signpost or marker along the way that points in the direction of the true Authority, namely God's own self.

Formal and Informal Spiritual Direction

Eugene H. Peterson writes,

> Spiritual direction is the act of paying attention to God, calling attention to God, being attentive to God in a person or circumstances or situation....It notices the Invisibilities in and beneath and around the Visibilities. It listens for the Silences between the spoken Sounds.[3]

Peterson's definition puts the emphasis where it belongs—on God—and also touches upon the difficulty of such attentiveness. Sometimes God is hidden for all of us, the silent presence who must be sought more than an obvious presence overwhelming us. Youth, like all of us, need help in the searching.

Tilden Edwards describes spiritual direction in an equally helpful way, though from a different perspective. Edwards differentiates the practice of spiritual direction from other types of personal therapy. He contends that spiritual direction is not problem solving focused on oneself.

> Rather, it is the opportunity to drop into the subtle, mysterious energy of the Spirit. With their guide, people seek to appreciate that living presence shaping their unique Christ-nature, and to discern its particular calling to share their gifts for ministry. It is also a time when they can look at their unique ways of noticing and inviting the Spirit's presence in and among them day by day, i.e., through personal spiritual disciplines. This ministry perhaps is the most intimate form of guidance: going through "the pain of childbirth until Christ is formed in you" (Gal. 4:19).[4]

Ours is the privilege of watching Christ take shape in the lives of young people and having a distinct role to play in the metamorphosis.

Soul Talk

Not long ago I led the memorial service for a remarkable young man. Dale was barely forty when he died, but his spirit through his life-and-death struggle remained unconquered. He had fought his way back from one bout with cancer several years earlier. When the disease returned again, it struck with a vengeance. I engaged in my own ministry of hand-holding with Dale through his last weeks in particular, but it was definitely a mutual ministry. Being with Dale and witnessing first-hand his faith and his courage moved me to tears on several occasions, making me wonder who was the pastor and who was the patient. His peace with dying and his joy for living well and fully inspired me to grow in new ways.

During our last months together, I got to know Dale at a much deeper level than the handshakes at the door on a Sunday morning or the occasional contact at a church meeting had previously allowed. In preparing for the service of celebration to remember his life, I talked at length with members of his family who shared their memories of him. His older brother, Jeff, told me that Dale would call him on his car phone every other day at 7:00 A.M. The conversation would take a rather predictable course. Dale would ask, "What are you doing?" to which Jeff would reply, "What do you think I'm doing? I'm driving to work." "And what are you going to do today?" Jeff would respond with a litany of appointments and projects. Then Dale would ask the best question: "But what are you going to do today that's *important*?"

Dale had the knack for pushing the significant people in his life to grow in positive ways. His repeated asking of that particular question— What are you going to do today that's *important*?—signaled his interest in going beyond idle chitchat or mere superficialities. He cared about the priorities in his brother's life and pushed him to use significance, not just busyness, as a barometer for his well-being.

We all would do well to ask ourselves that question on a regular basis: What am I going to do today that's important? Some of us have the self-discipline necessary to ask ourselves. Most of us need people like Dale to make sure the question gets asked at all. When we engage one another at this level, when we speak with youth about things that really matter, when we cultivate relationships in which others ask us what really matters, then we are participating in soul talk. Spiritual direction does not equate with psychological counseling. Its focus moves beyond emotions or problem solving or self-image (though all of these may be involved to lesser degrees). The intentional agenda of spiritual direction fosters an awareness of and an attunement to God. "Spiritual direction always keeps God in the picture," writes Marjorie Thompson.[5] That is its distinctiveness, and that is its strength. Godbearing guides do not shy away from soul talk; in fact, they always seek to bring the conversation to that level.

Most youth have a few (if not a battalion of) people in their lives to shoot the breeze with. They have friends with whom they can talk about sports or stay in touch with the latest gossip. They may have a best friend with whom to share more intimate secrets. Perhaps a teacher, guidance counselor, or parent offers them good advice about school or making plans beyond graduation. Each of these relationships is important in its own right. But none of them offers the intentional spiritual direction that a caring, committed Godbearer can as either a formal or an informal spiritual guide. To mature in faith, our youth need people to hold their hands gently and to point the way.

Leading Where You Go

We have tried to paint with broad strokes the art of spiritual direction with young people. Perhaps a more concrete description of what this might look like in our own ministries, without prescribing a single right way to do it, would be helpful. As we mentioned earlier, hand-holding and finger-pointing imply ways of being rather than doing. But our intentional behaviors will help young souls on their spiritual journeys connect with God.

We probably have neither the time nor the inclination to become the spiritual director for all the youth with whom we minister. Our suggestion: Don't try. In our circle of influence probably one or two or three youth have heightened spiritual sensibilities and a visible hunger to dig deeper into the ways of the Spirit. Perhaps a trial period of one-on-one meetings with an adolescent seeking spiritual direction (though he or she probably won't call it that) will illustrate the impact of spiritual guidance on both youth and adult. Or we may organize a small covenant discipleship group in which group members do the hand-holding and finger-pointing for one another, and the youth pastor acts as a facilitator.[6] Though spiritual direction or guidance may sound super spiritual or otherworldly, we can communicate to youth and youth leaders that at its core, spiritual direction is earthy indeed. It takes the ordinary stuff of our lives and the lives of teenagers, sorts it out, and refines it in the light of scripture, prayer, community, and the spiritual disciplines.

Several years ago, I heard a speaker offer some simple wisdom. He gently and directly cautioned us: "You can't teach what you don't know;

you can't preach what you don't show; and you can't lead where you don't go." We do not guide souls in order to create spiritual clones but to help light the path to God. This guidance implies enough familiarity with the way on the part of the soul tenders that we prove to be trust-worthy guides. It also assumes our own continuation down that path, having our own hands held and paying close attention to the spiritual finger-pointing offered by others. To be spiritual guides for others, we must intentionally seek direction in our own journeys, deepening our own firsthand experience of God's grace and discerning the ways of the Spirit. Whether working with a formal Spiritual Director, seeking the regular guidance of a mentor, or engaging in mutual hand-holding and finger-pointing with peers, we can best open youth up to receive spir-itual counsel by demonstrating a similar openness on our part as we seek to grow in faith.

Finding Their Way Home

Return with me to the two-year-old and her mother in the park. I pre-sumed that they were headed home, and the mother employed hand-holding and finger-pointing to ensure that the little girl got home as well. Our ministries with youth operate in much the same way. We may or may not have the privilege of escorting them up to and right through the door, as that little girl's mother probably did. Our best efforts may only help to put youth on the right path without any firm guarantees of a final destination. But if we are quiet enough to listen deeply, sensi-tive enough to care genuinely, and attuned enough to God to direct faithfully, our hand-holding and finger-pointing may well show the young people whose souls we tend the way home to God.

QUESTIONS AND EXERCISES

1. Which youth in your sphere of ministry are in special need of hand-holding? finger-pointing?

2. Who might be open to deepening their spiritual journey with you as their intentional guide?

3. How comfortable do you feel with the role of spiritual guide / director?

4. Where do you turn for direction in your own spiritual journey?

IDEA FOR THE ROAD

Do a variation of a trust walk with some other adult counselors. Announce that you are going to take them for a walk; they are to keep their eyes open and trust that you have a good destination in mind. Pick out a simple route (indoors or out) and lead them by hand-holding and finger-pointing only (no verbal communication). Talk about what it feels like to receive and offer gentle guidance.

FARE FOR THE SOUL

God be in your head, and in your understanding.
God be in your eyes, and in your looking.
God be in your mouth, and in your speaking.
God be in your heart, and in your thinking.
God be at your end, and at your departing.[7]

—Sarum Liturgy, England, 13th century

Notes

1. Douglas Steere, *Gleanings: A Random Harvest* (Nashville: The Upper Room, 1986), 83.
2. Both Marjorie J. Thompson's *Soul Feast* and Richard Foster's *Celebration of Discipline* are excellent primers on the classical spiritual disciplines.
3. Eugene H. Peterson, *Under the Predictable Plant: An Exploration of Vocational Holiness* (Grand Rapids: Wm. B. Eerdmans, 1992), 181.
4. Tilden H. Edwards, "The Pastor as Spiritual Guide," in *Communion, Community, and Commonweal: Readings for Spiritual Leadership,* ed. John S. Mogabgab (Nashville: Upper Room Books, 1995), 117.
5. Marjorie J. Thompson, *Soul Feast: An Invitation to the Christian Spiritual Life* (Louisville: Westminster John Knox, 1995), 112.
6. For a more detailed description of this model, see David Lowes Watson's "Covenant Discipleship Groups," *Accountable Discipleship: Handbook for Covenant Discipleship Groups in the Congregation* (Nashville: Discipleship Resources, 1984).
7. *The United Methodist Book of Worship* (Nashville: Abingdon, 1992), 566.

NINE

Youth Who Could Care More (or Less)

Practices of Compassion

*It's a shrunk-down planet. We'd better take care
of each other.*
—*Stan Grossfeld, "Camera at Work"*

J

S IT going to be on the test? That was the kind of question posed to Jesus on this particular day, the kind of question that seeks to establish the least we can do and still get by, the kind of question with which teenagers have an intimate familiarity in their day-to-day school lives. The asker, a well-intentioned, rule-keeping lawyer, has come to Jesus to discover the key to the kingdom. When Jesus turns the lawyer's question back on him, he answers Jesus well. He knows the right religious answer—love God, love your neighbor—but he's not sure he likes all the implications of Jesus' far-reaching affirmation. So now the lawyer asks one more question: "And who is my neighbor?" What he's really getting at is "Who is *not* my neighbor?" He is checking out the fine print, looking for loopholes. And Jesus slams the door shut with a story found in Luke 10:30-37, perhaps the best remembered of all his parables.

A man was going down from Jerusalem to Jericho, and fell into the hands of robbers, who stripped him, beat him, and went away, leaving him half dead. Now by chance a priest was going down that road; and when he saw him, he passed by on the other side. So likewise a Levite, when he came to the place and saw him, passed by on the other side. But a Samaritan while traveling came near him; and when he was him, he was moved with pity. He went to him and bandaged his wounds, having poured oil and wine on them. Then he put him on his own animal, brought him to an inn, and took care of him. The next day he took out two denarii, gave them to the innkeeper, and said, "Take care of him; and when I come back, I will repay

you whatever more you spend." Which of these three, do you
think, was a neighbor to the man who fell into the hands of
the robbers? He said, "The one who showed him mercy." Jesus
said to him, "Go and do likewise."

The accessibility, straightforward nature, and ease in retelling makes the
parable of the good Samaritan a powerful text for those who minister
to the young. Its familiarity brings both blessing and curse: blessing
because it is actually one story that may have lodged in the brains of our
youth from their early Sunday school lessons; curse because its familiarity may garner a "been-there, heard-that" response. However, when we
give the parable a fair hearing, its greatest value lies in helping Christians, young and old alike, get in touch with the dynamics and practices
of compassion.

Suffering with Another

At its root, compassion is the capacity or feeling of suffering with
another person (com, "with"; patri, "suffer"). It is a peculiar sort of iden-
tification, a sharing of another's pain, burden, injustice, or hurt. More
than feeling sorry for someone, a compassionate person cares enough to
take on some of the pain. In the stories where the text refers to Jesus'
being moved with compassion (such as the healing of the leper in
Mark's gospel or the healing of the two blind men in Jericho in
Matthew), we might translate the Greek better as "It hit Jesus in his
gut."[1] While it may begin as an emotional experience that strikes in the
pit of our stomach, mature Christian compassion moves beyond mere
sentimentality or pity to concrete acts of mercy and kindness. Compassion goes beyond simply feeling sorry for a brother or sister who is
thirsty (which may be the starting point) to taking the next step and
offering a cup of cold water (Matt. 10:42).

In the story of the compassionate Samaritan, the Samaritan man
takes on the suffering of his enemy whom he encounters beaten on the
road. In his act of caring—bandaging the wounds, taking the man to an
inn, seeing to his future well-being by striking an agreement with the
innkeeper—two strangers' lives become bound together. Rarely do the
circumstances so plainly present themselves; rarely is compassion so
freely given. As the parable accurately portrays, self-risk compassion—
the kind present in the suffering love of the crucified God—is the
minority approach to life: Two out of three in the parable choose dis-
engagement and detachment. In the real lives of teens, whether they live

on the safe side of the street or in a war zone, noninvolvement is the ticket to self-preservation and, in some cases, survival.

While many teens may act as if they could care less by copping an "I don't care" attitude about life in general, most of them really do care deeply for others. All of the data suggests that teens hunger for hands-on service projects. They display passion about social causes, moved in their guts by the plight of others. Youth do not lack compassion; they lack the opportunities to enact their gut reactions to people in need. They lack models of what it means to suffer alongside another. Godbearers draw out the latent potentiality present in youth who pretend to care less (and some who really do) and help form them into people who care more.

Birthed, Not Coerced

True compassion can never be coerced but always must be birthed in us through a reshaping of the heart and mind. Author Sue Monk Kidd remembers her own experience of being a reluctant twelve-year-old visitor in a nursing home with her church youth group. One of the residents recognized her discomfort and accurately named it with a phrase that Kidd remembers resenting at the time, but one she later came to appreciate: "You can't force the heart."

> You can't force the heart. Genuine compassion cannot be imposed from without. It doesn't happen simply by hearing a sermon on love, or being sent on a loving mission....Compassion, which is the very life of God within us, comes through slow and often difficult metamorphosis deep within the human soul.[2]

Compassion is a learned disposition and a practice of faith. Godbearers cultivate compassion in youth, knowing full well that compassion takes a lifetime of experience and practice to mature.

While compassion cannot be forced by coercing feelings that do not exist, forced starts are invaluable to the *practices* of compassion. A forced start is the head start gardeners give seedlings by encouraging their germination indoors before the planting season actually arrives. Planting these seeds outdoors too early in the season would be deadly; the environment is too harsh and cold to allow seeds to take root. The gardener makes use of an alternate, indoor environment in which the seed may begin to develop by placing it in a fertile dish on a protected window sill. Eventually the young plant is sturdy enough to transplant outdoors where it now can grow and flourish of its own accord.

Godbearing ministry with youth (and with all of us) patiently and persistently cultivates the compassionate life for which God created us, in spite of an environment unfriendly to caring. Engaging youth in practices of compassion is not about forced hearts but about forced starts, providing youth with the fertile and protected environment that helps all of us grow in our capacity to care for others.

Involuntary Voluntary Service

A growing number of states require high school students to perform a prescribed number of community service hours in order to graduate. In Maryland, where I reside, a lively debate initially occurred about the value of requiring voluntary service of students. Those who opposed the measure argued that making community service an obligation worked against the spirit of the educators' intent. Those who supported the requirement countered that we learn the *spirit* of community service by doing community service, even if we do not feel very charitable at the outset. As a Christian, I tend to favor the latter argument.

In the Christian community, youth learn compassion by practicing acts of compassion. The hands-on experience of caring for others shapes our hearts to care for our neighbor out of love as well as obligation. Additionally, as much as we like to think of compassion's flowing freely from the heart, practices of compassion possess a certain involuntary nature. The compassionate Samaritan acts as neighbor to the beaten man simply because he finds himself in a situation where someone needs him to be a neighbor. Jesus says little about the Samaritan traveler's *feelings* on the road to Jericho, mentioning only that he was moved with pity (v. 33). However, Jesus makes much about how the Samaritan *acts* in response to the need presented him and describes his assistance in great detail (several verses worth!).

One area in youth ministry in which churched and unchurched alike are primed for transformation is hands-on mission projects. The overwhelming interest in summer work mission camps indicates this potential. When youth receive the opportunity to act out their faith on behalf of another human being in need—painting houses, building wheelchair ramps, putting up drywall—they embrace their work willingly and with far more enthusiasm than many parents would dream possible given the condition of their rooms at home. This genuine fervor grows from the investment and sense of responsibility youth feel.

Often their work surpasses even their own expectations. Their enthusiasm also springs from the experience of an intense *esprit de corps,* an instant community that forms in these work camp environments.

We may attribute the balance (and largest measure) of their enthusiasm for this work to the sense of satisfaction that comes from helping another person in a tactile, specific way. They have been in ministry: They have served God and others and have experienced a change in themselves. This sense of ministry may not have been their motivation for signing on for the week, but almost invariably the strongest memory team participants carry home is that their service has transformed them into servants. When we empower youth to be ministers and not simply passive recipients of ministry, they come to see themselves as Godbearers in cutoffs and sweaty T-shirts. And Godbearing through the practices of compassion slowly forces the heart to bud. Youth who could care less learn to care more.

A Heart Stronger Than His Body

In the midst of completing a week of flood relief work in the Midwest with a volunteer mission team, I got the phone call. My sister was on the line explaining that our father had been involved in a serious accident while on vacation at the beach, a near drowning that left him lying in a coma in the hospital. My mind raced with fear and horror at this imagined scene. I pressed for details about his condition, which were sketchy and inconclusive at the time, and then she told me more fully what had happened. While I formally had been on the mission field for Christ, my father had been engaged more dramatically in compassionate self-giving.

My parents had just arrived in Ocean City, New Jersey, late on a Thursday afternoon in July. After checking into their motel, they headed straight for the beach to catch the waning moments of the day and to read by the water's edge. Shortly after 5:00 P.M. (just after the lifeguards had gone off duty) my father heard the screams of two young girls who had ridden their boogie boards out into the surf and were now struggling to make their way back to shore against a very strong undertow. My father, age sixty-one and not exactly the poster child for good health, knew only one thing to do: Go into the water to try to bring the girls in.

By one important measure, his efforts were successful. He helped the girls to a place where others could bring them the rest of the way to the shore. However, in the process, whether as a result of sheer exhaustion or a mild heart attack brought on by overexertion, my father began to struggle in the water himself. He went under, and the rescue efforts now focused on him. A shopkeeper and an off-duty policeman worked valiantly to bring him to a nearby jetty, where they pulled his body out of the water across the bodies of several other would-be rescuers so as not to drag him over the rocks. As my mother stood by helplessly, the paramedics worked unsuccessfully to resuscitate him. He remained in a coma for the next six weeks as we kept vigil by his bedside. None of the nurses in the hospital called him Dick or Richard—only the Hero. He finally died on September 1, and we wept proud tears. His heart had been stronger than his body.

Few of us are asked to sacrifice our lives physically so that others might live. However, all who claim to be Godbearers in the world, young and old, are invited into a kenotic lifestyle, a life of self-emptying. Compassion costs us more than emotional currency; it involves a genuine giving up of self, a putting aside of personal prerogatives, the real risk of loss. For my father, who made helping others a lifetime habit, his fatal plunge into the surf after those two young girls was a reflex action. None of us who knew and loved him could picture his responding in any other way. The good news is that in the losing, there is the finding of true life (Matt. 16:26). The compassionate spirit is sometimes a deadly disease; Godbearing ministry seeks to make it epidemic.

My father's compassionate last act has reinforced in my heart and mind the character of the Christian life. Following Christ is not just about being nice; it is about living heroically, compassionately. If we insipidly present the gospel as a matter of sterile "do-goodism," then not only do we miss the theological boat (by a long shot), but we surrender the compelling aspects of our faith that draw youth on board in the first place. Compassion is rooted in the life, death, and resurrection of Christ, the self-giving of God's own son. It is life lived on behalf of the other, life risked on behalf of the neighbor, love incarnated in sacrificial self-giving. Godbearers will name the true stakes and embody the self-giving spirit of the One who has claimed them. The challenge to live heroically has far more appeal than the admonition to be good.

Expanding the Question

Youth have an acute ability to sniff out hypocrisy and to name injustice. Early on they learn to observe the world and to judge whether or not something is fair. When as elementary school children we begin to gain the cognitive capacity to understand the perspective of other, we quickly charge, "That's not fair!" and to wage what we consider full-blown crusades for justice—namely, ours. In most instances, "not fair" really means it's not fair to me. As we grow and mature, so does our circle of concern. As young adolescents, "it's not fair" broadens to include the peer group; as in, "It's not fair that you parents get to set all these stupid rules, and we (me and my friends) have to follow them or be grounded."

Godbearing ministry expands the circle even further, making the critical link between compassion and justice. Micah, the prophet, reminds Israel of this integral and intricate connection that runs throughout the Bible: "What does the Lord require of you but to do justice and to love kindness, and to walk humbly with your God" (Mic. 6:8). Drawing upon the innate sense of fairness that many of our youth profess (or at least quietly possess), Godbearing ministry draws others into the circle of concern. We need to challenge youth to ask "Is it fair?" not only in reference to their own interests ("Is it fair for me?" meaning "Do I get what I deserve?") or even the interests of a select group of others ("Is it fair for us?"). Godbearers broaden the question for youth to: "Is it fair for all?" Put another way, compassion is the "sometimes fatal capacity for feeling what it's like to live inside somebody else's skin. It is the knowledge that there can never really be any peace and joy for me until there is peace and joy finally for you too."[3]

Thinking Globally: The Worldwide Web

In terms of global thinking, the current generation of youth has a tremendous advantage over the previous generation. They have grown up in an ever-shrinking, increasingly connected world. World beat is a viable category in the CD stores; satellite TV stations carry more and more international and ethnically flavored programming; school curricula are being adapted beyond Western authors and perspectives; youth go on-line and develop cyber-friendships with people halfway across the globe in chatrooms. Today's youth are growing up with a global consciousness due largely to the globalization of American youth culture.[4] The implications of this global consciousness—from the products youth use to the job opportunities that await them—are emotional and intellectual as well as economic. The world feels smaller, and people are thinking bigger.

Seeing and understanding the technological and economic links among geographically disparate peoples has become increasingly easy. Godbearing ministry attempts to help youth understand and feel the human connections. The worldwide web of connections can shape youth to live compassionately in a global context by embracing issues like ozone depletion, rain forest depletion, poverty in developing nations, and shoe factory child labor. Youth may become advocates for the disadvantaged through their acute awareness of our interrelatedness. Awareness is only the beginning. To see the pain is not enough; to feel the pain is a sign of sensitivity; to begin to act compassionately is the mark of faith.

Acting Locally: Next-Door Neighborly

Helping youth learn the practices of compassion requires more than a global mind set. Concrete acts of caring in their local context is where youth best learn the habits of compassionate living. When Godbearing adults model sensitivity and sincere caring—making themselves available to listen, to accept, to reach out in kindness—youth are encouraged to do the same for one another. The emotional climate of youth ministry extends far beyond the breadth of programmatic offerings. Empathy, concern for one another's well-being, and a mutual bearing of burdens signal that the lesson is being learned at home. By intentionally integrating and encouraging these behaviors, Godbearers seek to create a setting that encourages compassion. Trying on and testing out the practices of compassion with friends better equip youth to share the heart of God with strangers.

Serving meals at a local soup kitchen, visiting homebound members of the church, tutoring young children from the community, volunteering in a local hospital or nursing home: Each of these activities allows a young person to express compassion in a local setting. Where one-time experiences may make a short-lived impression, longer-term partnerships will more likely form habits and ongoing practices of compassion among youth.[5] Teens learn well experientially. Godbearers know this and tilt the tables toward compassion by offering varied and regular opportunities for hands-on outreach.

Looking beyond Themselves

On the subway to Battery Park in Lower Manhattan, a young boy and his older brother were looking into the mirror made of two-way glass that separated them from the engineer's cabin. After a few minutes, the older boy told his brother that he could see the tracks that lay ahead.

The seven-year-old, busily admiring his beautiful self in the mirror could see nothing but himself. "Where?" he asked. "I don't see anything."

His mother spoke up. "Spenser, look beyond yourself and you'll see it."

He did, and he did, just as we do when we look beyond ourselves: We catch a glimpse of the track ahead and the world around us.[6]

Godbearers know how to look beyond themselves and also have the gift of drawing others to join them in their compassionate gaze. The life stage of adolescents predisposes them to self-absorption but also opens them up to the feelings and experiences of others to "catch a glimpse of the work ahead and the world around them," as it were. Passing the practices of compassion on to youth is a gift that can literally change the world, one heart at a time.

QUESTIONS AND EXERCISES

1. When and how did you begin to develop the capacity for compassion in your own life? Which specific experiences were formative?

2. Whom do you know who has a genuinely compassionate spirit? What sets this person apart? How are you like him or her?

3. Where have you seen evidence of compassionate behavior in the lives of youth you know?

IDEA FOR THE ROAD

Surprise adult youth leaders who expect an information session on youth service projects with a servant activity of their own: cook a freeze-ahead meal for someone recovering from surgery, make a pot of soup to be divided into individual servings for elderly fiends, help make repairs at a local homeless shelter, or anything that suits your needs and time-frame. Begin the activity with prayer (perhaps use Mother Teresa's prayer on the next page) and scripture (perhaps read Luke 10:30-37 or John 13:1-20). After the project, reflect together: What kind of personal renewal do you find in practices of compassion? How does becoming a servant to others influence your ministry with youth?

FARE FOR THE SOUL

The work we do is only our love for Jesus in action.
And that action is our wholehearted and free service
    —the gift to the poorest of the poor—
to Christ in the distressing disguise of the poor.

If we pray the work...
        if we do it to Jesus
        if we do it for Jesus
        if we do it with Jesus...
that's what makes us content.

That is why I feel the Missionaries of Charity are real
contemplatives in the heart of the world.
        I do this because I believe I am doing it for Jesus.
        I am very sure that this is his work.
        I am very sure.
        I am very sure that it is he and not me.[7]

—Mother Teresa

Notes

1. G. Simon Harak, *Virtuous Passions: The Formation of Christian Character* (New York: Paulist Press, 1993), 4.

2. Sue Monk Kidd, "Birthing Compassion," in *Communion, Community, Commonweal: Readings for Spiritual Leadership*, ed. John S. Mogabgab (Nashville: Upper Room Books, 1995), 149–150.

3. Frederick Buechner, *Wishful Thinking: A Theological ABC* (New York: Harper and Row, 1973), 15.

4. Quentin J. Schultze et al., *Dancing in the Dark: Youth, Popular Culture, and the Electronic Media* (Grand Rapids: Wm. B. Eerdmans, 1991).

5. Peter L. Benson and Eugene C. Roehlkepartain, *Beyond Leaf Raking: Service: Learning & Youth Ministry* (Nashville: Abingdon, 1993).

6. Leonard I. Sweet, *Homiletics* 8, no. 1 (Jan.–Mar. 1996).

7. Mother Teresa, *Words to Love by...* (Notre Dame: Ave Maria Press, 1983), 22–23.

TEN
Breaking Water
Practices of Teaching and Nurture

Never lose a holy curiosity.
—Albert Einstein

IT TOOK Jesus' parents three days—*three days*—to find him. You know they were frantic. They asked all over Jerusalem: Had anybody seen him? Friends, neighbors, cousins must have swung into action, consoling and praying, caring for the other carpenter siblings so Mary and Joseph could return to the city to scour the marketplace for Jesus. Maybe they filed a missing person report; maybe the police came by looking for a recent photo for the blue and white mailers. But knowing that local authorities "have the situation under control" is small comfort to a mother and a father who cannot rest until every single child is tucked in and accounted for.

Jesus, on the other hand, seems completely oblivious to the ordeal he has just put his parents through (further confirmation that twelve-year-old Jesus is truly human as well as divine). He is incredulous that his parents would forget to look in the Temple. Where else would he be? There he is, sitting among the teachers, listening and asking them questions, amazing them with his precocious faith (Luke 2:47). He seems to be having the time of his life. According to the text, Jesus willingly returns to Nazareth with Mary and Joseph (and we can imagine that Mary's restrained reprimand recorded in Luke was probably saltier in the heat of the moment). Luke tells us that as Jesus grew, he obeyed his parents—although Mary still wonders what to make of the Temple Incident (as it undoubtedly became known at family reunions) years afterward (Luke 2:51).

However, for twelve-year-old Jesus the Temple tutorial marked a turning point. Young adolescents, then as now, push through the boundaries of home, neighborhood, and family in order to test their wings in the more expansive world of adult society. Primary relationships stretch to include peers and select adults. "Home turf" grows to include school and community. In early adolescence, youth move beyond peering through the back fence to dismantling it (which is what makes them so maddening) in order to explore the world beyond with eagerness and awe (which is what makes them so wonderful). The young man who returns to Nazareth is not the same boy who arrived in Jerusalem for the Passover celebration a few days earlier. His world has become larger. His boundaries have been pushed back. As a twelve-year-old Jewish male, Jesus now stands at embryonic adulthood.

Beyond Spandex: Expandable Faith

Funny how the Temple is the last place we look. Sunday school, someone once remarked, is the one place we can be absolutely sure nothing is going to happen. We do not expect boundary-breaking in church; yet growing in faith requires precisely this experience. Faith matures by *expansion*, not by progression. Sometimes the older we get, the more likely we are to cloud faith with competence. Western society's definition of mature adulthood can work against mature faith by closing us off rather than opening us more fully to mystery and grace. As "mature" adults we know how to fortify ourselves against metamorphosis. A little less passion here, a little more social conformity there, a little more listening to the boss, a little less listening to the heart: a formula for docile citizens and domesticated Christians. Under these conditions, children and people whose cognitive, emotional, and/or psychological development do not follow prescribed norms may have a distinct advantage when it comes to clearheaded, all-or-nothing obedience to Christ.

Still, human beings do develop—even if not according to plan—and, given the chance, so can our faith. The practice of Christian teaching is what others do *intentionally* on our behalf to expand our faith to fill the new spaces created by our growing cognitive, psychological, and physical awarenesses. My faith expands whenever I realize, gradually or all at once, that God loves me enough to die for me—me personally. My faith expands whenever I discover a greater sense of belonging in a community of faithful others, whenever my life more completely enacts what I say I believe about the Father, Son, and Holy Spirit.

Typically these discoveries take place when I am a little off balance, a little uncertain, a little more punctured and vulnerable than I care to admit. Christian teaching artfully fosters this creative disequilibrium, seeking an intentional loss of footing for the sake of reorganizing the self's structure. Whenever life throws me off balance, a little or a lot, my carefully erected boundaries of who I think I am tumble down. There I lie in the rubble, forced to reckon with the person God is calling me to be instead. Christian teaching repositions life's Legos to allow us to see new possibilities in the gentle reconstruction of self.

At this point, throwing rocks is instructive. Toss a rock in a pond, and you get ever-expanding ripples moving out toward shore from the spot of the rock's impact. Teaching for faith is like that. Teaching breaks the water's surface, creating a disturbance that calls forth new rings of faith. We can think of disturbances in our faith life as growing pains, times of stretching beyond our present self toward a deeper and more profound relationship with God. Of course, life creates plenty of "teaching disturbances" without our help, and our faith expands and contracts accordingly. Teaching, however, is made up of intentional moments that create "faith ripples," which take us beyond our limitations toward the awesome expansiveness of God.

Breaking water is a midwife's term, referring to the tear in the amniotic sac that precedes childbirth. Some mothers (and fathers) recall the moment "the water broke" as high drama; others barely remember it at all. Usually the water breaks on its own because accommodations inside the womb become too cramped. The baby needs more room and, not unlike young adolescents stifled by childhood, finally decides, "I'm outta here." Sometimes the breakage is induced for the youngster who, like the young adult who still brings her laundry home, has grown dangerously comfortable in the womb and cannot see that to stay there is to die.

Catechesis: Handing on Faith without Handouts

The aftermath of breaking water is almost always pain. Breaking water signals the coming of new life. The learner works hard to push past the once-necessary boundaries into a new, larger, frightening, and exhilarating world. Another word for this process in Christian faith is *catechesis* (kat-ah-KEY-sis). Catechists are those who assist us amidst the birth pangs of growing faith. They are the midwives of Christianity, gracious gardeners who disturb the soil to loosen its grip on new roots, healing practitioners who urge us to push and relax at appropriate times, demolition experts who know just where to place the explosives so the structure caves safely to make way for new construction—and who know where to point us for the resources to rebuild.

Catechists know Jesus Christ well enough to introduce him to their friends with or without the questionable advantage of printed Sunday school leaflets. *Catechesis*—a word familiar to Catholics but largely lost on contemporary Protestants—means "oral teaching." It implies an intentional act of transmission (teaching) in the most accessible way possible (talking about faith). Catechesis has nothing to do with handouts, flannel boards, dry erase markers, interactive teleconferencing, or any other form of educational technology, although it has nothing against these things, either. Simply put, catechesis means telling others about the Christian tradition. Roman Catholics understand catechesis as a category of ministry rather than of education. Catholic educator Michael Warren contends that effective catechesis with youth "must attend to the multiple needs of youth, balancing the ministries of the Word, of worship, of guidance and counsel (including education), and of healing."[1]

Since passing on faith means expanding the boundaries of our openness and our obedience to God and not just completing crossword puzzles on the back of the Bible study workbook, Godbearing youth ministry involves handing on the practices of our faith and not Bible verses alone. Catechists constantly interrupt the flow of perfectly good lives with God's boundary-busting good news. They set new birth in motion. They throw rocks. They break water.

As a practice of teaching and nurture, catechesis falls somewhere between private contemplation of scripture (where God tutors the heart directly) and public acts of caring (governed by images of healing more than birth and growth). Catechesis can happen in a variety of settings: Sunday school, small or large group studies, camps, mission trips, mentoring relationships. Whenever we pass the baton in what Barbara Brown Taylor calls "the ancient relay of the faith"[2]—the intentional handing on of those basic pieces of Christian tradition that allow us to grasp what God has done for us in Jesus Christ—we are catechists. And while all of us need catechesis, normally the runner with the baton focuses most intently on the next runner, assessing how best to hold and release the baton so the next sprinter will seize it with confidence and ease. Since teenagers are already on the track waiting for someone to hand them the baton, catechesis is crucial for adolescents poised for the next leg of the relay of faith.

Boiling Water versus Breaking Water

A generation ago, Desi Arnaz (on screen and off) got as close to the birth of Little Ricky/Little Desi as the hospital waiting room. For generations before that, husbands waited outside their bedrooms, wincing as they heard their wives moan in their travail. Husbands helped by boiling water, a practice with questionable medical relevance at best. Mostly it got husbands out of the way while giving them the impression that they were doing something useful.

Much of what we chalk up to Christian educational practice with teenagers amounts to boiling water at the birth of our children. It keeps us busy but often is irrelevant to their growing faith. As Christian educators, we have learned many of our strategies from the great educational movements of our century that have influenced our schools, colleges, and corporations; and we have learned them well. For instance, the Religious Education movement of the early twentieth century set out to reform archaic and haphazard practices of Sunday school by providing more age-appropriate strategies to help children master religious material. Faith, however, is not a subject to master. Faith is a life to be lived in light of the God who saves. When we learn faith the same way we learn geography, we push God out of the delivery room. It is as if we say to God, who is mopping the holy brow attending to the faith-birth of a stubborn ninth-grader: "Go boil some water, God! I'll take it from here!"

Catechists face a major doctrinal dilemma: If faith is the gift of the Holy Spirit (Eph. 2:8-9)—if faith ultimately comes in God's time and in God's way to each of us—then what in the world is the catechist's job? To practice midwifery, that's what. Midwives/catechists attend to the birth of faith, which is the Great Physician's responsibility. Midwives/catechists check our faith progression and show us how to accommodate each awkward stage along the way, observing, reassuring, providing comfort and wisdom, helping us focus on the job at hand—and, when necessary, breaking water. Their greatest gift may be their utter confidence that in all the pain and the pushing, something marvelous is taking place. Midwives know the struggle is worth the effort, and they encourage us to see it through.

Catechetical Stages of Labor

Since all metaphors have their limits, we will admit up front that this explanation of catechesis will not survive medical scrutiny. Instead of addressing teaching techniques(which many others before us have done well), this chapter will outline four catechetical moments for which a variety of teaching techniques could be appropriate. So put on your scrubs and imagine yourself a midwife, at least for the next few minutes.

Four Moments of Midwifery

PACK YOUR BAG.
Study of scripture
Practice of prayer
Exegesis of adolescence
Exegesis of culture

NAME THE PAIN.
Listen closely for signs of labor
Interpret the discomfort
Reassure the one who is struggling
Identify helpful strategies for
managing the awkwardness

BREAK WATER.
Naturally
With minor assistance
With decisive intervention

BE READY FOR THE CATCH.
Wait expectantly
Stay close to the ball
Remind the youth of your
presence and readiness
Make opportunities for faith to grow

Pack your bag.

Since we never know the exact moment birth/growth will occur, we have to be ready at all times. Give up on a "sterile" birth environment; faith never grows in a vacuum, and youth ministry in particular operates more like a M*A*S*H unit than a hospital. Today midwives are involved in pregnancy as well as childbirth with standard regular checkups and prenatal care. But everything points to the moment we grab our bags and go, making do with whatever portable skills we have acquired in our years of education and experience.

People pack differently, but the properly equipped catechetical bag has a few essentials. The first essential is *un*packing, owning up to biases and seeking redemption for baggage left over from previous experiences that we may project onto young people. We cannot rid ourselves of our history, and we shouldn't. But we do need to confess prejudices that poke their way into our ministries uninvited. For instance, maybe I resent a restrictive upbringing with fundamentalist parents, so I discourage theological language because it sounds like the "God-talk" that took place in my home. Or maybe Aaron in Sunday school reminds me of a college boyfriend. Unless I am careful, latent feelings for my former boyfriend can color the communication patterns I use with Aaron, perhaps even pushing the relationship past appropriate adult–youth boundaries.

Once we have unpacked, we need to polish up four essentials and have them ready to go: the study of scripture, the practice of prayer, the ability to interpret culture, and the ability to interpret adolescence itself. Chief among these tools is profound respect for scripture and prayer. These two resources nourish every Christian practice (including catechesis). Adult youth leaders do not need to be Bible study or prayer "experts," but we do need to practice them reverently and regularly in the context of a supportive and challenging faith community.

In addition, we must recognize what is going on in young people because of their "social location," which includes their gender, racial and ethnic background, and economic place in society as well as their geography and generation. Just as important is the ability to interpret the developmental nuances of the adolescent life stage. Careful exegesis of culture and adolescence allows us to enter the world of youth to encourage faith on their "turf" as well as on ours. These four resources improve our ability to discern accurately when and where to break water for a particular adolescent and to avoid one-size-fits-all formulas for fostering faith maturity.

Name the pain.

Catechists must monitor the pain and discomfort associated with growing faith. Sometimes discomfort can be a good sign. It means labor is progressing. But it takes a skilled leader to know the difference between helpful discomfort and immobilizing terror. Especially for first-time births, the signs of impending labor are not always clear. In catechesis, as in childbirth, false labor—suffering that does not move faith along—is common. We accompany many youth as far as the hospital, expecting a larger faith any minute only to realize it is not yet time. Drew's drug problem does not improve. Erin can't trust her own giftedness to let go of her insecurities. The hard-looking group of youth who hang out near campus have familiar faces, but no point of connection has presented itself. We don't give up on these youth; on the contrary, we watch them more closely. The pains will return, and the next time they may signal the imminent arrival of a larger faith.

Catechists help youth understand that life struggles are faith struggles. God uses the family, social, and theological environments in which we live as canvases of creativity, not determiners of destiny. As catechists, our job is to *affirm* adolescents' deep-seated yearning for a God who can recreate them and to *confirm* their instinct that God wants to work through them to change the world. Catechists help young people express this embryonic faith, for we cannot claim what we do not name. The naming might be verbal, nonverbal, or ritual. Altar calls, for instance, help some youth articulate their faith with the risky gesture of coming forward while other youth scramble for the exits. The point is not to avoid altar calls or their functional equivalents; public profession of faith is a time-honored Christian practice in which youth should participate. What's more, some youth respond positively to the drama of high risk, uncomfortable situations that ask for a "total" response of the self, physically as well as socially and emotionally.

However, catechists also help those youth whose confidence in God has not yet gathered public momentum find ways to claim their growing relationship with Jesus Christ. Invitational teaching is one catechetical method that offers youth multiple opportunities to profess their faith at different levels of risk. They might name this faith privately (through silent prayer or written responses), implicitly (through public but low-risk acts of profession like wearing a Christian T-shirt or singing a meaningful hymn), or explicitly (public, high-risk, and often one-time professional acts like testimonies, confirmation, or believer's baptism). All of these forms of expression are variations on practices of witness that gradually expand our faith capacity, but they do so incrementally and at the discretion of the attending catechist.

Naming the discomfort that often accompanies growth spurts in our faith encourages us to own what God has done and is doing on our behalf. The humbling conviction that Jesus Christ has died for me *personally* is what educator John H. Westerhoff III calls "owned faith"; Christian tradition calls it "conversion."[4] After his reluctant (but pivotal) visit to a prayer meeting on Aldersgate Street, John Wesley wrote about owning his faith after hearing Martin Luther's "Preface" to the Epistle of Romans read aloud:

> While he was describing the change which God works in the heart through faith in Christ, I felt my heart strangely warmed. I felt I did trust in Christ, Christ alone for salvation; and an assurance was given me that he had taken away *my* sins, even *mine*, and saved *me* from the law of sin and death.[5]

We might better construe such "conversions" as faith "growth spurts" rather than "births" (John Wesley, after all, had been an active Anglican priest for years before his experience on Aldersgate Street). Sudden or gradual, dramatic or undramatic, emotional or intellectual, conversions always involve a major change in a person's thinking, feeling, and willing—in short, in their total behavior. Due to the serious struggle with doubt that precedes owned faith, conversion often appears as a great illumination. In any case, our actions and new deeds provide evidence of our changing heart.[6] Conversions are transformations, and catechesis aims for nothing less.

Break water.

Sometimes our faith journey gets stuck. We press our noses against the glass peering into another room where God seems to dwell, and we wonder how to get in. We stretch what we know about God and about ourselves to their absolute limits and then spin our wheels. We push against the membranes that have held us until they practically burst. At this point catechists free faith from its confines by breaking water. Unless the water breaks, contractions can only push new life so far. The safe, secure womb in which the baby has resided happily until now needs to give way for the child to grow beyond the womb itself. The midwife's one decisive act of intervention is to break water—to discern if and when to burst the soul's confines to make room for faith to grow.

These are heart-in-mouth moments for most of us. The stakes are extraordinarily high. When we break water, we know new life will follow in short order; and we must be ready to care for this new life properly for it to survive. Breaking water is an act of discernment, for the timing and appropriateness of direct engagement in growing faith depends upon the particulars of the young person involved. Much of the time gentle prodding is enough: Does it matter whether Jesus walked on water? How can Christians go to war?

Sometimes breaking water requires a more pointed question: Is something happening at home that you'd like to talk about? Is God calling you to take a new step? Or breaking water can mean shedding a mask: You're kidding yourself if you think you can cut class and still graduate, or if you think suicide will stop the pain. God loves you too much to see you self-destruct, and I believe God has put me here to stop you. Sometimes the midwife's prodding accompanies active labor: staying up all night with the boy in the police station, mediating a long-overdue conversation with parents, accompanying a teenager on a terrifying trip to the doctor. Every time we break water, a new life is called forth by God, and no two situations are the same.

Most of us try to avoid having our water broken. It is much easier simply to stay away from sharp objects, to quit rather than risk rupturing the comfortable walls of self. The massive exodus of youth from churches begins around age twelve and accelerates throughout adolescence, meaning that youth are leaving church at the very ages researchers tell us they are likely to experience their first faith "crisis."[7] Parents unwittingly conspire in this avoidance when they make church attendance "optional" for teenagers over a certain age. Often, of course, youth drop out of church simply by imitating the example of their elders. Rather than struggle with the parable of Jonah or with issues raised by homosexual Christians, many adults dismiss Christian education as children's fare to avoid having their water broken around difficult issues.

James W. Fowler describes the particulars of how "stages" of human development affect the way we interpret faith as we mature.[8] While catechists cannot "move" people from one stage of human development to another, we can prod the limitations on our faith and make openings that give faith more breathing room. We adults get stuck in faith as often as youth do, and breaking water expands our faith as well. Just watch the way grown-ups perk up during the children's sermon. While less intimidated by religious abstraction than teenagers, adults rediscover an invigorating reality when they—like their children—see, smell, touch, hear and taste God's concrete presence. One study of adult cognition found that 40 percent of American adults *never* develop the ability to think abstractly,[9] which helps explain why people sometimes need to whittle faith down to literalism in order to fit it into their existing cognitive framework. It also explains why Jesus Christ—a person who could be seen, heard, touched, smelled, and tasted—is such a powerful window to God for people at all stages of cognitive growth.

Be ready for the catch.

Our daughter Shannon was born in twenty-nine minutes. By some miracle, we were already at the hospital, but there was no time for much in the way of preparation: no time for an epidural and no time for a doctor to arrive. The nurse, forever an angel in our family lore, stood at the foot of the bed and cheerfully postured herself like a quarterback waiting for the hike. "Good catch!" exulted the staff as a huge groan and a baby flew at her simultaneously. Despite the unbelievably quick delivery, everything was ready. Moments after greeting our howling little girl, the nurse moved her to a waiting baby warmer (which looked like it could also handle french fries) and soon had her bathed and bundled for the photo shoot.

Like children, faith generally needs time as well as space to emerge —but the how and when of its arrival depends entirely on God. Catechists are not the ones doing the pushing. Butterflies obtain the strength for their brief survival through the effort involved in hatching.

Our faith must push hard against its boundaries if it is to burst through them with vigor enough to survive the real world. God has planted seeds of grace in all of us long before we show any signs of sprouting. Certainly some youth experience the gift of faith as an explosion, a sudden event that changes everything about them. But most of the time faith, like an elm tree, grows one ring at a time. And so we wait, ready for the catch.

Being "ready for the catch" means staying close to the ball, being available to teenagers whenever faith begins to crown. It means we care for youth even before they claim an identity in Christ, and we celebrate the arrival of this identity with joy and generosity. Being ready implies that we pray for young people's faith and nourish its possibility with friendships and mentors; opportunities for community, study, worship; and other practices that expand our faith boundaries. Catechists ask young people about their faith the way old friends ask about the children. We want to know the details about how teenagers' faith is growing, where it is taking them these days, and how it has changed since last we talked.

There are hundreds of ways to "be ready"—to prepare for the expansion of young people's faith before it actually happens. I know a Lutheran congregation that sends birthday cards to young persons on the anniversary of their baptism, even to those who have dropped out of church since being baptized. "Happy birthday!" this church says to these youth, reminding them that their birth into the life of the Christian community is worth celebrating again and again.

A mother of two daughters remembers when, as a teenager, she anguished over the acne on her face. One day she was so depressed she felt unable to leave the house. Her father led her to the bathroom and asked if he could teach her a new way to wash. He leaned over the sink and splashed water over his face, telling her, "On the first splash, say, 'In the name of the Father'; on the second, 'in the name of the Son'; and on the third, 'in the name of the Holy Spirit.' Then look up into the mirror and remember that you are a child of God, full of grace and beauty." Today this woman reenacts those words at her daughters' bath time, making every bath a baptismal act, a reminder that they are made in God's image.[10]

In our congregation, women honor fifth- and sixth-grade girls with a spiritual life retreat (designed to coincide with the year many girls start menstruation, which is also when girls tend to "go underground" in terms of self-confidence). The retreat invites girls to view the changes in their bodies as God's special invitation to grow into their faith as young women. During the retreat, each adult woman covenants to pray for and mentor one of these girls throughout the year.

All of these people—the Lutheran congregation, the father washing his face, the women on the girls' retreat—are catechists, people who hand on basic elements of our Christian tradition purposefully and aloud (even with cheers and birthday cards) to youth. They do all of this with little evidence that faith will come of it. But they believe something wonderful is happening amidst the pushing and the tears. As catechists, they are confident that the struggle is worth it, and they sidle up alongside these youth to encourage them to see this struggle through.

Cranking Up the Coals

Thinking all is lost after the crucifixion, some of the disciples go fishing on the Sea of Tiberias—a dismal, depressing fishing expedition. Hot, naked, and exhausted, the disciples try valiantly to return to the way things were before they met Jesus. Suddenly a voice from the shore (big rock thrown here): "Catchin' anything?" "Nah," they shout back, more depressed than ever. "Then try the other side of the boat!" the voice yells again. Peter stands up to see who this wise guy is. Wait—no, it can't be—but, yes, it is: the Lord! Suddenly Peter can't move fast enough. He leaps into the water, and swims to shore, leaving the others to haul in a miraculous catch. His faith grows three sizes in a matter of minutes. The boundaries of what he thinks God can do explode, and his love and gratitude for what God is doing in Jesus Christ, the Lord of Life, is simply too large to fit in the boat any more.

Jesus anticipates his arrival. As Peter stands dripping wet on shore, he smells something....breakfast? The coals are already hot. Fish are already frying in the pan; bread already laid out; the disciples' places already set. "Come and eat!" Jesus calls to them (John 21:1-14). Before the disciples even arrive ashore, everything is ready. Jesus is expecting them, just as he is expecting us.

Godbearing youth ministry is expectant ministry. We know that every young person comes equipped with God-given, embryonic grace that can potentially grow into viable faith. In the face of the retreat gone bad, the relationship gone sour, the teenager gone astray, we lose track of the fact that soul tending matters even for faith too small to detect with the naked eye. But Jesus sees it. Jesus expects our faith long before he has any good reason to do so. We forget that the pushing is not up to us. What we can do is crank up the coals, fry the fish, set the table. And then throw some rocks into the lake—and wait.

QUESTIONS AND EXERCISES

1. Remember your favorite teacher in high school. In what ways was he or she a midwife?

2. Think of a rock thrown in the middle of your life—a disturbance (positive or negative) that resulted in "faith ripples." Was it an intentional or an unplanned disturbance? What happened to your faith as a result?

3. How have you "broken water" for others on their faith journeys?

IDEA FOR THE ROAD

Gather adults by a pond or a lake (a full wading pool will do). Give each person a stone. Play some meditative music and allow time for reflection. Invite persons, as they are so moved, to throw their stones into the water. As they watch the ripples circle out from the place of impact, invite them to share aloud the learning they will take home with them and silently to ask God's guidance to break water for a youth whose faith needs room to grow.

FARE FOR THE SOUL

A woman dreamed she walked into a brand-new shop in the marketplace and, to her surprise, found God behind the counter.

"What do you sell here?" she asked.

"Everything your heart desires," said God.

Hardly daring to believe what she was hearing, the woman decided to ask for the best things a human could wish for. "I want peace of mind and love and happiness and wisdom and freedom from fear," she said. Then as an afterthought, she added, "Not just for me. For everyone on earth."

God smiled. "I think you've got me wrong, my dear," [God] said. "We don't sell fruits here. Only seeds."[11]

—Anthony de Mello

Notes

1. Michael Warren, *Youth, Gospel, Liberation* (San Francisco: Harper and Row, 1987), 10.

2. Barbara Brown Taylor, *Gospel Medicine* (Cambridge, Mass.: Cowley Publications, 1995), 8.

3. Bob Stromberg, *Why Geese Fly Farther Than Eagles: Tales That Ignite the Imagination* (Colorado Springs: Focus on the Family, 1992), 102.

4. Westerhoff, in *Will Our Children Have Faith?* (New York: The Seabury Press, 1976), 98, describes the process of growing in faith as analogous to a tree adding rings as it grows. He describes moments in the expansion of faith as "styles" of faith and believes they typically incorporate one another: experienced faith, affiliative faith, searching faith (a style of faith he ascribes to many teenagers), and owned faith, which "historically has been called conversion."

5. John Wesley, *Works*, vol. 18 (Nashville: Abingdon, 1988), 249–50.

6. Westerhoff, *Will Our Children Have Faith?*, 98.

7. Peter Scales et al., *The Attitudes and Needs of Religious Youth Workers: Perspectives from the Field* (Minneapolis: Search Institute, 1995), 13.

8. James W. Fowler, *Stages of Faith: The Psychology of Human Development and the Quest for Meaning* (San Francisco: HarperSanFrancisco, 1981).

9. Lawrence Kohlberg and Carol Gilligan, "The Adolescent as a Philosopher: The Discovery of the Self in a Postconventional World," *Daedalus* 100 (Fall 1971): 1071.

10. Stephanie Paulsell, "Honoring the Body," in *Practicing Our Faith: A Way of Life for a Searching People,* ed. Dorothy C. Bass (San Francisco: Jossey-Bass, 1997), 19.

11. Anthony de Mello, *Taking Flight: A Book of Story Meditations* (New York: Image Books, 1988), 103.

ELEVEN
Stick Holding
Practices of Witness

*To communicate the Gospel means putting it
before the people so that they are able to decide
for or against it....All that we who communicate
this Gospel can do is to make possible a genuine
decision.*
—Paul Tillich, A Theology of Culture

J REMEMBER THE day in seminary when David Steinmetz, one of
my favorite professors, broke away from his notes and proceeded to
preach with passion about our role as theologians-in-residence in
parish ministry. His words reinforced the importance of our knowing
our theology and our church history, the fine-tuning of the faith that
has gone on for centuries, in order to proclaim the gospel faithfully in
a local church.

Dr. Steinmetz was right. By virtue of our training, title, or position,
like it or not, people often view us as the ones who know about the
things of God—or at least as the ones who should know how to talk
about matters of faith in a credible way. Being theologians-in-residence
means we take seriously the responsibility of talking about God coher-
ently, of witnessing to the ways we have seen the risen Lord with our
own eyes. It does not necessarily mean that we have a seminary degree
or a bunch of letters after our names to validate our credentials. What it
does mean is that in our various settings for ministry, as Godbearers we
will have some understanding and vocabulary to speak consistently and
compellingly about God.

Dr. Steinmetz's job was to translate the issues and contexts of historical church debates and personalities into accessible, contemporary language for us. People who pastor youth receive the daunting task of translating the gospel. In no other way can we be both faithful and relevant,
and this ability to translate the gospel is critically important for the cross-
cultural communication that is part and parcel of ministry with youth.

Malls, Mirrors, MTV, Madison Avenue, and Microsoft

Witnessing to the gospel takes witness and gospel seriously. Witnessing means telling others what we have seen and experienced in Christ in a way that makes sense to the person with whom we are speaking. Witnessing to the gospel means attempting to maintain the integrity of our faith as it has been handed down to us through scripture and the collective tradition of living Christian communities. Without attention to the integrity of the gospel, witnessing can slip into mere advertising. Conversely, preserving the integrity of the gospel is pointless unless we tell others in intelligible fashion how it has made a difference to us.

The practices of witness or claim staking in youth ministry include a lot more than preaching: Teaching, modeling, raising a prophetic voice, and advocacy can all be forms of witness. No matter what form these practices of witness may take, only conscious attention to building bridges of connection between faith and the real world of youth will allow the witness to have any significant impact. So where do we turn to mine the everyday life experience of teenagers? Probably to the same places that teenagers turn: malls, mirrors, MTV, Madison Avenue, and Microsoft. By no means is this list exhaustive, but it serves as a good starting point.

Godbearers take Christ to the streets. Go to the local mall where teenagers hang out together, and let them give you a tour. Take note of the places where they shop, the styles of clothes they wear, the comments they make along the way. The mall is an icon of late twentieth-century America; it speaks volumes about the values of consumerism, current trends, and lifestyles of the population. The mall as gathering space itself is worth delving into with youth. What are they looking for? What do they actually find? What is the attraction?

One of the things you will notice while walking through the mall with adolescents is that every store window also serves as a mirror, sometimes figuratively in terms of the values that it presents, sometimes quite literally as youth steal sideways glances at themselves walking past. Mirrors are strong forces in identity formation: the light-reflecting mirrors that reinforce feelings of self-worth or self-loathing; the mirrors of peers who offer approval or disapproval, acceptance or rejection; the mirrors of heroes or idols who project a longed-for image of self. When we pay attention to the mirrors in the lives of youth, we can better help them turn to Christ for a truer reflection of themselves.

MTV offers another rich insight into the lives of youth. Music is a driving force of youth culture. The power of MTV lies in its ability to combine image and sound in a world that dips in and out of reality, merging fantasy, feeling, sexuality, violence, success, love, and self-expression into a potent brew. Overt and subliminal messages creep through this realm. Listening to the music of our youth (and in the case of MTV, watching it too) gives us a valuable window to their souls and a current language with which to critique, challenge, and explore values—and the possibility of offering a bridge for youth to claim their faith.

Music videos have their place, as do the other worlds of visual art: movies and television. We try to stay in touch with the movies our youth are going to see, the TV shows they watch, the videos they rent again and again. Although a number of good resources help us stay current with youth culture, the best resource of all is our youth who will tell us what's hot (and what's not) if we take the time to ask. As Godbearers, we do not have to pretend to live in their world—to love their music, to see all their favorite movies, to buy the same CDs, to hang out at the mall with them every Friday night—but we do need to be in touch with their world to share the message of Christ effectively.

Microsoft is an appropriate icon of the cyberspace that many teenagers frequent. Chat rooms, hyperlinks, interactive games, CD-ROM encyclopedias, and on-line access to savory and unsavory sites make computers a driving force in the lives of youth. With more and more information available literally at a point and click of their fingertips, images and data bombard youth at an unprecedented rate. Godbearers-as-translators provide filters to deal with the barrage of bytes through the lens of Christian community, while borrowing words, phrases, and symbols from the multimedia vocabulary of cyberspace to make the gospel current. Listen to the language of cyberspace, and you will hear a cry for community in muted and explicit ways: Youth meet people in chat rooms, use hyperlinks to connect with others through worlds and domains of information, buy interactive video games that mimic the presence of other human beings. The options available in this virtual reality are seemingly endless.

The Perils of Being a Bridge

Knowing the icons of media culture is only the first step in bridging the gap between adolescents and the Christian tradition, and bridging the gap can be difficult work. Few acts of translation offer one-to-one correspondence. Translation from one language to another is an imprecise science at best, complete with competing options, nuances, and choices.

From time to time multinational corporations have paid dearly for this imprecision. Coca-Cola could not figure out why their sales had not soared as projected in China until someone pointed out that their transliterated Coca-Cola logo read something like "Bite the wax tad-pole." Similarly, Pepsi tried to translate their "Come to Life with Pepsi" campaign into Korean only to discover that their advertising claims implied that Pepsi brings your ancestors back from the dead. Chicken magnate Frank Purdue's trademark tag line, "It takes a tough man to make a tender chicken" inadvertently metamorphosed into Spanish as "It takes a virile man to make a chicken affectionate."[1]

The peril of being translators of the gospel is that we might miss the mark and say something we don't intend, something irrelevant, or something that just does not matter. The yawns of youth, the dangers of disseminating less-than-faithful images of God, and the risk of failing to communicate with passion the passion of God make the role of trans-lator a dangerous one. The art of good translation is imperative if the gospel is to have any credence and gain any sort of hearing among youth with whom we minister. In the spirit of the prophet Isaiah (Isa. 58:12), Godbearers self-consciously see themselves as "repairers of the breach," a vital link in passing on faith to a new generation in faithful and vital ways.

The Power of Getting It Right

But fear not! As difficult as giving the gospel an honest and appealing hearing among youth is, the fruits of such labor are rewarding. Think for a moment about the young people throughout your ministry who have had the call of Christ take root in their lives. Think of their faces, their faith, their passion. For me, vivid images come to mind. I can see Kelly, singing her heart out in praise to God; Pat, a high-school senior, think-ing about a call to youth ministry; Jennifer, a freshman in college taking next steps toward the mission field; five-year-old Tyler telling and inter-preting the story of David and Nathan (my morning sermon topic) at the Sunday lunch table to his open-mouthed parents; Katie, preparing for her first Communion, who told me that her upcoming Sunday experience would mean that "I'm like one of his disciples."

When God becomes real, when faith takes root, when youth make commitments to Christ with unabashed zeal, the Godbearers who have had a hand in pointing young people toward God are humbled and affirmed. Effective practices of witness make a difference. The power of getting our witness right, or at least finding the appropriate words or images, is worthy of our best efforts to bring Christ's message alive in such a way as to pass it on. When youth come to faith or take their next step in their faith journeys, we cannot claim sole responsibility. The power of the Holy Spirit plants the seeds that take root and grow. Usually many have had a hand in the nurturing.

Nevertheless, those of us given the mantle of theologian-in-residence or youth pastor must offer a compelling and articulate witness to Christ. Translating the gospel well is more a delicate art than a precise science. However, we can develop some skills that will help us perform our task more faithfully and more forcefully: eavesdropping for the sake of gospel; doing double, invisible exegesis; knowing the difference between rocks and sand; learning our faith ABCs; sneaking in backdoor theology; and remembering our audience.

Eavesdropping for the Sake of the Gospel

Looking at life homiletically—learning to attend to the people, the situations, the movies, the magazine articles, the conversations, the everyday ordinary stuff of our lives with an eye toward the gospel of Christ and the ways of faith—is a lifelong skill we can practice and sharpen. Belton Joyner, a former pastor, used to describe one of his sermon preparation techniques as "eavesdropping for the sake of the gospel." He used as an example a conversation he overheard at a fast-food restaurant one day that dovetailed into the scripture texts he was dealing with that week, which found its way into his preaching. Joyner encouraged us (a group of fledgling preachers), not to become intrusive spies into the lives of strangers, but to develop an active ear and eye that filters our life experiences through the lens of the gospel.

Eavesdropping for the sake of the gospel means being in touch with the teenage world of music, values, images, icons, fashion, heroes, and magazines, and finding implicit connections with the message of Christ. That doesn't mean we have to like all the music or condone all the heroes or agree with all the images. But to communicate in a real and vital language with teenagers, we will do primary research on MTV, on-line, at the mall, and at the video store, where we can start making connections between the world of the Bible and the world in which our youth actually live. Unless we can converse in the language of popular culture, we have little chance of being a bridge between our youth and Christ.

Doing Invisible, Double Exegesis

Communicating the gospel effectively with people in general, and with youth in particular, requires an invisible, double exegesis: simultaneous interpretation from both sides of the fence. On the one hand we have to be faithful to the biblical texts and use all the resources and tools available to us to draw out their meaning. We have to be serious students of the stories of Jesus, the message of the prophets, the history of Israel, the teaching of Paul to pass on a biblically informed faith to this generation. We must listen to the texts on their terms and not simply lift them out for our personal use or their fitting key word.

Maybe this guideline seems too obvious even to mention. Yet we often use the Bible too casually in our ministry with adolescents. We detach texts to emphasize a certain point or perspective and pay little attention to context or the big picture of the biblical authors. We're short on time and the water balloon volleyball game still needs setting up; we'll "get by" without studying the scripture in advance for tonight. Yet a serious, sensitive study of scripture transforms those who teach as well as those to whom we pass on biblical insights.

On the other hand, presenting ourselves as biblical experts probably won't fly with youth either, which is why we need invisible exegesis. We do our homework, learn the context, and find out what various scholars have to say about particular texts. Youth probably don't want to hear the seven variant meanings of the Greek word, but knowing the subtleties of the text helps us translate it faithfully into their world. In the end, we let our research rest comfortably in the background and try not to get overly technical in presenting the meaning of the biblical passages.

What we are really after in translating the gospel for youth is "dynamic equivalence," a phrase borrowed from one of the stated goals of the New Living Bible. The translators weren't after a word-for-word translation ("formal equivalence") but sought instead to use contemporary language with faithfulness and clarity to bring the power of the original text project into the present.[2] Being a student of the Bible is not enough in and of itself. The other side of the interpretation equation rests in drawing out the gospel's meaning for the theological struggles at work in the lives of teenagers. Translation works both ways. Youth need people to interpret, critique, and make sense of the potpourri of images and value systems that invade their lives on a daily basis. The skillful communicator will make connections, build bridges, and do invisible double exegesis. To paraphrase Karl Barth, Godbearing translators work with the Bible in one hand and a mouse and remote in the other.

Knowing the Difference between Rocks and Sand

A college professor held an empty glass jar before his class one day. Methodically, he filled it to the top with several large rocks. Then he asked his students, "How many of you think the jar is full?" About half of them raised their hands. "No, it's not," he replied. He then proceeded to pour a beaker of gravel into the jar. "Now is it full?" Beginning to catch on, only one or two students raised their hands. "Right, it's still not full." He then took a small cup of sand and poured it into the remaining crevices. "Now is it full?" A few students nodded yes; a few shook their heads no. "No, not quite." He took a container of water and filled the jar up to the very top and concluded his exercise by saying, "Now it is full, or at least as full as I can make it. But what would have happened if I had put the water or the sand in first? Would there have been any room for the rocks or the gravel?" Of course, the answer was no.

So how does this illustration help us understand youth ministry and communicating the gospel to teenagers? Everything, we think. If we picture the rocks as the four or five most important things that we want to pass on to youth about God and about who they are as children of God, the gravel as the next most important, and so on, we see a clear focus for our best efforts. For this reason distilling our personal theologies into their most foundational form is not just an idle exercise. It is the first step that allows us to find the most lively, highly charged ways to communicate our core convictions.

One temptation in youth ministry is to cover all the bases, to say something about every aspect of the Christian life. While we certainly favor a balanced and holistic approach to youth ministry, in our roles as translators it is important to narrow the focus. Do we want youth to take away the big rocks of the faith? Or are we busy filling their jars with water and sand? What three or four things do we most fervently want to communicate about God, about the gospel, about humanity in relationship to God?

Learning Your Faith ABCs

Frederick Buechner has been one of the most refreshing Christian translators of this generation. His lively writing and style engage and provoke. In his book *Wishful Thinking: A Theological ABC*, Buechner takes theological jargon and unpacks it in conversational ways. For example, he describes a miracle as

> A cancer inexplicably cured. A voice in a dream. A statue that weeps. A miracle is an event that strengthens faith. It is possible to look at most miracles and find a rational explanation ....It is possible to look at Rembrandt's Supper at Emmaus and find a rational explanation in terms of paint and canvas.
>
> Faith in God is less apt to proceed from miracles than miracles from faith in God.[3]

Godbearers would do well to imitate Buechner's gap-bridging style. The church has a language all its own, much of it helpful and useful. With youth, church jargon can look like the communicative equivalent of the Great Wall of China. Only when translated into a familiar vernacular will theological language gain power and meaning for youth. How do we take the language of justification, born again, grace, forgiveness, and draw out the depth of meaning of these fundamental concepts with youth? Not by slipping into a secret code language for insiders only but by carefully and creatively translating these rich terms into contemporary images and phrases.

Again Buechner is instructive. Moving in the opposite direction in *Whistling in the Dark: An ABC Theologized*, Buechner takes ordinary, everyday words and imbues them with theological meaning and reflection. One favorite is his exposition of what he calls tourist preaching.

> English-speaking tourists abroad are inclined to believe that if they only speak English loudly and distinctly and slowly enough, the natives will know what's being said even though they don't understand a single word of the language.
>
> Preachers often make the same mistake. They believe that if only they speak the ancient verities loudly and distinctly and slowly enough, their congregations will understand them.
>
> Unfortunately, the only language people really understand is their own language, and unless preachers are prepared to translate the ancient verities into it, they might as well save their breath.[4]

Unless those of us who minister with youth are willing to translate, we might as well save our breath too.

Backdoor Theology

I once had a group of teenagers stop by the church after school to help with a bulk mailing. Because of their various extracurricular activities, they arrived in a somewhat staggered fashion. A few got to work at 2:45

P.M. Another joined us at 3:30 P.M., and the last person didn't arrive until nearly 4:00, just as we were wrapping up. We drove to get ice cream, which led to an interesting *en route* conversation about justice (it just wasn't *fair* that everyone got the same thing) and grace (everyone got the same thing). What a perfect entree into the parable about the laborers in the vineyard and the nature of grace. I retold the story briefly, tied the two events together; and they made their own connections. With the cookies and cream and mint chocolate chip, I mixed in a little theology, a natural outgrowth of the situation at hand. They didn't even notice, and a scoop of theology often tastes better that way.

Sometimes the best translating happens spontaneously when we can reframe our immediate context. The situation preaches the gospel, and our role is to sneak in a little backdoor theology, an interpretation that allows youth to recognize the cross standing right there before them. If this sounds a bit subversive that's because it is. Jesus knew that theology does its best work when our guard is down and we least suspect it. If we stay alert to youth who keep the back door open to God, we possibly may weave God or Jesus or the kingdom into the conversation quite naturally. Rather than a frontal assault of the gospel, Godbearing youth ministry looks for opportunities to smuggle God into the room from the rear before youth can erect the normal defenses.

Remember Your Audience

A few final words about our role as translators. Youth live in that in-between world of no longer a child, not yet an adult. Even though startlingly sophisticated and growing up faster than ever in some ways, youth still long to be kids. One of the gold mines I have discovered in my own ministry with youth is the wonderful world of Disney. Particularly with middle highs, but even with senior-high girls, Mickey Mouse communicates powerfully. The Disney films are full of images that lend themselves to theological interpretation. The whole story line of *Beauty and the Beast*, complete with its final scene of transformation (hints of resurrection?), centers around the power of love to free us from the prison of self by putting off our beastly nature and putting on a new heart and life. *The Lion King* overflows with baptismal imagery (the opening scene) and probes the discovery of true identity (Simba's listening to the voice in the night sky that reminds him who he is) and regeneration (the rebirth of the pride land). Pocahontas sings about the "Colors of the Wind" and calls attention to creation's intricacy and interrelatedness. Mulan draws strength and guidance from her ancestral faith to challenge oppressive traditions. Godbearers might weave any of these images into a message or a program, either by allusion or use of the actual video clip.[5]

Another technique that takes into account the in-between cognitive development of adolescence is the use of simple object lessons to imprint a message. Unlike young children who have not yet developed the cognitive skills to deal in metaphors, adolescents are in the beginning stages of formal operational thinking and therefore can think abstractly. Although abstract thinking is a relatively new skill for young teenagers, it becomes more manageable with a tangible object to which they can attach concepts.

I took a message that came straight from our fourth-grade Sunday school lesson to a high-school Bible Club. On the heels of some episodes of racially motivated violence, I brought in six containers of vanilla pudding each of which I had dyed with different food coloring. The results with the sixteen- and seventeen-year-olds did not differ that much from those I had witnessed with the fourth graders. My taste testers were convinced that the blue pudding tasted like blueberry; the red was cherry or strawberry; the green was lime. In reality, all of the samples were exactly alike (save for food coloring), which led to a stimulating conversation about stereotyping others and prejudging based on outward appearance. Visual aids and props from children's ministry provide valuable insights for youth when used in ways that respect adolescents' potential for maturity and that acknowledge they are only a stone's throw away from childhood.

Sometimes We Get to Hold the Stick

Translating the gospel with and for youth is an arduous and at times frustrating task. I once heard Episcopal priest Barbara Brown Taylor describe her experience of going into a primitive antique store and being drawn to a strange creation of twisted metal and glass. She picked it up, tried it out, and proceeded to inquire of the store owner about its function.

> "Why it's a lightning rod, of course," she replied. No wonder I liked it. It was a mediator's stick, a sign of office for anyone foolish enough to stand between God's word and God's people. We do not create the live current, of course. We merely consent to bear it, which makes us assistant mediators at best. The real mediator is the Holy Spirit, that white hot crack of

lightning that connects heaven to earth. Without that spirit, no encounter takes place. We cannot make God known. Only God can make God known, but if we are lucky we get to hold the stick.[6]

Our effective translation allows us the exhilarating privilege of standing between heaven and earth, serving as assistant mediators in a young person's journey toward God. On the days when we wonder if we've misread our call from God, we may receive reward enough simply knowing that sometimes we get to hold the stick.

QUESTIONS AND EXERCISES

1. Who helped translate the gospel for you during your own faith development (particularly when you were a teenager)?

2. How would you define the following terms in youth-friendly language?

   • *Grace*:

   • *Justification*:

   • *Forgiveness*:

3. To what other sources (beyond those mentioned in this chapter) do you turn to help you in your translation of the gospel for youth?

IDEA FOR THE ROAD

Get together with some other youth leaders (from your church or colleagues in other settings) and physically reenact the rock, gravel, sand, water exercise on page 179. Talk about one another's "core rocks" for Godbearing ministry with the young.

FARE FOR THE SOUL

Who speaks the things that Love him shows
Shall say things deeper than he knows [7]

—Coventry Patmore

Notes

1. *Homiletics*, January-March, 1993 (Communication Resources, Dayton, OH).

2. Rusty Wright, "New Life for Old Words," *Duke Magazine* 83, no.5 (July-August, 1997).

3. Frederick Buechner, *Wishful Thinking: A Theological ABC* (New York: Harper and Row, 1973), 63.

4. Frederick Buechner, *Whistling in the Dark: An ABC Theologized* (New York: Harper and Row, 1988), 107.

5. Using short segments of commercial videos for teaching purposes is allowable, provided that you erase the clips within an appropriate time frame. Copyright laws prohibit the public showing of most films and videos to a group (like a youth group or Sunday school class) without special permission.

6. Barbara Brown Taylor, "The Three Lives of the Sermon," a lecture delivered at the Hickman Lectures, Duke University, October 29, 1996.

7. Quoted in Sweet's *SoulCafe* 1, no. 6–7 (October–November 1995).

TWELVE
Sacred Spacemaking
Practices of Dehabituation

*All those college football coaches who hold dress-
ing room prayers before a game should be forced
to attend church once a week.*
—Duffy Daugherty, football legend and coach

GODBEARERS SEEK sacred space, and we try to help create it for
youth. Our firsthand familiarity with sacred space equips us to
draw others into the *kairos* experience of sacred space. *Kairos* time
refers to those moments in space and time when we no longer measure
time *chronologically* (in minutes and hours) but *qualitatively*. In *kairos* time
an individual or community experiences the spirit of God filling up the
time to its fullest measure. *Kairos* time is full of God-consciousness, not
bound by clock-consciousness. Too often youth and adults will find themselves simply going with the flow of their culture and time. Sacred
spacemaking provides a way out.

Breaking the Rhythm

We might best describe the practices of dehabituation as rhythm breaking. While Christians need a rhythm of life available in the practices of
faith, we also need to vary these rhythms from time to time if we are to
stay fresh in our faith and open to the new and energizing ways Christ
calls to us. We all fall prey to the powers of habit, circumstance, and
acculturation. Enter a room where music is playing loudly, and we find
it almost impossible not to move to the beat, become accustomed to the
volume, and adjust to the rhythm within a few minutes. Lives lived
without intentionality work the same way. Unless we consciously
decide to live otherwise, we may drift aimlessly with the currents of
daily routine rather than deliberately choose to live as part of God's
kingdom.

Sacred spacemaking breaks the rhythm of the ordinary and punctuates it with moments of God-consciousness. This does not suggest a sharp discontinuity between ordinary time and God-time. Certainly the spirit of God is in the midst of the ordinary; we do not have to escape our ordinary, everyday existence in order to ascend to a higher, more spiritualized plane. If incarnation means anything at all, it means that God is in the detail, moving in our midst moment-by-moment: in the traumatic breakup of the sixteen-year-old; the joyful self-discovery of the thirty-year-old; the hallway, day-to-day conversations of a group of middle highs; the eating/sleeping/working/studying/playing ordinary experiences of our lives.

Yet few of us live with a constant awareness of God's presence. That awareness comes only as we place ourselves in settings more attuned to the God-beat and less to the pulsating cadences of our contemporary culture. Sacred spacemaking helps us do precisely that. The practices of dehabituation reprogram our frequencies, reduce the clutter of background noise, and redirect our hearts to the composer of a cosmic melody. To get a better handle on the practices of sacred spacemaking, we turn to an unlikely tutor: the realm of sport.

A Surprising Tutor

When I was a college junior taking a class on the sociology of sport (much more rigorous than the title would suggest!), the professor introduced me to an intriguing description of a field of play, whether it be a baseball diamond, a football field, an ice-hockey arena, or a basketball court. As the class members discussed common elements among these various action-soaked venues, our professor referred to them collectively as sacred spaces. The heavy religious overtones were intentional.

Now I had been an athlete all my life but had never thought of my cherished basketball court or soccer field in quite those terms. The professor quickly convinced me of the appropriateness of the language. In a limited sense, all of these sites are sacred spaces. Much like an ancient temple whose boundaries clearly demarcated the sacred and the profane, the various chalk lines and field markings set special turf apart for play. The field of play exists for the players. On those rare occasions when a disruptive fan crosses the magical line, security personnel summarily escort the interloper out. All of the action takes place within these prescribed boundaries, and what happens beyond is out-of-bounds or doesn't count.

An artificial accounting of innings, time clocks, quarters, and periods suspends and replaces ordinary time. The priests and priestesses (umpires and referees) officiate over the recreational rituals and pass judgment on what is fair and foul, what is in and out, what constitutes rule keeping and rule breaking. They serve as guardians of the game, keepers of the sacred space.

The longer I have sifted through this analogy, the more its accuracy convinces me. The deification of professional athletes, the worshipful and zealous loyalty of fans, and Saturday and Sunday (Sabbath Days within the Judeo-Christian tradition) rituals/games further reinforce that notion. The religious image of sacred space opened up my understanding of American sport, but the analogy contains an interesting boomerang effect: Traipsing on the athletic turf sharpens this significant religious phrase in its own context as well. The concepts of godly play, alternative timekeeping, and pick-up games—all borrowed from sports jargon—inform our understanding of sacred space for God.

Recreation as Godly Play

At their core, baseball, football, basketball, hockey, and soccer games are just that: games. Admittedly, they are games invested with great significance for some and with economic rewards or losses for others. But they are still games. Little children play them in various forms. Millions of adolescents hone their skills on the athletic fields after school. Collegians compete with one another on interschool and intramural levels. Even in the surreal culture of multimillion-dollar contracts, shoe endorsements, and inflated egos, most professional athletes explain their vocation as playing a game they love and being lucky enough to be paid for it. At a basic level, then, sacred space is space set apart for fundamentally recreational purposes, purposes of play.

In his book *Godly Play*, Jerome Berryman writes about the holiness of play and its potential for recreating or shaping souls.[1] Sacred space provides room in our lives and in the lives of our youth for godly play, an intentional contrast to the work of our jobs, our schools, or our household chores. Offering youth sacred space means going beyond providing wholesome recreation or one more game of blob tag. Godbearing ministry with youth is more than fun and games, but we dare not minimize the significance of godly play. If it breaks the rhythm of our drivenness, if it relieves the accumulated stress of our lives, then it has the potential to serve as true recreation, a renewing of body and spirit.

On another level, anthropologists and philosophers understand play as a symbolic representation of a larger reality. Football is a national passion in the U.S. not just because of the game itself but because it represents cultural values dear to American life: strength, competition, getting up and starting over after being tackled. While cheering in the stands or racing down the field, we may not consciously acknowledge this representation; in fact, one of the qualities of play is our getting lost in the play itself. Worship with youth is a special kind of play, a symbolic representation of a larger reality that allows us to get lost in the play.

I create a sacred space in my life by playing basketball at the YMCA. I will allow few things to deter me from driving the twenty-five minutes (twenty-three on a good day) to be on the court twice a week to engage in a few games of pick-up hoops. I play basketball for a number of reasons, the vain attempt to slow the aging process being chief among them. I play for the exercise and to counterbalance all the junk food that I love to eat. I know I still play for the rush of competition. But most significantly, I play to break the rhythm of my work week so that my job will not consume me. I schedule this interruption in my calendar of meetings, counseling appointments, hospital visits, sermon preparation. The interlude of godly play helps recreate my body and spirit.

Alternative Timekeeping

In a sense, basketball functions for me on one level the way Sabbath keeping does on another. The distinction is somewhat artificial; our bodies affect our souls and vice versa, and we neglect this important connection to the detriment of both body and soul. In practice, Sabbath keeping intentionally binds our physical work-a-day world with the state of our souls. A life of unbridled activity and constant striving misshapes our souls; a life of balance between work and play, doing and resting releases us from the idolatrous bondage of believing that the salvation of the world depends upon our own busyness rather than on God's active presence.

Ancient Israel tied the practice of Sabbath observance to two foundational events: the Creation and the Exodus. According to the Exodus account (Exod. 20:8-11), God ordained the theological grounding for Sabbath observance in the creation rhythm. In the Creation story in Genesis, God labors for six days bringing light, stars, moon, sun, animals, plants, trees, birds, and finally humanity into being. On the seventh day, God rests. So Israel marks its days accordingly. The enactment of the

Sabbath ritual comes as part of the Decalogue, the identity-forming code of ethics that shapes the Israelites and distinguishes them among the nations. The alternate explanation of the Sabbath observance (Deut. 5:15) asserts Israel's remembrance of a time in Israel's history when the Israelites were forced to work, a time when they could take no rest. Now that God has brought them to freedom, they are to commemorate their release with a day of nonwork, a day of doing nothing.

Over the past two to three millennia, keeping the Sabbath has come to mean a variety of things: abstaining from any form of work at all (in Orthodox Judaism), refraining from commerce or shopping (the old blue laws in many states), no card playing, and going to church all day long (some American Protestant traditions). Yet for most of us, the notion of Sabbath keeping is a thing of the past, an obsolete practice whose time has come and gone. We would do well to reconsider this position. The question for Godbearers is not *should* we but *how* shall we reclaim Sabbath keeping in way appropriate to our time and context?

Today the seven-day-a-week rhythm shapes most of us, and we try to squeeze everything we possibly can into our already overbooked calendars. In many churches, rather than being a day of Sabbath keeping, Sunday is the most frenetic and activity-laden day of the week, offering little sense of rest. Godbearing youth ministry lays claim to the value of Sabbath rest. This may mean simplifying things on the church calendar on Sundays—even the youth schedule. It may mean changing our own personal habits so that Sundays once again become a day of rest and not the last-gasp attempt to finish all our weekend tasks we neglected because we were too busy with other things—soccer games, grocery shopping, yard work—on Friday night and Saturday.

Or more likely, it may mean keeping Sabbath on another day. For many of us reading this book, Sunday plainly is not our best option for Sabbath rest because of the nature of our positions and the realities of our own church/work schedule. (I know it is definitely not my Sabbath!) Godbearers intentionally interrupt the schedule with time for reflection, renewal, and prayer in order to refresh their souls and to reorient themselves Godward, which sets Godbearing ministry apart from rat-race ministry. Godbearers know that Sabbath means quit. Stop. Take a break. Cool it. The word itself has nothing devout or holy in it. It is a word about time, denoting our nonuse of it; what we usually call *wasting time*.[2]

Sometimes our own passion works against us in this regard, and we easily cloak our workaholic tendencies in religious garb to justify all the hours we are putting in. After all, we're doing it for God, aren't we? Clearly God's intention does not include broken-down vessels for ministry, weakened by fatigue. Jesus' own modeling in this area frees us. As urgently and passionately as Jesus preached and lived the kingdom of God, scriptures suggest that he honored the spirit of the Sabbath (sans the frivolous legalities some had tied to it). He knew the value of time away from the crowds and the disciples, and he regularly built it into his regimen to renew his own spirit. Often we read about his going off to a quiet place to pray, claiming mini-Sabbaths along the arduous road he traveled.

Keeping Sabbath involves rhythm-breaking as well as falling into God's rhythm and developing a new rhythm altogether.

> Sabbath-keeping often feels like an interruption, an interference with our routines. It challenges assumptions we gradually build up that our daily work is indispensable in making the world go. And then we find it is not an interruption but a more spacious rhythmic measure that confirms and extends the basic beat. Every seventh day a deeper note is struck ...(and) creation honored and contemplated, redemption remembered and shared.[3]

Keeping Sabbath then, like a scoreboard clock at a football or basketball game, is an alternate way of timekeeping, a different way of framing and demarcating life's moments.

Another related but distinct practice of sacred spacemaking is retreat. Whereas Sabbath keeping is built into the weekly cycle of days, retreats come with less frequency—perhaps on a quarterly, semiannual, or yearly basis. Many of us have experienced the powerful effects of a spiritually charged weekend away with youth. Many reasons explain the significance of retreats in the life of youth groups: the high-energy, action-packed agenda; the discovery of new and deeper friendships. The water balloon fights and shaving cream battles usually make the highlight reel. Once in a while a dynamic speaker comes in and lights a fire with lively, inspirational messages. Juiced-up worship with guitars, drums, and a good sound system can leave its imprint. Many youth will point to a retreat experience as the moment in their spiritual journey when they were first able (or best able) to make a commitment to God.

While all these factors add to the potency of retreat experiences, we would suggest that the simple act of breaking the rhythm of the ordinary—removing ourselves to a separate setting, imposing an alternate schedule and claim on our time, bracketing the time and space for

God—is what most significantly opens the door for spiritual transformation. We have no guarantee that what we fill the time with will really make a difference; we can pull off a rip-roaringly fun retreat (which may be fine if that is its purpose) that does little to spark anyone's spiritual growth. However, Godbearers recognize the potential of such sacred space and intentionally seek to open fresh doorways to God in and through the unique possibilities that retreat settings offer.

Our task goes beyond planning and carrying out life-changing retreats for youth: We also must claim time for personal retreat. Godbearers need incubation periods, times of active waiting on God's spirit, whether it be a weekend away with a group for our own spiritual well-being (a time when we are *pastored*, not *pastor*), a one-day or partial-day silent retreat at a nearby monastery or convent, a guided retreat with a spiritual director or several close companions. Each of these retreat types and settings has gifts to offer Godbearers. We may have difficulty claiming this sacred space for ourselves, feeling that we can't take time away from our families or work. Yet we may best be able to offer the people we cherish the gift of caring, attentive presence only after a period of absence.

Pick-up Games

At my house growing up, first base was the spindly birch tree that adorned our front lawn. A frisbee became second base, and third base was the corner of a garden bed marked by a coiled hose. The fourth square of our front walkway served as home plate. The grassy area on the other side of the street was the outfield wall, and the U.S. mailbox on the corner was our built-in foul pole. This area was sacred space for our endless round of neighborhood pick-up games of whiffle ball.

Our front yard had nothing particularly sacred about it. In fact, it bore only the vaguest resemblance to Camden Yards or Yankee Stadium with their manicured outfields and precision-marked baselines. The players framed the field using ordinary stuff—a tree, a frisbee, a hose, a mailbox—to set apart the space for special purposes. So it is with the sacred spaces of our lives that refresh our souls. Occasionally the place itself evokes a sense of the sacred because of its incredible beauty or expansive view. A bench by a lake, a house along a shoreline, a mountain overlook might all fall into this category. More often, however, a place becomes holy because of the experience we bring to it, the emotional and spiritual framing we offer it.

One familiar technique suggested for a personal time of prayer is to designate a regular space for this part of our day, perhaps a particular chair by which we light a candle to symbolize God's presence. If we're more the outdoor type, we may find ourselves most at home turning to God in our gardens or taking a walk through a nearby woods or park. The point is that we help create the space for God, and God fills it with God's presence. The *where* matters little, though regular place for prayer does seem to have some power. The *who* matters immensely. Making ourselves present to the God who is already present to us renders any space sacred.

As Godbearers among youth, we can help frame ordinary places and times and transform them into sacred spaces. Going for a walk with a teenager and intentionally bringing God into the conversation; beginning a youth meeting with three minutes of silence or meditation; lighting a candle that burns for the length of a meeting; bracketing a lesson with prayer, scripture, and song; moving out of the church building to the edge of the cemetery and lying in a circle head to head: All of these simple but potentially profound ways allow us to become sacred space-makers for youth. In a pick-up game of baseball or football, we set the boundaries with what we have at hand, and it doesn't take much because of the larger reality of the game itself, which gets thrown into the mix. Godbearers have a similar capacity to use what is available to frame the time and space for God, to be sacred spacemakers.

Quenching Our Thirst

I came into the kitchen one sweltering summer's day, dripping with sweat after another session of cutting the lawn. I had my heart set on one thing and one thing alone: a tall, chilled glass of water. Opening the fridge, I spotted my goal: the clear rectangular pitcher that we use to filter our well water. I picked it up and noticed that it felt awfully light. Sure enough, it was empty. It gave the appearance of being able to satisfy my thirst, but one of us (probably me) had failed to refill it when last used. I walked over to the sink, refilled the pitcher and made a mental note to be a little more diligent as I drank my glass of lukecold, mildly satisfying tap water.

As Godbearers, we must intentionally carve out sacred space in our own lives, times of replenishment and renewal, times of intentionally filling ourselves with God. Otherwise we will discover on a hot, draining day that we have no cold water to restore our parched souls; and subsequently, no refreshing drink to offer the souls of youth either. Jesus promises us living water. The regular practices of sacred spacemaking insure that we do not leave the pitcher—or our ministries—high and dry.

QUESTIONS AND EXERCISES

1. Look over your calendar for the last two months: How many scheduled interruptions have you built into your schedule?

2. Pick four days in the coming month where you will make and keep an appointment with God. What will you do to create the sacred space for your meeting?

3. What might you do to offer youth more sacred space?

IDEA FOR THE ROAD

Plan a one-day (or half-day) retreat for yourself. Find a setting where you can enjoy uninterrupted quiet space—as formal as a retreat center or as informal as a friend's house at the beach. Take along a Bible, a journal, maybe a book or two. Breathe deeply. Enjoy the silence and solitude. Listen lots. Refresh your spirit.

FARE FOR THE SOUL

Making space for God takes some discipline. At first it may sound like one more thing you have to do in your already hassled life. But, as you know, it takes discipline to do anything well, and it is no different with prayer. We make appointments with everyone. Maybe we should make an appointment also with God.

> I used to write in my daily calendar 7–7:30 A.M.—Prayer. But many times I passed that up. It was one more thing to pass by that day. Now I write 7–7:30 A.M.—God. Somehow that's a little harder to neglect.[4]

—Don Postema

Notes

1. Jerome Berryman, *Godly Play: A Way of Religious Education* (San Francisco: HarperSanFrancisco, 1991), 2.

2. Eugene H. Peterson, *Working the Angles: The Shape of Pastoral Integrity* (Grand Rapids: Wm. B. Eerdmans, 1987), 87.

3. Ibid., 70.

4. Don Postema, *Space for God: The Study and Practice of Prayer and Spirituality* (Grand Rapids: CRC Publications, 1983), 17.

THIRTEEN

From Awful to Awe-full

Practices of Worship

We have Kids Time for the little kids and the rest
of the service is geared to the adults. Most youth
tend to lose interest.
—A fifteen-year-old

ONE DAY I spent an hour talking with the members of our senior-high Sunday school class about their experience with worship. I had designed a simple questionnaire asking them such things as: What do you like best about our worship services? Can you describe a time when you felt that you really worshiped God? If you were in charge of our worship services, what would you change?

Their answers offered somewhat typical insights. They expressed feelings of connection to the broader faith community, and yet a sense that worship was not for them but for the adults. One of our youth went so far as to name a feeling of in-betweenness about worship: "We have Kids Time for the little kids and the rest of the service is geared toward adults. Most youth tend to lose interest."

The youth threw in a number of positive responses as well, ranging from the humorous ("I feel good when I pray with the pastors because they are like mega-close to God") to the predictable ("I feel closest to God...when I understand something about [the worship service]") to the profound ("Worship helps us build and maintain a bridge to God, and worship helps persons know who they are"). The questionnaires garnered a fair share of helpful critiques ("I would shorten the sermon because when it's too long, sometimes people forget what it's about," and "I would not sing old songs"). If the youth had been a little bit more honest (and not quite so polite), I think a few more "borings" might have surfaced along with their muted praise. In fact, as we discussed the responses, the overall consensus was that the main Sunday worship experience had little in it for them. Admittedly, this less than scientifically gathered data confirmed my intuition: Many youth experience worship as a bland and uninspiring event, and I can't say that I blame many of them.

I am equally convinced that youth long for and are open to worship that genuinely moves them toward God by allowing them to lower their defenses to the divine. Adolescents struggle to define themselves in relation to an Other greater than themselves; they can reason abstractly and are in a position to think of God in new and rich ways. The dramatic hormonal and social changes of adolescence make it an intensely emotional period of life; often youth feel vulnerable and fragile. All of these developmental factors predispose youth to the power of corporate worship. There windows to the soul are thrown open, and youth become fertile ground for Christ's transformation. Godbearers know it is possible to move from awful to awe-full in worship with youth, so we approach worship with young people expectantly and with great hope.

Playing Some Theological Cards

Here we pause and play our theological hand, at least some main cards, before venturing further into the possibility of transforming worship with and for youth. We view worship as the *primary* act of the Christian community (hence, its significance for ministry with youth). The worship life of a congregation fundamentally sets the Christian community apart from the Kiwanis Club or the local recreation council. Worship is a peculiarly religious act. It is not something that we add to the church program or tack on to the youth ministry agenda: Practices of worship, the intentional space set apart for the reorientation of life Godward, comprise the starting point for spiritual transformation. Put another way, "The proper relationship between creature and Creator is, in Christian eyes, the relationship of worship."[1]

Worship is always a *communal* act; while individuals participate in the worship experience, they always do so in the context of the broader Christian community. Both the primary worship service of a congregation and the private devotional time a person may set apart for God involve the broader context of Christian community. That community shapes and shares the experience of worship, framing the Christian story in language, song, and symbol. As we speak about youth and worship, our strong bias is that worship is primary for youth ministry, including the integration of youth into the worship life of the congregation.

Godbearers also recognize the importance of providing alternative worship settings and experiences that focus more uniquely on the sensibilities of youth and supplement the intergenerational worship of Sunday mornings. In the course of a seminar I was teaching, one participant voiced the concern that if his Wednesday night worship experience with the youth came to be viewed as real worship, his church might run the risk of youth discounting the need to participate in the *real* worship (his emphasis, not mine) of the church (Sunday morning worship). For this reason, he wanted to call the Wednesday night singing, praying, and teaching "practice" for worship—or something along those lines so as to not confuse the two. Furthermore, he argued youth were not the whole body of Christ (the assumption being that the Sunday morning crowd somehow was), and therefore worship among teenagers did not constitute *real* worship.

While I acknowledged some of his concerns, I countered that we run a far greater risk by telling youth that their worship somehow does not count, either in the church or before God, and that in their gathering they are not the real body of Christ. When it comes to worship with youth, we may best answer the question of integration (into the worship life of the congregation) or segregation (via alternative worship experiences apart from the rest of the congregation) with "Yes, both!" For worship to transform truly, youth need to feel included as part of the larger whole, and they need to be given their own holy space in which to express their faith creatively. Youth are not just miniature adults; they live uniquely between the world of adults ahead of them and young children who follow behind. Youth need their own space where they can worship in their own style within the life of the congregation, and that constitutes real worship too.

One other disclaimer. As an adolescent, I actively participated in a United Methodist Church in suburban Philadelphia. I went to Sunday school, sang in the youth choir, took part in youth fellowship, and attended worship most every Sunday. While my level of church involvement exceeded that of many of my peers, like most teenagers I found myself engaged at some points of the worship service and lost completely at others. One of my family's favorite extra-ecclesial activities was doing "the count." During the sermon, my sister, brother, and I would count the number of alliterations that our well-loved, like-letter-liking pastor Reverend Beale would weave into his sermon.

Though we gently mocked Reverend Beale's technique, to this day his favorite pet phrase ("the power, the passion, and the promise") still echoes in my heart and mind. My own description of transforming worship in alliterative style may have developed as a belated tribute, or perhaps this alliterative use puts me in touch with the worship of my own adolescence, which on the whole was a positive experience. Then again, maybe I've chosen this alliterative path in hopes that some of these characteristics might stick to your brain a little more forcefully. So start the count, for Godbearers seek to engage youth in worship experiences that are translated traditional, always awe-full, musical and mystical, inwardly invasive, and God-grounded. May the Lord be with us (and also with youth).

Translated Traditional

About eight years ago on a walk down a country road, my wife and I and our two cocker spaniels ran into one of the youth who had been at our worship service the previous Sunday. He and his family occasionally graced our pews; but in general, worship was not a regular experience for him. That does not indicate a lack of interest in worship on his part. In fact, the question he asked that day seemed to suggest that he was paying attention with a great deal of curiosity: "Why did you throw water on that man's head?" We had celebrated the baptism of one of our new adult members, and this strange ritual made no sense to the young man. I explained a little bit about baptism and how the water marks us, kind of like an invisible tattoo that says God loves us and claims us as part of the family. He seemed pretty satisfied by my response. We moved on to something else, but I have never forgotten his honest confusion.

More recently as I drove our baby-sitter home one Saturday night, we passed by a new synagogue in town. Shannon commented that she had attended several bas mitzvahs there for some of her friends. While much of what was done in the service seemed foreign to her, she had also observed some similarities between this Jewish worship experience and her own at our church. "Like, we both say Amen at the end of our prayers. But what does it mean?" Without knowing it, Shannon was asking me as her pastor to translate the tradition for her.

Responding with a traditional answer such as "Amen means 'so be it' [a fair summary of the *Strong's Bible Dictionary* version] or 'may it be so,' a humble affirmation at the close of the prayer that speaks to the desire of the petitioner to pray in the will of God" just didn't seem to cut it at the moment. In my attempt to convert this "churchy" word into language that Shannon both would comprehend and relate to, I simply said (with the appropriate bent elbow swooshing downward), "Yes!"

These two examples struck me then and now as a microcosm of the larger task of theological reflection with youth. Effective communication in this manner involves a continual act of translating the Christian tradition into contemporary, fresh, and age-sensitive language and images that at the same time remain faithful to tradition. Worship with youth is a matter of presenting the Christian tradition with fidelity and creativity through the liturgy, however simple or complex. We cannot stress the matter of continual translation enough. Many of the post-Christian era youth we pastor have had little formal connection to the worship life of the church. Church schedules that provide an either/or experience of concurrent worship and Sunday school tend to isolate children and youth from the liturgical life of the church. Couple this with the fact that many youth and their families are simply unchurched, and the need for basic instruction is enormous. If we seriously undertake the task of teaching youth the tradition of faith, we must be able to explain it in their vernacular. Youth cannot learn language—even and especially holy Godspeak—without a common referent.

The contemporary trend toward seeker-sensitive services (such as Willow Creek Community Church, Saddleback Community Church, and other megachurches) recognizes the fact that we have to begin where people are for worship to have any significant impact. Youth ministry has been dealing with a seeker crowd for years. We don't want to simply hook them with contemporary images but to invite them, through these images, into the worshiping tradition of the congregation. It is not enough simply to throw youth into the predominantly adult-oriented worship experience and hope that they catch on. Direct experience is only valuable when it allows participants more than onlooker status, which is precisely how many youth experience worship without some translation of tradition. Youth need to be schooled in the fundamental shape and flow of the worship service and, given the worship inexperience of most of them, we can take very little for granted. While the contemporary sociological reality may exacerbate the problem, this age-old dilemma is not unique to our time in many respects. The process of initiation into any religious community is a matter of explaining the symbols, inviting participation and personal engagement, and ongoing translation.

Godbearers approach the practice of worship in a proactively youth-sensitive manner. Engaging youth in the worship of God in a way that connects their world with the story of salvation takes a concerted effort. To make this connection, youth need to be part of the broader worshiping community as active participants, planners, and leaders. Making Sunday morning worship more youth-friendly (in terms of musical styles, language, locus of illustrations, up front and regular involvement) is possible only insofar as the pastoral and music leadership take youth seriously as disciples of Christ in the *now*, not just in the church of the future.

Always Awe-full

Developmental psychologist Erik Erikson contends that adolescents need to be moved physically, emotionally and existentially. Adolescents thrive on movement—active games, fast cars, thrill-laced movies. But equally important is being moved existentially: the ecstasy of celebration, the deep awe of worship. "Transportation" is another way to describe transcendence, the idea being to get beyond where we already are.[2] If the concert or the drugs move a youth and the church does not, then the church loses; and the rock musicians gain a young person's allegiance.

Static worship does not offer transcendent experience for youth (and only marginally offers it to adults). Worship with and for youth requires creativity, fun, and occasionally downright rowdiness in volume, playfulness, and style. Sometimes worship should be a high-voltage experience, tapping into the energy that youth bring to the table. At other times, worship calls for silence and stillness, an atmosphere of holy hush. But no matter what form it takes, transformative worship with youth always must be awe-full. This aspect of youth worship prevents it from lapsing into mere entertainment (albeit, godly stuff) and grounds it in the reality of the absolute God of the universe.

But how do we inculcate a sense of awe? How do we tap into or recreate a sense of wonder among the been-there, done-that generation, a generation of youth who, by and large, isn't impressed by much, certainly not a domesticated God. Godbearers might see ourselves in the business of holy leisure. In the Latin, *leisure* means "to be permitted" or "to be given license or freedom" to do or to be something. Holy leisure: the sacred space not bound by time or measured by performance, the permission to simply be in God's presence. In many cases, the youth to whom and with whom we minister are as overextended as their helter-skelter parents, sometimes more so. Life is a blur of continual activity and images, from school to sports to TV to church to clubs to movies to malls. Godbearers may offer youth on the fast track the gift of sacred, leisurely, reflective space that allows them to recollect themselves, to imagine new ways of being, to sort through confusion, to regain perspective in a God-not-me-centered universe.

Watts Wacker is a marketing consultant and futurist to many of the top Fortune 500 companies. His unorthodox style and methods may have him one day posing as a panhandler in New York City, riding the range in Montana, or busing tables at Taco Bell. The next day he'll be hobnobbing with high-powered CEOs, offering his expertise. When asked to describe his job, he responded by telling a story.

> A traveler encounters the Buddha on the road and asks him, "Are you a deity?" Buddha says no. "Are you a saint?" Buddha says no. "Are you a prophet?" Buddha says no. Exasperated, the traveler says: Then what are you? Buddha answers: "I'm awake."
>
> Says Whacker: "I get paid to be awake."[3]

Transforming worship sensitizes youth to the reality of the vastness of the universe, the immensity of God, the complexity of the world, the intricacy of self, and the sacredness of their souls. Developmentally, youth need to experience transcendence; and creative worship can offer this soul transportation with a capital *T*. If youth leave with yawns and glazed eyes, we have missed the mark badly. Godbearers plan for worship that keeps youth awake (in the very best sense of that word), that inculcates a sense of awe and wonder. Innovative and instructed prayer, guided meditations, contemporary readings of the psalms, holy-ground experiences of barefoot worship, well-selected settings (whether your own sanctuary or a cliff overlooking the ocean): All contribute to the art of awe-full worship.

Musical and Mystical

Youth live in a world filled with music. They wake up to the sound of tunes coming out of the radio (several times over, depending on how many times they hit the snooze bar), do homework with the stereo or headphones on, hang out with friends watching MTV. In the malls they spend their allowances and part-time job earnings on tapes and CDs. Music has always been an integral part of youth culture: a symbol of rebellion, a voice for hopes and dreams, the soundtrack to the drama of their growing up. Music functions as a surrogate language for teenagers, giving them a way to articulate—through a tune and a beat as well as lyrics—deep feelings that accompany growing up, which they often have difficulty expressing in other ways. The degree to which music permeates their lives—in part because of the portable technologies, in part due to the changing cultural norms—has never been greater.

Given the pervasiveness of music in their lives, why do we sometimes fail to connect with youth through music in the church? The most obvious answer: The church's music is not their music. The message teenagers receive from many of the church's musical selections is: We are an alien culture, speaking a language you do not speak. The hymns sound old, the lyrics archaic, the organ an instrument of a previous generation. Yet the potential to engage youth in worship through music is enormous, and the resources available to us are better than ever before.

By 1995, Contemporary Christian was the fastest growing sector of the music industry, with sales topping one billion dollars. In the same year, *Billboard* magazine began reporting on Christian music sales (including Christian bookstore outlets) in their biweekly accounting of market trends.[4] These statistics demonstrate that the world of Christian music for youthful audiences has moved light years beyond "Kum Ba Yah" and "Pass It On" and now embraces a potpourri of pop, rock, alternative, rap, heavy metal, and country. Most musical genres offer high quality Christian music that teenagers can relate to and claim as their own. Youth worship can involve these resources and put them into service.

Amy Grant's album *Songs from the Loft* in 1993 popularized a new wave of music resources for youth ministries—Christian music designed specifically for youth group use. Split-track CDs (with instrumental accompaniment on one track—vocals on the other), ready-to-go overheads, Christian music videos, and the Christian Copyright Licensing agreements make integrating music into youth worship easier than ever, whether or not you have a guitar player. We have found that singing along with contemporary Christian music allows even nonsinging youth and small groups to sing confidently and less self-consciously.

If the contemporary Christian music scene does not suit you or the youth in your congregation, try working from the opposite direction. A surprising number of songs that our youth listen to from their favorite artists (even the ones that grate on your nerves) deal with spiritual themes or name the deep heart longings and needs of adolescence. Explore their music with them in light of the gospel; discover, baptize, and put secular music into service for Christ.

The musical inclination of youth stems from their mystical inclination. Just as music names inner stirrings too deep for words, sacred symbols and holy space provide similar forms of expression. Their active curiosity with New Age artifacts (crystals, incense) signals their fascination with mystery. The Christian liturgical tradition spaciously allows for the mystical (though the Eastern Orthodox and Roman Catholic Churches have done a better job of maintaining these parts of our tradition than have we in most mainline Protestant circles). The youthful impulse toward mystery makes the use of candles a powerful technique in worship. A midnight worship service filled with the light of twenty candles to punctuate the darkness will engage youth. The mystery of fire has a way of drawing youth into the mystery of God.

Inwardly Invasive

Transforming worship with youth is inwardly invasive; it is sensitively soulful, not manipulative. Worship, by its very nature, invades our personal space. Coming into God's presence has a way of stripping away the false veneers of self we hide behind and helping us see ourselves more honestly and truly. Christian ethicist Stanley Hauerwas is fond of saying that the church's job is not just to make us feel good. In fact, quite the opposite: the church, through its liturgy and teaching, is to help us feel bad about the right things. In a sense, youth should feel confronted by God in worship, and as Godbearers we should not shield them from the holy fire of the Holy Other.

At the same time, we should never pressure youth into false commitments or corner them with guilt and fear. Adolescents may experience life-changing decisions for Christ only if made freely in contexts where "no, thank you" or "not yet" are equally permissible options. Adolescents possess the emotional capacity and developmental predisposition to put their whole lives on the line, to give themselves fully to something or someone who captures their trust. If we avoid manipulating the heartstrings and hormones of youth and allow enough space for genuine response, we may discover that tapping into their affective side offers a window to the soul.

God-Grounded

Finally, transforming worship is always God-grounded. An intentional God-consciousness in the planning and experience of worship can prevent it from slipping into entertainment, the feeding of narcissistic needs, or child's play. Those of us entrusted with developing worship experiences with youth would do well to etch Annie Dillard's description of the holy ground we tread upon in worship in our brains.

> On the whole, I do not find Christians, outside of the catacombs, sufficiently sensible of conditions. Does anyone have the foggiest idea what sort of power we so blithely invoke? Or, as I suspect, does no one believe a word of it? The churches are children playing on the floor with their chemistry sets, mixing up a batch of TNT to kill a Sunday morning. It is madness to wear ladies' straw hats and velvet hats to church; we should all be wearing crash helmets. Ushers should issue life preservers and signal flares; they should lash us to our pews. For the sleeping god may wake someday and take offense, or the waking god may draw us out to where we can never return.[5]

Godbearers not only make worship a primary practice for ourselves, but maintain a healthy reverence for the practice of worship itself, an unwavering sense of who constitutes our primary audience: not youth or even our congregation—but God. Our intentionality, creativity, and openness in worship may draw us to places from which we can never return. And of course, Godbearers always graciously have a hand out to the youth with whom we worship, gently inviting them to that transcendent place too.

QUESTIONS AND EXERCISES

1. Think about your experience of worship as a teenager. What made worship boring for you? What captivated your heart and imagination? What differences can you identify?
2. How well-integrated are youth into the worship life of your church? How might your congregation do more to include them?
3. What approaches to worship mentioned in this chapter will help you in your ministry?
4. Think of a time when you had a positive worship experience with youth. What elements made it so?

IDEA FOR THE ROAD

Gather with several youth, other leaders, and maybe your pastor. Pass around copies of several recent worship bulletins at your church. Evaluate the services through the lens of youth. Make comments and suggestions about what might change and what should remain the same in order to engage youth more fully in the worship life of the church.

FARE FOR THE SOUL

A Call to Worship

Come together, joining hands and hearts.
Let our hands be links of a chain
which hold our lives together—
not a chain of bondage but a silver cord of strength,
a ribbon of love and faith and community,
giving us slack to sail the wind,
yet holding us in a mystical embrace,
that we may be alone, but never lonely,
that we may be together, but never lost in the crowd,
that we may be one without forfeiting uniqueness.
Come together, joining hands and hearts,
and let the spirit of God and the human spirit
flow in each one and through us all
as we gather here to share this time and space
and as we walk together on the journey.[6]

—John W. Howell

Notes

1. Geoffrey Wainwright, *Doxology: The Praise of God in Worship, Doctrine, and Life* (New York: Oxford University Press, 1980), 16.

2. Erik H. Erikson, *Identity: Youth and Crisis* (New York: W. W. Norton & Co., 1968), 243–44.

3. David Diamond, "What Comes after What Comes Next?" *Fast Company*, no. 6 (Dec.-Jan. 1997): 80.

4. Deborah Evans Price, "Pop Goes the Gospel," *Billboard* 108, no. 17 (April 27, 1996):34–35.

5. Annie Dillard, *Teaching a Stone to Talk: Expeditions and Encounters* (New York: Harper and Row, 1988), 40–41.

6. John W. Howell, in *Touch Holiness: Resources for Worship*, ed. Ruth C. Duck and Maren C. Tirabassi (New York: The Pilgrim Press, 1990), 173.

Benediction

Be God's.
—Rich Mullins, Christian musician and poet

O NE OF the significant Godbearers in our lives has been Rich Mullins, a man who made God real and present to us through his ability to meld faith, imagination, and music into songs that feed the soul. Deemed by many the poet laureate of the contemporary Christian music world, Rich Mullins wrote with passion and honesty about the holy, fiery love of God and the claim this God makes on those who would follow Jesus. Rich Mullins was a Godbearer, someone who helped bring to birth Christ in the lives of saints young and old alike. With his tragic and untimely death in 1997, we lost a good friend, someone who drew us closer to God.

Though his musical legacy won him quite a following over the years, Mullins never drew attention to himself. And whenever fans would ask him to sign a picture or CD, he had a trademark way of keeping things in focus. In life, as in his music, Mullins pointed to Christ. He would simply pen: *Be God's, Rich.*

Be God's. In many ways, that phrase serves as a fitting close to this book, as well as being a blessing for the journey for all would-be Godbearers. One of the temptations in ministry is to "be gods," to intentionally or unconsciously place ourselves at the center of things, living with the mistaken notion that it all depends on us. The good news of the gospel is that it doesn't. Godbearers get the capitalization and the punctuation right and know that all authentic ministry points to the Source of our lives, never to ourselves. Our encouragement to all who would read and use this book is simple: *Be God's.*

This book intentionally closes with a benediction rather than a conclusion. To close with a conclusion might suggest that we have Godbearing ministry all figured out, and we don't. Just as the blessing at the close of a worship service sends us back to our work, our friends, our families, and our communities to live the faith we have heard, sung, and prayed about, so the benediction at the close of this book sends us out with blessing to resume the journey. We have suggested a route by which we can deliver God's good news to the world and to young people in particular.

You Are a Love Letter from Christ

In 1980, eight-year-old Andy Bremner was diagnosed with cancer. During his first hospitalization, he received a deluge of cards and letters from his classmates and his Scout troop. Letters poured in for five days—and then they stopped. His mother, Linda, noticed that in that brief span of time those letters had become a kind of a lifeline for Andy, so she decided to pick up the slack quietly. Every few days she sent him a note, signing it "Your Secret Pal."

She didn't think Andy suspected anything. Then one day she found her son sketching at the kitchen table. He wouldn't let her see what he was drawing. "It's for my secret pal," he explained. After Andy fell asleep, Linda sneaked a peek at the picture he had drawn for his secret pal. What she found drove an arrow into her heart: a child's picture and below it these words: "I love you, Mommy."

For the next four years, Linda Bremner wrote to her son. When he died in 1984, she found every letter she had written him stashed like treasure in the back of his closet, along with an address book from a camp he had attended for children with cancer. Linda kept the address book, and one by one wrote to every child listed there. The response was enormous. "Thank you, thank you, thank you," one child wrote back. "I didn't know anybody knew that I *lived*."

Linda posted a sign-up sheet at Children's Hospital in Chicago, where Andy had been treated, for terminally ill children who might like a secret pal. She was inundated with names. When writing each child became too much for her to handle alone, she enlisted the help of her family. As more and more names poured in, to meet the demand Linda eventually founded "Love Letters," a Chicago-based nonprofit organization now staffed by sixty-five volunteers who write 1,100 notes every week to children they have never met.[1]

That story kept pestering me until I did something about it. I called Linda Bremner to get some more information. I asked her what gave her the fortitude for such an undertaking, still going strong fourteen years after Andy's death. "We don't call it ministry," she said. "But that's what it is. Society has taught us that touch—physical or emotional—is dangerous, and I understand the concern. But we're out to touch people." And then she added for my benefit: "If you choose not to volunteer to write Love Letters for us—and we can use all the help we can get—then go home and write a love letter to *somebody* in your life. Something as simple as a card or a letter can change a day. Or a life."

What kind of logic could explain this brazen courage, the inner strength that voluntarily relives the death of your own child day after day through the names of other terminally ill children whose stories flood your office? On the other hand, isn't that what God does for us? It's not logical that God can take the inexplicable death of a twelve-year-old boy and use it to bring hope to more than a thousand children every week. It's not logical that God can use people who never imagine themselves ministers and use them to deliver "love letters" from God, however unwittingly, to people desperate for a touch of transformation. It's not logical that God can use unlikely people like Mary and Moses, ordinary people like you and I to bear Christ's love to the world again and again. But then nobody becomes a Godbearer out of logic. We are Godbearers because two thousand years ago in a stable in Bethlehem, God delivered a Love Letter addressed to us.

The Address Matters

Most young people today will tell you they are on a spiritual "journey" of one kind or another. The image of the spiritual voyager remains a popular description of youth who consider life a spiritual journey to be valued whether or not they reach a destination. Journeying authentically interprets the Christian life; Jesus, after all, told his disciples, "*Follow* me." And leaving boat and business, brothers, sisters, and parents behind, they did.

But Jesus also told his disciples: "Follow *me*." Christians stake their hope on the fact that the life of the spirit does lead somewhere, specifically to the cross of Jesus Christ, which reveals the profound depth of God's love for us. The address matters. What sets the Christian journey apart from all other routes is that our destination involves both receiving God's love letter in Christ and carrying this love letter to others. We seek the One who both "addresses" us *in* love and "delivers" us *to* love others in Christ's name. As Paul told the Christians in Corinth, we are love letters of Christ, "written not with ink but with the Spirit of the living God" (2 Cor. 3:3). Whether in the contexts of our families, our congregations, or simply in the daily relationships we count as sacred in our lives, ministry with young people addresses youth with the good news that God loves them and God desires to send them—signed, sealed, and delivered in the cross of Jesus Christ—as love letters to others whose faith has yet to take root.

When we become Godbearers—when we seek to embody Christ, to convey through the power of the Holy Spirit an unconditional love and a sustaining, guiding presence—our lives become epistles from God, love letters of Christ. The practices and friendships available in the Christian community mark us with God's return address. And in a world where youth literally are dying to know who they are and to whom they belong, where youth desperately need to know that someone notices they are still living, becoming a love letter of Jesus Christ can change a day—or a life. And not just for youth.

Dismissal with Blessing

Go now to smuggle God into your world,
Holding tight the hands of those with whom you share the way:
Youth, parents, friends, colleagues, Christ.
May your life show forth God at every turn;
May your heart and your road be
ablaze with holy fire.
Amen!

Notes

1. We are grateful to Carol Antablin Miles of Lamington, New Jersey, whose use of this story in a sermon on Acts 2 inspired us to include it here. See Penny Falcon, "Mother's Letters Are a Labor of Love," *USA Today* (September 4, 1996), 3. For more information on the nonprofit organization "Love Letters," call 630-620-1970.

APPENDIX A

A Historical Snapshot of American Youth Ministry

For most of the twentieth century, youth ministry was conceived as a defensive measure: It defended youth against the wiles of culture, and it defended the church against extinction. In the 1890s, Christian Endeavor—a coeducational, interdenominational, interracial, and international Christian "youth club" model of youth ministry that virtually all major denominations copied—sought to protect rural and small-town youth from the evils of urban life through "meetings" that encouraged teenagers to practice the Christian behavior they might later employ as adult church members. Although the liberal Religious Education movement of the early twentieth century urged churches to involve youth in the reconstruction of society directly, the Depression and World War II cut short this brief attempt to empower youth. These historical forces empowered youth, not for the social gospel but for wage earning and war fighting, an empowerment that robbed a generation of youth of a protected adolescence altogether.

Following the 1940s, parents grieving the loss of their own "carefree" adolescence to poverty and war sought desperately to reclaim a protected space for their children's teenage years. Parachurch youth movements relocated evangelism in the high school and pioneered relational ministry as a means to disciple youth—technically alongside congregations but in practice often in place of them. These leader-centered movements called youth to conversion and provided "clubs" where youth could wait out their adolescence. Most denominations during this period developed "fellowship movements" to socialize young people into loyal church members. By the 1960s, both "fellowship groups" and "clubs" appeared laughably inadequate against a background of social protest; teenagers who came home from Vietnam were no longer adolescents, and friends who buried friends were no longer content to be sidelined in the church (or anywhere else) until adulthood.

In the late 1960s the World Council of Churches argued that youth ministry was not properly the responsibility of churches' educational programs but rather should be construed as "mission" and integrated into the life of the church as a whole. Furthermore, in an effort to acknowledge the agency of young people that churches had ignored for so long, the WCC heralded an age of peer-leadership in which adults stepped back and allowed youth real, rather than surrogate, leadership opportunities. Budget-stressed denominational offices seized upon the WCC's recommendations and proceeded to slash their youth education departments, which up until that point had provided local churches with program possibilities, resources, and leadership for their ministries with youth. When no structure replaced the "youth departments," youth ministry became almost exclusively a matter of local talent and "good instincts": a place where seminarians and new pastors "did time" until they got a "real" job; where youth hung out until something larger caught their attention; where volunteers and staff alike spent an average of eighteen months before they burned out, threw in the towel, or both.

For a long time, congregational youth ministry languished, while the noninstitutional, parachurch youth ministries hit their peak. Then in the late 1970s churches briefly noted that post-Christian culture was upon them. Conservative evangelical churches, convinced of the theological urgency of "saving" youth from both sin and cultural assimilation, redoubled efforts and personnel in youth ministry and recalled youth ministry's defensive roots. Roman Catholics, whose youth ministry had focused on parochial education for more than a century, began an intentional effort to "catch up" with Protestants in offering parish-based youth programs. Meanwhile, mainline Protestants continued to eliminate such programs in their own churches. A decade later, almost all of these efforts leveled off or began a serious decline. In retrospect, a 1991 report of the Carnegie Council on Adolescent Development summarized the 1980s as an era of massive cuts in programs and personnel in Protestant, Catholic, and Jewish religious youth programs alike.

The tension in youth ministry between protecting youth and empowering them still exists. The most promising models seem to be those that combine the protection of adolescents from premature adulthood with the empowerment of adolescents for ministry in their own right. We see hopeful signs among ethnic-minority congregations who historically have viewed the salvation of their youth as a matter of physical and economic as well as existential protection and who therefore have balanced protective ministries with ministries of social empowerment. They have pursued this balance without adhering to the patterns of youth ministry found in Euro-American congregations.

Parachurch youth ministries have modeled relational styles of youth leadership that congregations increasingly adopt; and while these leader-centered ministries are overtly protective in intent, they also offer youth the one variable consistently identified by research as the single most important factor for overcoming "developmental deficits" in adolescence: the presence of a significant, caring adult. The enormous popularity of youth mission projects, which predate the "service-learning" movement by decades, continues. Youth mission projects are by far the most likely existing vehicle for empowering youth for ministry through their own congregations.

As media culture and globalization expand the scope of youth ministry and bring the far reaches of the world closer together, youth ministry cannot defend youth from the galloping pace of cultural change. Youth ministry in the future will require a public theology, an understanding of the gospel that takes us into the world and not out of it, as well as models that both protect and empower young people for the sake of Jesus Christ.

APPENDIX B

Guidelines for Healthy Adult Leaders of Youth

(Adapted from Charles M. Shelton, *Pastoral Counseling with Adolescents and Young Adults* [New York: Crossroad, 1995], 9–14.)

1. Can I model for youth the meaning of a happy, healthy, and whole adulthood, including
   a. self-competence?
   b. adequate interpersonal functioning?
   c. capacity for commitment?
   d. a developed philosophy of life?

2. To what extent have I been able to forgive my own parents?
   a. How do I reflect my parents' positive attributes?
   b. What experiences with my parents impeded my growth or were painful?
   c. What feelings do I associate with my parents' shortcomings?
   d. Does my work with youth evoke some personal characteristics that mirror my parents' behavior?

3. How do I deal with "loss"?
   a. To grow means to let go. How well do I do this?
   b. Can I speak openly and appropriately with young people about my own experiences of loss?

4. What is my theology of friendship?

   a. Do I have healthy friendships?
   b. How do my friendships reflect my faith commitment?
   c. How do I speak to youth about friendship?

5. Do I find time for solitude?
   a. What do I do when I am alone?
   b. How do I experience myself when I am alone?
   c. What feelings and reactions does my solitude elicit?

6. Do I maintain adequate boundaries?
   a. Am I a compulsive caregiver?
   b. How much do I need these adolescents?
   c. How much do I feel I *have* to be with them?

    d. What need might I be satisfying in my own life by working with adolescents?

7. Have I realized and accepted the fact that I can't save every adolescent?

    a. What are my reactions to the above question?

    b. Do I feel I have to be at every function?

8. Do I focus on experiences of gratitude and cultivate a sense of being grateful?

    a. What good things are happening in my life?

    b. For what am I grateful?

    c. To what actions do my feelings of gratitude lead?

9. Can I accept not doing everything right?

    a. Do I view mistakes in terms of what I have learned or in terms of what I did wrong?

    b. Can I reframe failure in myself and others?

10. Am I able to maintain a sense of integrity?

    a. What does my integrity call me to do?

    b. How do I discern which sacrifices to make in difficult decisions?

APPENDIX C

Resources for Professional Development

Note: This list is incomplete in part because no comprehensive national network exists to link persons involved in youth ministry. We welcome your additions to this list for future use. The theological base noted identifies the program's original source of support, not the audience the organization hopes to address. All of these organizations are either ecumenical in scope or welcome contacts from persons of many faith perspectives, and most have mailing lists.

Association for Women in Youth Ministry (AWYM). Professional network founded to support women in youth ministry. Benefits include networking, resource development and distribution, speaker's bureau (open to interested women), bimonthly *Journey* newsletter, discounts to selected conferences and events, free advertising in the newsletter. *Theological base:* Evangelical. *Contact:* Youth Leadership/AWYM, 122 W. Franklin Ave., Suite 510, Minneapolis, MN 55404 (fax 612-874-4656); E-mail:YTHLEAD@aol.com..

Augsburg Youth and Family Institute. Outstanding resources and training events for integrative ministries which focus on families as well as youth. *Theological base:* Lutheran (ECLA). *Contact:* Executive Director, Augsburg Youth and Family Institute, Campus Box 70, Augsburg College, 2211 Riverside Avenue, Minneapolis, MN 55454 (612-330-1624); E-mail: hardel@augsburg.edu.

Black Methodists for Church Renewal. BMCR youth ministry is directed primarily toward youth themselves, but it also offers training for adults, especially those working with youth in African-American United Methodist churches. *Theological base:* United Methodist. *Contact:* Southeast Jurisdiction Youth Coordinator, United Community Centers, Inc., 3617 Hickory Ave., SW, Birmingham, AL 35221 (205-925-2944 or 925-3683); E-mail: kennethharris@yahoo.com.

Boys' Town. Outstanding resources and training for ministries related especially to youth and families at risk, stressing faith skills and relationships. Sponsors the Boys'Town Center for Adolescent and Family Spirituality. Good source for multicultural materials and resources for parenting and pastoring deaf children. *Theological base:* Roman Catholic. *Contact:* Director, Religious Education, Boys' Town, Father Flanagan's Boys' Home, 13803 Flanagan Blvd., Boys'Town, NE 68010 (402-498-1885).

Center for Youth Ministry Development. Excellent resources and short-term or sustained training opportunities offered regionally, usually through a diocesan office. *Theological base:* Roman Catholic. *Contact:* Center for Youth Ministry Development, PO Box 699, Naugatuck, CT 06770 (203-723-1622; fax 203-723-1624); E-mail: http://www.cmnon-line.com/cmd/home/htm.

Center for Youth Studies. Particularly helpful source for youth culture resources, especially the Encyclopedia of Youth Studies (now on CD-Rom from NavPress Software) which was developed by the CYS. Physically located at Gordon Conwell Theological Seminary, CYS networks information about youth and culture around the world as well as in the U.S. *Theological base:* Evangelical. *Contact:* Director, Center for Youth Studies, PO Box 720120, Norman, OK 73070 (Dean Borgman, 978-468-7111, E-mail: cys@gcts.edu; or Kathryn Q. Powers, 405-321-3324; E-mail: k2p@aol.com).

Denominational training events. Many denominations offer denominationally-sponsored training events for practitioners on national and regional levels. Check with your regional or national denominational office's youth staff person.

Forum for Adults in Youth Ministry (FAYM). Professional organization for youth workers dedicated to increasing the professionalism of the field of youth ministry in the eyes of the church. Benefits: networking, FAYMpaks (tri-annual mailing of relevant spiritual and programmatic resources for youth workers, announcements of upcoming events of interest, recommendations for mission projects, speakers, etc.), discounts at bi-annual United Methodist youth ministry training events. $50 membership (discount for students). *Theological base:* United Methodist. *Contact:* Methodist Theological School of Ohio, 3081 Columbus Pike, Delaware, OH 43015 (740-363-1146; E-mail: etrimmer-@mtso.edu).

Group Publishing. Skills-based training events both nationally and regionally, and youth ministry resources galore. Group resources and curriculum are the most widely used youth ministry resources in the U.S. among both evangelical and mainline denominations. *Theological base:* Interdenominational. *Contact:* Group Publishing Co., 1515 Cascade Avenue, PO Box 481, Loveland, CO 80539 (970-669-3836, 800-635-0404); E-mail: http://www.grouppublishing.com.

National Network of Youth Ministries. Professional network founded to support fundamentalist and conservative evangelical youth ministries. Started the "See You at the Pole" movement. Benefit: national interchurch events, communication networks with other youth ministries. *Theological base*: Fundamentalist/evangelical. *Contact*: Executive Director, National Network of Youth Ministries, 17150 Via Del Campo, Suite 102, San Diego, CA 92127.

National Institute of Youth Ministry. Sponsors brief skills-based training events nationwide, with particular attention given to counseling issues, drug and alcohol abuse, and parenting. *Theological base*: Nondenominational. *Contact*:

President, National Institute of Youth Ministry, 940 Calle Amanecer, Suite G, San Clemente, CA 92673 (714-498-4418); E-mail: www.NIYM.org.

Nyack College Institute of Urban Youth Ministry Studies. Sponsors conferences offering specialized training in urban youth ministry. *Theological base*: Christian and Missionary Alliance. *Contact*: Chair, Department of Christian Education and Youth Ministry, or Ron Bellsterling, Program Director, Nyack College, 1 South Blvd., Nyack, NY 10960 (914-358-1710); E-mail: Leonard@J51.com.

One to One. Training and resources for developing mentoring programs in churches, especially in urban settings. *Theological base*: None (One to One is a secular organization that recently developed mentoring initiatives in churches). *Contact*: One to One Mentoring Partnership of Greater Philadelphia (215-665-2467).

Perkins School of Theology Youth Ministry Institute. Annual week-long, university-style training event in January at Perkins School of Theology. In-depth training for local church youth ministry for both youth ministry beginners and veteran professionals. Other opportunities include one-day workshops, summer seminar in youth ministry, on-site youth ministry coaching, and leadership training for human sexuality education. *Theological base*: United Methodist. *Contact*: Continuing Education, Perkins School of Theology, Southern Methodist University, PO Box 750133, Dallas, TX 75275-0133 (800-THE-OLOG, ext. 3, fax 214-768-2117); E-mail: perkins@mail.smu.edu).

Presbyterians for Renewal Youth Ministry. Resource for junior and senior high conferences, short term missions and wilderness camping. PFR Youth Ministry also trains youth workers, conducts family life seminars, and assists youth pastors in relocation. *Theological base:* Presbyterian (PCUSA)/evangelical. *Contact:* National Director, PO Box 3100, Chattanooga, TN 37404 (423-624-2495; fax 423-624-7482); E-mail: pfrym@chattanooga.net.

Presbyterian Youth Connection. Presbyterian initiative to develop local, regional, and national continuity in youth ministry programs, including conferences and resources. *Theological base:* Presbyterian (PCUSA). *Contact:* Presbyterian Youth Connection, 100 Witherspoon Street, Room 2001, Louisville, KY 40202-1396 (502-569-5497); E-mail: http://www.pcusa.org.

Princeton Theological Seminary Institute for Youth Ministry. Theological education for persons pastoring youth, including degree and nondegree programs as well as ongoing programs of research. Conferences held across the country emphasize the theological significance of youth ministry and the need to integrate youth into the total mission of the church. Certificate in Youth and Theology possible. *Theological base:* Presbyterian (PCUSA). *Contact:* Director, PO Box 821, Princeton, NJ 08542-0803 (609-497-7910; fax 609-279-9014); E-mail: kay.vogen@ptsem.edu.

Rock the World YouthMission Alliance. Dedicated to evangelism, discipleship, and leadership development among youth. Includes direct youth ministries with students, training for adults working with young people, and training with college students. *Theological base:* Episcopal. *Contact:* Operations Officer, P. O. Box 43, Ambridge, PA 15003 (724-266-8876; fax 724-266-5916); E-mail: rock tworld@aol.com.

Search Institute. Research organization with resources and training emphasizing community collaboration and interfaith initiatives on "asset development" in adolescents. *Theological base:* none (technically secular, Search has focused much of its research on youth in mainline Protestant churches). *Contact:* Search Institute, Suite 210, 700 S. Third Street, Minneapolis, MN 55415 (1-800-888-7828; fax 612-376-8956); E-mail: search@www.search-institute.org, http://www.search-institute.org.

Youth Leadership Graduate School of Youth Ministry. Multifaceted training in youth ministry ranging from continuing education opportunities to master's degrees through Bethel Seminary or Luther Seminary. Provides direct ministries with youth as well as support for leaders, including a new urban youth worker training program. *Theological base:* Lutheran (ELCA) and Reformed. *Contact:* Executive Director, 122 West Franklin Ave., Suite 510, Minneapolis, MN 55404 (612-870-3632, fax 612-870-4656); E-mail: ythlead@aol.com).

The Youth Ministry and Spirituality Project. Based at San Francisco Theological Seminary, works with congregations to develop youth ministry that is integrated into the practices of congregational life (currently they are involved in congregationally-based research on such youth ministry). *Theological base:* Presbyterian (PCUSA). *Contact:* Program Manager, San Francisco Theological Seminary, 2 Kensington Road, San Anselmo, CA 94960 (415-258-6553); E-mail: YMSP@SFTS.edu.

Youth Ministry Educators Forum. Meeting of professors of youth ministry at the NAPCE (North American Professors in Christian Education) conference each fall. *Theological base:* Evangelical. *Contact:* (for more information) TIU, 2065 Half Day Road, Deerfield, IL 60015 (847-317-7165); E-mail: jsun dene@tiu.edu.

Youth Specialties, Inc. Skills-based resources and training, available both regionally and nationally. Excellent media resources. Publisher of the only professional journal in youth ministry, *Youthworker Journal.* Founded by Wayne Rice and Mike Yaconelli, Youth Specialties was the pioneer entrepreneurial youth ministry organization in the U.S., responsible for training youth leaders in more than 70,000 organizations worldwide (including the U.S. Air Force). *Theological base:* Nondenominational. *Contact:* Youth Specialties, 1225 Greenfield Dr., El Cajon, CA 92021 (fax 619-440-4939).

APPENDIX D

Certificate and Certification Programs

Note: This list is incomplete in part because no comprehensive national network exists to link credentialing programs in youth ministry. We welcome your additions to this list for future use.

Associates in Ministry Certification. Evangelical Lutheran Church of America. Youth ministry specialization through Certification Schools at Wartburg Theological Seminary. Contact Center for Youth Ministries, Wartburg Theological Seminary, 333 Wartburg Place, Dubuque, IA 52003-7797 (319-589-0220); E-mail: CYM@ECUNET.ORG.

Certificate in Youth and Theology. Princeton Theological Seminary Institute for Youth Ministry and School of Continuing Education. Contact Princeton Theological Seminary, PO Box 821, Princeton, NJ 08542-0803 (609-497-7910; fax 609-279-9014); E-mail: kay.vogen@ptsem.edu.

Certificate Program in Youth Ministry. Roman Catholic. Developed by the Center for Youth Ministry Development, sponsored by universities/dioceses from around the United States. Contact Center for Youth Ministry Development, PO Box 699, Naugatuck, CT 06770 (203-723-1622); E-mail: cmd@cmnon-line.com).

Certification in Youth Ministry. Perkins School of Theology Youth Ministry Institute. Contact School of Continuing Education, Perkins School of Theology, Southern Methodist University, Dallas, TX 75275-0133.

Certification in Youth Ministry. The United Methodist Church. Contact annual conference Board of Ordained Ministry, or General Board of Higher Education and Ministry, section of Deacons and Diaconal Ministries, PO Box 871, Nashville, TN 37202-0871 (615-340-7375); E-mail: SDDM@GBHEM.ORG).

Educator Certification (no specialization in youth ministry available). Presbyterian Church (USA). Contact Presbyterian Church (USA), 100 Witherspoon Street, M003, Louisville, KY 40202-1396 (502-569-5751).

ABOUT THE AUTHORS

Kenda Dean and her husband, Kevin, are the parents of Brendan (family humorist, guitarist, and pop culture critic) and Shannon (art aficionado and resident critter expert). An ordained elder in the Baltimore-Washington Annual Conference and graduate of Wesley Theological Seminary, Kenda serves as Assistant Professor of Youth, Church, and Culture and Director of the School of Christian Education at Princeton Theological Seminary. Kenda's other published books include *Practicing Passion: Youth and the Quest for a Passionate Church* and *Starting Right: Thinking Theologically about Youth Ministry* with Chapman Clark and David Rahn. She is serving as an investigator for the Religious Practices of American Youth project sponsored by the University of North Carolina at Chapel Hill. Her hidden talents include soaking up the sun on any beach and singing "The Good Ship Lollipop" in pig-Latin.

Ron Foster is the heart-wrapped-around-their-not-so-litte-fingers father of two daughters, Christine and Sara. He and his wife, Holly, live in Rockville, Maryland in an old farmhouse with a great white oak (complete with tire swing) in the front yard. Ron has been an ordained United Methodist pastor since 1985 and has served churches in Boonsboro, Reisterstown, and currently Bethesda, Maryland. He has been active in youth ministry for the past twenty years as a youth director, retreat speaker, pastor, and workshop leader. Ron graduated from Princeton University (1983) and Duke Divinity School (1986) and has been a regular part of the faculty of Princeton Theological Seminary's Institute for Youth Ministry since its inception. His other loves include basketball, coaching soccer, writing, and music of all kinds.